The Catholic Biblical Quarterly
Monograph Series
34

The Lord of the East Wind

BY

Aloysius Fitzgerald, F.S.C.

The Catholic Biblical Quarterly
Monograph Series
34

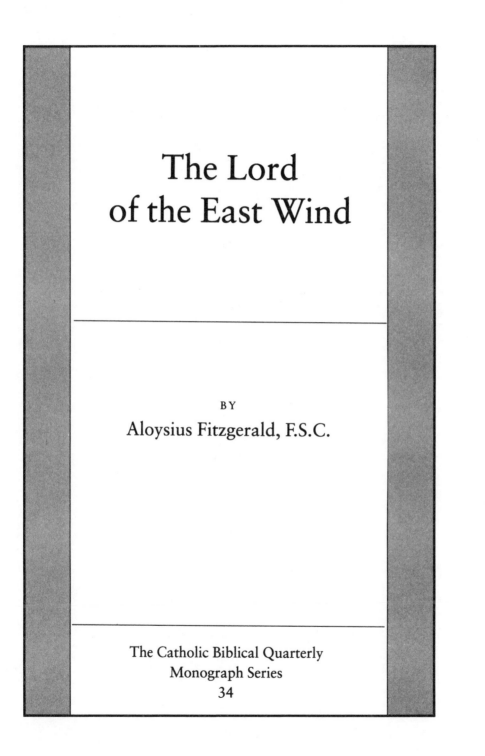

Produced in the United States of America

Library of Congress Cataloging-in-Publication Data

Fitzgerald, Aloysius.
The Lord of the East Wind / by Aloysius Fitzgerald.
p. cm. — (The Catholic Biblical quarterly. Monograph series ; 34)
Includes bibliographical references and index.
ISBN 0-915170-33-7
1. Sirocco in the Bible. 2. Theophanies in the Bible. 3. Bible. O.T.—Criticism, interpretation, etc. 4. Bible. O.T.—Geography. 5. Palestine—Climate. I. Title. II. Series.
BS656.5 .F57 2002
221.9'1—dc21

2002007068

Contents

INTRODUCTION • *1*

PART I: THE PALESTINIAN SIROCCO • *11*

PART II: SIROCCOS THAT DRY UP WATER SOURCES • *24*

1. Hos 13:14–15 • *24*
2. Nah 1:2–8 • *27*
3. Isa 19:1, 5-7 • *35*
4. Isa 50:2-3 • *37*
5. Jer 51:34-37, 42-45 • *38*

PART III: SIROCCOS WITHOUT DIRECT MENTION OF WATER SOURCES DRYING UP • *44*

1. Isa 13:2-22 • *44*
2. Jer 4:5-31 • *46*
3. Jer 25:30-38 • *52*
4. Deut 32:21-25 • *56*
5. Lamentations 2 • *59*

PART IV: THE MIRACLE AT THE SEA, EXOD 15:1B–18 + 21B • *66*

PART V: COMBINED SIROCCOS AND RAINSTORMS • *71*

1. Isaiah 34-35 • *72*
2. Isa 30:27-33 • *79*

3. Hab 3:2-19 • *82*
4. Ps 18:8-10 (= 2 Sam 22:8-10) • *97*
5. Isa 29:1-8 • *100*
6. Psalms 96-97 • *104*

PART VI: JOEL 1–4 • *110*

PART VII: VOCABULARY AND MOTIF STUDIES • *129*
1. *ybš/ḥrb* Used of Bodies of Water • *129*
2. Disease (*dbr, qṭb, ršp*) and the Sirocco • *131*
3. *swph* • *133*
4. *sʿr* (*śʿr*) / *sʿrh* (*śʿrh*) • *136*
5. *ʿnn* • *139*
6. Flying Dust • *141*
7. Withering Vegetation • *141*
8. *zʿm* • *142*
9. *ḥrwn* (*ʾp*) • *150*
10. *ḥmh* • *159*
11. Flying *qš, mṣ, glgl, tbn* • *168*
12. *ʾš* + *ʾkl* • *170*
13. The Dead or Frightened Fish • *175*
14. The Chariot in Sirocco Contexts • *178*
15. Agricultural Land Becoming a Desert • *179*
16. The Darkening of the Heavens • *182*
17. *tnyn* in Sirocco Contexts • *182*
18. The Sodom and *gpryt* Motifs • *185*
19. *ʿbrh* • *189*
20. The *ywm Yhwh* • *192*
21. *bʿr* • *200*
22. *lhṭ* • *201*

CONCLUSION • *202*

BIBLIOGRAPHY OF WORKS CITED • *210*

INDEX • *217*

Introduction

This study is the result of personal befuddlement occasioned by the different approachs, taken by geographers and a minority of exegetes influenced by them on the one hand and the majority of exegetes on the other, to storm theophanies in the OT—and to OT meteorology more generally.

The situation can best be illustrated by a typical example, Nah 1:2-8. Writing of the theophany here, G. Dalman, whose concern is meteorology and whose *Arbeit und Sitte in Palästina* I is the classic presentation of the unfolding stages of the Palestinian climate through the agricultural year, says simply, "Nahum's description of the angry God (1, 3f.) . . . is developed on the basis of the east wind."[1] By that he means the sirocco from the desert which blows in the spring and the fall.[2]

The analysis of J. Jeremias, whose 1965 monograph *Theophanie* is devoted to the subject, is different. He shows little concern for details of weather and his whole presumption is that meteorology as experienced in Palestine is not the take-off point for the analysis of Nah 1:2-8.

[1] Dalman, *Arbeit und Sitte in Palästina* I (Gütersloh: Evangelischer Verlag, 1928) 108.

[2] "Sirocco," Arab. *šarqīyah*, connected with Arab. *šrq*, Heb. *śrq* (Sir 50:7) = "to shine" (of the sun), simply means "east (wind)." It is used by Dalman and others of the hot, dry, sometimes violent and dangerous, desert wind of the spring and the fall. The word is always used in what follows in this specialized sense.

He recognizes that the storm here "is not eo ipso a thunder storm (Gewittersturm, 3)."[3] Nonetheless, there is an *ʿnn* in the picture (v 3) which he apparently regards as a rain cloud. That is to be viewed as "nur Begleiterscheinung." Jeremias remarks: "The Lord stirs up the cloud with his footsteps; he rules it with sovereignty." Dalman understands the cloud as the dust blown by the sirocco. Jeremias attributes the drying up of the waters (v 4) to the Lord's angry command. Dalman regards it as the effect of the sirocco. According to Jeremias, the result of the Lord's coming, the withering of the vegetation (v 4), is "that of the sirocco;" and the shaking of the mountains and hills (v 5) he explains as an earthquake.[4] Dalman regards the former as the direct effect of the sirocco and, though he does not say so, possibly the latter also.[5]

These contrasting analyses raise the question: Who is right? The question is hardly posed that way, if at all, but a frequent presumption of modern scholarship is that the approach of Jeremias to the text is in general right. That does not necessarily mean the details of Jeremias' form-critical analysis are accepted or of general concern. Nor does it mean that with differences in detail some exegetes will not explain aspects of theophanies on the basis of nature to a greater degree than Jeremias—though even when that is done, there is a recognizable tendency to combine elements from nature in unnatural ways. These differences in detail are presumed unimportant because in only a more or less limited way is something with a significant contact with nature being described. In other words, these theophany presentations are not sketched under the control of nature as experienced in Palestine, as Dalman presumed, and so patient of analysis on that basis. Instead, for Jeremias these are the product of various grades of free-wheeling imagination, outside borrowing or whatever.

At the same time it is not unreasonable to suggest, if one is willing to grant that by poetic hyperbole sirocco becomes super-sirocco in theophany contexts (no sirocco ever dried up the sea), Dalman could possi-

[3] J. Jeremias, *Theophanie* (WMANT 10; Neukirchen-Vluyn: Neukirchener Verlag, 1965) 32.

[4] Ibid., 33.

[5] For similar hyperbole in a Palestinian context, see the Arabic proverb cited by Dalman, *Arbeit und Sitte* I, 315: Wind when the grain is in ear knocks over (*hdd*) mountains.

bly be right. This sort of exaggeration is not unknown in modern descriptions of weather. A hot summer day in Washington can be described as hot like a furnace or hot enough to fry eggs on the sidewalk or hot as hell.

The present study aims to test that hypothesis on the basis of one specific meteorological phenomenon, the sirocco, in its meteorological context in Palestine. The conclusion that will be reached is that the Dalman approach is the right one.[6] This is not to say that all references to meteorological phenomena can be explained meteorologically, as Dalman himself recognized.[7]

The immediate problem that presents itself in beginning a study of this kind is that for all practical purposes there is little base to start from. That does not mean we lack adequate descriptions of the weather of Palestine, both the strictly scientific kind composed in large part of charts and numbers and the more descriptive kind that records what the eye saw, the ear heard and the body felt. The latter type is the more helpful for the analysis of OT texts since that is what is recorded there. Descriptions of both kinds we have in abundance and the best for interpreting OT texts is still Dalman's first volume. But from the OT side there is almost no area of research more neglected than the area of meteorological vocabulary.

I know of only two significant exceptions. The first is an all too brief treatment of directly meteorological words by R. B. Y. Scott, "Meteorological Phenomena and Terminology in the Old Testament," *ZAW* 64 (1952) 11-25; and the second, P. Reymond's 1958 monograph, *L'eau, sa vie, et sa signification dans L'Ancien Testament*,[8] where the focus is

[6] There is much to be learned from Jeremias' painstaking and stimulating study. But to make the issues at stake evident from the start, it will become clear in what follows I regard Jeremias' form-critical analysis of storm theophany as something in large part imposed upon the texts by an academic working in a library. It could never be explained to the OT writers who as members of an agriculturally based society knew their weather well and give abundant evidence of that knowledge. With necessary adaptations I make the same criticism of other analyses of storm theophany that do not begin with the meteorology of the Syro-Palestinian litoral as the key to the analysis and take that meteorology seriously.

[7] Dalman, *Arbeit und Sitte* I, 216.

[8] Reymond, *L'eau, sa vie, et sa signification dans L'Ancien Testament* (VTSup 6; Leiden: Brill, 1958).

different from what is attempted here and the discussion insufficiently rigorous and too general to be of help.

Scott clearly knew things which Jeremias fails to take into consideration. For example, the *ʿnn* (Nah 1:3) is "seldom if ever cloud bringing rain," but can be the "*dust-filled air* of the Scirocco" which he specifically identifies in Nah 1:3;[9] the *swph* (Nah 1:3) is a "destructive storm wind . . . specifically the Scirocco."[10] Apart from Scott's study the identification by the geographers (Dalman included) and by the exegetes of reflections of nature in these materials is very much ad hoc with little attempt to work out a typology of the vocabulary or motifs involved in these reflections of Palestinian meteorology in OT texts. Without making any serious effort to catalogue how the vocabulary and motifs divide, for example, one storm will be identified as a rainstorm, another as a sirocco, simply on the basis of a greater or lesser knowledge of the weather of Palestine and what the text seems to say. That can lead to right answers or to wrong answers or to the noncommittal, a storm.

There are two kinds of storm common in Palestine, the rainstorm and the sirocco, and this situation is reflected in the OT texts. As might be expected, western commentators do much better with the former, a phenomenon with which they are quite familiar. In part for that reason the sirocco is the storm selected for analysis here. The whole point is to isolate typologically distinct pieces of vocabulary and motifs which are characteristic of the sirocco storm and do not occur in rainstorms. That may sound like a silly exercise, but it is badly needed. Behind many a western analysis of this material there seems to lie the unspoken prejudice that a storm is a rainstorm, and quite often lists of storm texts with descriptions of rainstorms and siroccos are presumed to represent a unified package of materials with no distinctions to be made.

The isolation of rainstorm and sirocco materials here follows the outline of the procedures by which they were isolated in the first place. The study is divided into seven parts. Part I is a brief description of Palestinian meteorology with emphasis on the sirocco in its climato-

[9] R. B. Y. Scott, "Meteorological Phenomena and Terminology in the Old Testament," *ZAW* 64 (1952) 24.

[10] Ibid.

logical context, when it occurs and how it alternates with rainstorms in the spring and the fall interchange periods between the wet and dry seasons and vice versa. In Part II are brought together five texts which seem to reflect characteristics of the sirocco as described in Part I and in which a storm dries up bodies of water. The presumption here is that if any motif is going to distinguish the sirocco from the rainstorm, it is this one. On the basis of these five texts the first steps are made in the attempt to identify the distinctive vocabulary and motifs involved in the literary representations of siroccos. In Part III are brought together another five texts in which appear the same vocabulary and motifs that appeared in the texts studied in Part II and are never met in a rainstorm context, but without the specific motif of bodies of water drying up. Part IV deals with Exodus 15. The storm here is the sirocco and as in Part III, where it could have been treated, without the specific motif of bodies of water drying up. This text is given a treatment apart because it presents the opportunity to discuss the problem of the miracle at the sea and Yahweh versus the sea in the OT as a reflex of Baal versus Yamm at Ugarit. Here, I think, some meteorological distinctions must be made.

In Parts II–IV, a series of eleven texts, for the most part theophanies, will have been isolated through which a series of motifs and characteristic vocabulary runs and in which not a drop of rain falls. It will have been shown that these texts are not descriptions of rainstorms and that they are a group of texts apart with their own typical vocabulary and motifs. They reflect the characteristics of the sirocco as described in Part I, though it is also clear that they manifest features, generally in theophany contexts, beyond the possibility of any ordinary sirocco. These exaggerations can all be regarded as hyperbole that befits sirocco become theophany. They can also be understood to undercut the whole argument to this point. We are not dealing here with theophanies sketched on the basis of Palestinian meteorology and capable of being rationalized on that basis, but with the supranatural, the irrational, in which nature appears but exercises no controlling role over the presentation.

This problem would be all but irresolvable save for one fortunate aspect of Palestinian meteorology. Siroccos and rainstorms alternate in the spring and fall interchange periods. In Parts V and VI are studied a series of seven texts, six of which on *purely meteorological* grounds can be meteorologically located in the fall interchange period. In all these texts are met alternating and contrasting siroccos and rainstorms of the interchange periods. The point to be made is that it is more generally recognized the rainstorm descriptions are precisely that and capable of being rationalized on this basis. The way these rainstorms are played off against the sirocco in a way that is typical of Palestinian meteorology in a period when this can be expected to happen indicates that we are dealing here with sirocco become super-sirocco in a theophany context. The motifs and vocabulary characteristic of sirocco descriptions met in Parts V and VI are the same as in Parts II–IV. That guarantees we are dealing with sirocco descriptions there too.

In Part VI Joel 1–4 is studied apart because the key to the whole book is to recognize its meteorological setting in the fall interchange period and because the book moves through two such periods, one normal, one eschatological, in which these storms are played off against one another in the fall interchange period. These contrasting storms of the spring and the fall are the essential elements in the whole argument to be unfolded in what follows. We are not limited here to seven texts studied in Parts V and VI; more will be added in the vocabulary and motif studies of Part VII.[11]

The discussion of Parts I–VI is followed by Part VII, "Vocabulary and Motif Studies." There are 22 such studies, 19 of which treat in detail motifs and pieces of vocabulary identified as characteristic of sirocco contexts and not met in rainstorm contexts. The remaining three are present for other reasons. It is understood that these vocabulary and motif studies are capable of refinement and being added to, but that goes beyond the goals of an initial investigation. Part of the material collected in these studies is without surprises. Bodies of water

[11] Express mention must be made here of J. C. de Moor's monograph, *The Seasonal Pattern in the Ugaritic Myth of Baᶜlu* (AOAT 16; Neukirchen-Vluyn: Neukirchener Verlag, 1971), which first called my attention to rainstorms, siroccos and interchange in a serious way. If little reference is made to de Moor in what follows that is because the biblical material stands on its own, is more abundant and easier to deal with than the very difficult texts de Moor handles. Acknowledgment must also be made of J. H. Eaton's study, "The Origin and Meaning of Habakkuk 3," *ZAW* 76 (1964) 144-71, which first taught me that alternating siroccos and rainstorms are not just something geographers talk about, but can be found in biblical texts. Till that lesson was learned the characteristic vocabulary and motifs of sirocco texts were significantly more difficult to isolate and the split between the language of the sirocco and the rainstorm less clear.

dry up in siroccos, never in a rainstorm (Study 1). Part of it is surprising. The phrase, *ḥrwn ʾp*, never occurs in a rainstorm context, is typical of sirocco contexts (Study 9) and helps identify that storm. The accurate isolation and collection of the materials gathered in these studies are intended as the primary goals of this investigation. They are meant to provide a firm foundation for the identification of the sirocco in an OT text. In a sense the discussion of Parts I-VI is simply intended as background to make readable the studies of Part VII, where the discussion is presented necessarily in more summary fashion.

A certain lack of logical order enters the presentation when a statement like "*ḥrwn ʾp* (see Study 9) is never met in a rainstorm, typically in a sirocco context," is made in Parts II–VI and then the support for the statement is relegated to the reviews of Part VII which are meant to be read as a unit in the order in which they follow after Parts I–VI. To put the issue of order another way, the purely inductive procedures of the original investigation, where the texts examined *gradually* wrote the concluding studies of Part VII, are sacrificed in the presentation of the results. While concessions are made to ease the reader by degrees into the material, the discussion of the first text in Part II already presumes the completed Part VII. The only excuse for that manner of presentation is the attempt to keep the order of the argument simple, the need for avoiding excessive repetition and the difficulty inherent in ordering any demonstration that a series of motifs and pieces of vocabulary in a significantly large body of texts is all part of a literary presentation of a specific meteorological phenomenon. That difficulty is enhanced by the fact that no modern person can have an initial "feel" for the overtones and undertones of words and motifs associated in context in a language that is so foreign as OT Hebrew. The substitute for that "feel" which comes from "living the language" can only be developed out of the concordance, and it is a poor one. The experience throughout this study of groping and scratching toward "discoveries!" that any ten-year-old in Isaiah's day knew without reflection has been humbling.

There are a number of other methodological problems that call for further discussion. This has been postponed because they are best handled in conjunction with appropriate texts and the intention is to face them at various stages in both Parts II-VI and in the vocabulary and motif studies of Part VII. The points made here about the general development of the argument will be reviewed in the course of the discussion in an attempt to keep that argument in clear focus as it unfolds.

The prime intention of this study is simply to show that it is possible to analyze and make distinctions in the OT language of siroccos and rainstorms (often in association with theophanies), and to show that Palestinian (or better Syro-Palestinian) meteorology is the ultimate source of these presentations. To accomplish this is to rationalize a not insignificant bulk of OT text.

There are some secondary gains. The material is pure Palestinian and alternating siroccos and rainstorms in the fall interchange period combined with the assumption that agriculture depends on rain, not irrigation, eliminates both Egypt and heartland Mesopotamia as a source of possible borrowing.

Though Yahweh is patently no nature god, the study without paying much direct attention to the matter, gives a relatively clear insight into the sources and the millennia-old origin of meteorological nature myth in Palestine and how the relics of this mythological world-view survive in the religious *language* of the OT. It also affords the opportunity to make some refinements in—at least to ask some questions about—how this OT material is related to the Baal material from Ugarit, the oldest significant literary reflection of this Syro-Palestinian meteorological mythology otherwise available. The correct meteorological analysis of some texts makes it possible to give them a temporal setting. This can be combined with other time indications in the text and all of a sudden a text which seems at first to have a static stance takes on a temporal movement and the whole becomes clear. The best example of this is Joel (Part VI), but there are others. In some texts, both primary and editorial units, particularly in the prophetic corpus, the imagery patterns are based on the contrasting storms of the fall interchange period. The Lord's enemies are blasted by the sirocco; his friends are rained on and the agriculture flourishes. Once the pattern is recognized, the intent of the juxtaposing becomes evident, and units that are usually or sometimes studied in isolation become parts of a broader structure. A clear example of this is Isaiah 34-35 (Part V, 1), and there are others. There are, in addition, individual gains to be made in individual texts which are too random to categorize.

A further area of potential gain to be made on the basis of the meteorology analyzed in this study is in the discussion of Sukkoth, the Israelite New Year, the Autumn Festival or whatever name one wishes to give to the feast(s) of Tishri, initiated by P. Volz (1912)[12] and especially S. Mowinckel (1922).[13] Not a few texts to be studied reflect the interchanging siroccos and rainstorms of the fall interchange period which opens toward the middle of Tishri. Other sirocco texts which on meteorological grounds cannot with certainty be assigned to that period belong meteorologically either to the fall or the spring interchange periods. That this sort of meteorology and the mythology derived from it could be expected to be reflected in a festival of a Palestinian agricultural community celebrating the successful conclusion of one agricultural year (or lamenting its failure) and looking forward with anxiety to the coming of the first rains and the beginning of the next agricultural year seems natural. That is to say, there is so much of this material and it is so stereotyped that it almost has to have a common *Sitz* in the life of the community. The liturgy of the feast of Sukkoth suggests itself as that *Sitz*.

The point to be made is that, without being concerned in any way with the criteria Mowinckel used to assign texts to his *Thronbesteigungsfest* or to view others as reflecting the materials of that feast and attempting only to isolate meteorology certainly located in or characteristic of the fall interchange period, this study isolates many of the same texts used by Mowinckel and his followers. There are too many texts involved for the connection to be happenstance.

If Mowinckel's criteria were brought into consideration, the meteorology of numerous other sirocco texts could be assigned to the fall and the spring-fall option could be resolved. Some thought was given to proceeding this way, but eventually the idea was rejected. The meteorological material to be handled is sufficiently difficult in itself. The whole problem of the Israelite New Year is likewise not an easy one.[14]

[12] P. Volz, *Das Neujahrsfest Jahwes (Laubhüttenfest)* (Tübingen: Mohr, 1912).

[13] S. Mowinckel, *Psalmenstudien II. Das Thronbesteigungsfest Jahwäs und der Ursprung der Eschatologie* (reprint of 1922 ed.; Amsterdam: Schippers, 1961). John Gray, *The Biblical Doctrine of the Reign of God* (Edinburgh: Clark, 1979), reviews the whole question in the light of the subsequent scholarship.

[14] H. Cazelles, while sympathetic to Mowinckel's views, gives a more complete picture of the problem than the Gray study noted in n. 13. See "Le Nouvel An en Israël," *DBSup* 6 (1960) 620-45.

To keep the argument in what follows as simple as possible, it was thought best to limit this study to meteorology. In what follows reference will be made to texts concerned with "an agricultural new year" or on occasion "an eschatological, agricultural new year"—without capitals. For example, if a text affirms that the Lord's enemies will be blasted by the sirocco, Israel will be rained on, the grass will start to grow and the agriculture will prosper through the harvest, that is described as an agricultural-new-year text because it starts with the meteorology of the fall interchange period and the beginning of the agricultural new year. The only affirmation directly intended is a meteorological one. The relation between the texts studied below and Mowinckel's texts will be evident in any case. In a few isolated instances where the text cries out for a different approach, the general policy adopted has been violated and I speak of Sukkoth or the like. That will serve as a reminder of the further possibilities inherent in the meteorological materials being studied.

Two final introductory remarks. This study would be better served if it were to be done by a professional geographer who like Dalman sat in Palestine for years and observed the weather with scrupulous attention. The excuse for a non-professional undertaking the task is the geographers have been reluctant to undertake it. The hope for success lies in using the eyes of the Dalmans and in working out a clear typology of the motifs and vocabulary. Both, I think, can be done.

Secondly, what has been written to this point and what will follow has been penned with full knowledge that it must be regarded by many as an even more primitive view of the matters treated than that of H. Gressmann, *Der Ursprung der israelitisch-jüdischen Eschatologie* (1905).[15] The prime defense against this potential perception is the typology and the way siroccos are played off against rainstorms in a period when this can be expected to happen. Both facts demand an explanation and the one offered here is the control exercised by the meteorology of Palestine. The details of the argument are left to the body of the study.

[15] H. Gressmann, *Der Ursprung der israelitisch-jüdischen Eschatologie* (Göttingen: Vandenhoeck und Ruprecht, 1905).

PART I

The Palestinian Sirocco[1]

Westerners are inclined to think of the climate of Palestine as particularly dry. That is, of course, in part true, Beersheba receives about 10 in. of annual rain; the Dead Sea area, 2-4 in. But the average yearly rainfall in Jerusalem, 25 in., is about the same as in London or Minneapolis–St. Paul; and that of the Galilean hills, up to 40 in., is about the same as the annual rainfall in New York City. What distinguishes these more favored areas of Palestine from their western counterparts, where the climate is not considered particularly dry, is the feature of Palestinian meteorology most significant for life, the fact that all the rain falls in half a year. The rest of the year is completely dry. The sirocco storm of concern here is characteristic of the interchange periods from the dry to the rainy season and vice versa, i.e., from mid-September through October and from April to about mid-June. The rainy season runs essentially from mid-October through April. The months of the heavy concentration of rain are November through March. It is understood that variations in detail may occur in a particular year. Even charts reflecting averages based on a scientific gathering of the evidence over different periods of years reflect minor deviations.

[1] Convenient treatments of the material presented here can be found in G. Dalman, *Arbeit und Sitte in Palästina* I (Gütersloh: Evangelischer Verlag, 1928) 103-9, 314-29; D. Baly, *The Geography of the Bible* (New York: Harper, 1957) 67-70.

The meteorology of Palestine is significantly influenced by its location between Arabia Deserta on the east, Sinai on the south and the Mediterranean on the west. All the rain that falls is brought by the moisture-laden west winds off the Mediterranean which during the rainy season are cooled as they meet the land and let loose the rain. The dry winds from the east and south bring no rain. It would be possible to distinguish E, NE, SE etc. winds; but the OT has no words for the in-between points of the compass and the distinction is of little practical importance for present purposes. The essential point is that a wind coming from any westerly direction in the right season of the year can bring rain; a wind coming from an easterly direction or from the south can develop into a sirocco during the interchange periods. Despite its etymology, the term "sirocco" is also used for southerly winds that betray its characteristics.

In the fall periods of sirocco or the related *samūm*[2] typically precede the coming of the first rains. Thus the Palestinian saying: "the east wind arouses the west wind"; or: "the east wind brings the west wind";[3] or: "at the beginning of the year the east wind is good."[4] In the spring such storms can continue beyond the close of the rains into June.

An important point for the discussion to follow is that siroccos and rainstorms can alternate in the fall and spring interchange periods. For the fall Dalman[5] presents his observations in Jerusalem in 1908 as typical:

> Oct. 24 east wind; humidity, morning 36%, noon 39%, evening 45%. Oct. 25, noon 45%, evening 52%. Oct. 26, noon 27%, midnight 18%. Oct. 27, morning only 18%, evening 19%. Oct. 30 [wind from the west], morning 82%, midnight 100%. Nov. 1, evening 100% and a heavy rain, the first significant one. In the preceding days the temperature varied from 27° [C; 81°F] to 17° [63°F]; it now descended to 14° [57°F] and 12° [54°F]. After 8 cool days there came another east wind

[2] A heat wave with almost no wind in an east-wind period; Arab. *samūm* connected with *samm* = "poison" and *sammam* = "to poison" and probably reflecting the deleterious effects of the sirocco on human health (see below). Dalman, *Arbeit und Sitte* I, 103.

[3] Ibid., 103-4.

[4] Ibid., 107.

[5] Ibid., 105-6.

(*smūm*). On the 10th-12th the humidity fell to 26% and the thermometer rose to 26.5° [80°F]. On Nov. 13 the wind switched to the west, the humidity reached 100% and in three periods 15.5 mm. of rain fell between the 15th and 17th. The temperature at night descended as low as 3.5° [38°F]. There followed a third period of east wind between the 19th and 22nd of Nov. The temperature was cooler and reached only 22° [72°F] at midday. The west wind and the east wind battled between the 23rd and 25th. On the 26th there was calm. The 27th and 28th brought the west wind again and 46.5 mm. of rain, the third of the season, with the thermometer at 9° [48°F].

For the spring Dalman,[6] using W. Georgii's Beersheba observations, cites the period between May 12-18, 1916 as an example of a severe sirocco:

> In the preceding days the maximum temperature reached a high of 26°-29° [C; 79°-84°F]; the minimum fell to 10° [50°F]. On the 12th the maximum reached 34.5° [94°F]; on the 17th, 43.1° [110°F]; on the 18th 42.1° [108°F]. Thereafter the temperatures became normal. Correspondingly the minimum temperatures rose during the sirocco from 12° [54°F] to 25.6° [78°F] on the 18th so that the nights were likewise unbearably [for a north German] hot. The humidity during the month ran between 89% and 38%; during the sirocco period, between 23% and 2%. How quickly the situation can change with a change in the wind is illustrated by the following. On the evening of the 18th the east wind ceased, the temperature fell 20°, the humidity reached 88%, and a thunderstorm with rain followed. During the sirocco the troops suffered from heart problems and fainting. Everyone experienced nervous tension. The whole of Palestine must have experienced this sirocco. Baruch (Rosenstein) names the period from May 14-19, 1916 as the worst sirocco period in Tel Aviv near Jaffa during which the temperatures went as high as 36° [97°F] and 46.5° [116°F].

The characteristics of the sirocco, which has been described as the storm that brings desert conditions to Palestine,[7] are generally known and a lengthy discussion is unnecessary. The storm is extremely hot and dry, and typically produces abnormally low humidity and high temperatures. The winds can reach velocities up to 60 mph. In the fall the siroccos contribute to the loss of the leaves from the trees. In the

[6] Ibid., 319-20.

[7] Baly, *Geography*, 67.

spring they bring to an end the green of the winter and early spring, and give Palestine its dusty-brown summer color. This can happen in a severe sirocco in the course of several hours. They dry up shallow bodies of water. Though spring siroccos contribute to the ripening of the grain, if they blow too early or too severely they can also destroy the grain crop. Siroccos can also raise great clouds of sand and dust which sting the face and blot out the light of the sun and moon.

There is, however, one characteristic of the sirocco that in the present context needs to be emphasized for the non-native, the effect of the sirocco on human health. Dalman speaks of the high incidence of nervous disorders, skin sores, malaria, heart problems, fainting and sunstroke in sirocco periods.[8] De Moor has culled from the literature: nervousness, headaches, inflammation of the mucous membranes, fever, malaria, dysentery, sunstroke, heart attack.[9] Baly adds the odd fact that the newcomer is frequently less affected by sirocco periods than the native.[10] And Ashbel speaks of "hamsinopaths (*ḥmsynwp'tym*)" as those most afflicted.[11]

The attempt to set the sirocco in its meteorological context in Palestine has to this point purposely not been in the terms of the professional meteorologist. At the same time it has been pretty much bare-bones description. To attempt to match this bare-bones description directly to the literary presentations of the sirocco in the OT is possible, of course, but the attempt is made easier if the presentations being compared are closer. For that reason there are added here several descriptions of siroccos experienced in Palestine. None of these descriptions can be termed literature, but they generally strive for a vividness characteristic of many OT descriptions of the storm; like their OT counterparts they attempt to enable the reader to experience vicariously the sirocco and ease the effort to identify the storm there.

[8] Dalman, *Arbeit und Sitte* I, 106-7, 319-20.

[9] J. C. de Moor, *The Seasonal Pattern in the Ugaritic Myth of Baʿlu* (AOAT 16; Neukirchen-Vluyn: Neukirchener Verlag, 1971) 175.

[10] Baly, *Geography*, 68.

[11] D. Ashbel, *Bio-Climatic Atlas of Israel* (Hebrew and English; Jerusalem: Hebrew U., n.d. [1950?]) 133. The word is derived from Arab. *ḫamsīn* = *ḫamāsīn* = "fifty," the "fifty day period" between the Coptic Easter and Pentecost, the Egyptian parallel to the sirocco which is characteristic of that period and does not necessarily come from the east. See Dalman, *Arbeit und Sitte* I, 320-21.

Unfortunately the modern descriptions come mostly from travelers caught by a late spring sirocco, who make it their business to complete their travels before the fall interchange period and the first rains. But the fall sirocco is very similar to one in the spring save for the fact that the spring sirocco is frequently more severe.[12] With that limitation these descriptions can serve as the basis for comparison with OT fall siroccos too.

It will be noted that these descriptions have been culled from sources dating from roughly the last half of the 19th century and the earlier years of the 20th. The present more scientific age eschews such impressionistic presentations of Palestinian meteorology probably because technology has reduced man's exposure to the elements and because they are unscientific. That is from one point of view, at least, regrettable. As will become immediately clear, echoes of the biblical text itself can be heard in the following citations in a way that is not true of the charts and numbers of scientific meteorology. To be noted throughout is the tendency toward intentional exaggeration—"perfect tempest," "as from a burning oven," "blistering hurricane," "blast of a furnace," "burning Sirocco"—a tendency met in modern popular descriptions of the weather and, as will become clear, in the biblical texts. E. Robinson, *Biblical Researches in Palestine, Mount Sinai and Arabia Petraea* I (Boston: Crocker and Brewster, 1841) 287-89; April 11, south of Beersheba:

> During this time we were exposed to a violent Sirocco, which continued till towards evening, resembling the Khamsîn of Egypt. The wind had been all the morning N.E. but at 11 o'clock it suddenly changed to the South, and came upon us with violence and intense heat, until it blew a perfect tempest. The atmosphere was filled with fine particles of sand, forming a bluish haze; the sun was scarcely visible, his disk exhibiting only a dun and sickly hue; and the glow of the wind came upon our faces as from a burning oven. Often we could not see ten rods around us; and our eyes, ears, mouths, and clothes, were filled with sand. The thermometer at 12 o'clock stood at 88°F, and had apparently been higher; at 2 o'clock it had fallen to 76°, although the wind still continued. . . .
> We encamped at 3 3/4 o'clock in the Wady. . . . The tempest now seemed to have reached its greatest fury, and had become a tornado.

[12] Baly, *Geography*, 69.

It was with the utmost difficulty that we could pitch our tent, or keep it upright after it was pitched. For a time the prospect was dreadful; and the storm in itself was probably as terrific, as most of those which have given rise to the exaggerated accounts of travellers. Yet here was no danger of life; though I can well conceive that in certain circumstances, as where a traveller is without water and is previously feeble and exhausted, such a "horrible tempest" may well prove fatal. Most of our Arabs covered their faces with a handkerchief, although we were travelling before the wind. After 5 o'clock the wind fell; the air became less obscure; a breeze sprung up from the N.W. which soon purified the atmosphere, restored the sun to his splendor, and brought us a clear and pleasant evening, with a temperature of 66°F. It was no little labor to free ourselves from the casing of sand in which we were enveloped.

E. Robinson, *Palestine* II, 429-30; May 23, near Hebron:

The Sirocco wind which we had felt all day, now increased to a violent tempest, bringing up the dust and sand from the desert, and filling the air so as to obscure the sun. The whole atmosphere became of a deep dun or yellowish hue. . . . The guide said immediately, this would blast the grain. . . . We found great difficulty in pitching the tent, as the Sirocco had now become almost a tornado; the ropes were several times broken, and had at last to be doubled on the windward side. The air became dark, almost like night, from the sand and dust. After a short time, however, the tempest abated; and we had at evening a fine cool wind from the N.W. The actual heat was not unusually great; the thermometer rose only to 86°F.

E. Robinson, *Palestine* II, 504; May 30, south of Dead Sea:

Finding here no convenient shade, we set up the top of our tent, to shield us from the intolerable heat of the sun. The South wind, which at early dawn was cool and pleasant, had already become a burning Sirocco; the thermometer, as we stopped, stood in the shade at 96°F. The violence and glow of the wind increased; so that at 12 o'clock the thermometer had risen to 102°F. It being difficult in such circumstances either to write or sleep, and our Arabs wishing to go on, we concluded to proceed; and found ourselves actually less uncomfortable in traveling, than we had been in lying still.

W. M. Thomson, *The Land and the Book* I (New York: Harper, 1880) 142-43; April 14, on the road from Ekron to Ashdod:

The sirocco to-day is of the quiet kind [*samūm*] and they are often more overpowering than the others. I encountered one, years ago, on my way from Ludd to Jerusalem. Just such clouds covered the sky, collecting, as these are doing, into darker groups about the tops of the mountains; and a stranger to the country would have expected rain. Pale lightnings played through the air like forked tongues of burnished steel, but there was no thunder and no wind. The heat, however, became intolerable; and I escaped from the burning highway into a dark vaulted room at the lower Beth-horon. I then fully understood what Isaiah meant when he said, "Thou shalt bring down the noise of strangers, as the heat in a dry place; even the heat with the shadow of a cloud [Isa 25:5]"; that is, as such heat brings down the noise and makes the earth quiet; a figure used by Job when he says, "How thy garments are warm, when he quieteth the earth by the south wind [37:17]?"

We can testify that the garments are not only warm, but hot.

This sensation of dry, hot clothes is only experienced during the siroccos; and on such a day, too, one notices the other effects mentioned by the prophet—bringing down the noise and quieting the earth. There is no living thing abroad to make a noise. The birds hide in thickest shades, the fowls pant under the walls with open mouth and drooping wings, the flocks and herds take shelter in caves and under great rocks, the laborers retire from the fields, and close the windows and doors of their houses, and travellers hasten to take shelter in the first cool place they can find. No one has energy enough to make a noise, and the very air is too languid to stir the pendant leaves even of the tall poplars. Such a south wind, with the heat of a cloud, does indeed bring down the noise and quiet the earth.

W. M. Thomson, *The Land and the Book* II (1882) 262:

But there is another wind . . . the dry, hot sirocco. . . . I have felt its greatest power on the plain of Aleppo, and in the wadys about Hâsbeiya. The air becomes loaded with fine dust, which it whirls in rainless clouds hither and thither at its own wild will; it rushes down every gorge, bending and breaking the trees, and tugging at each individual leaf; it growls round the houses, runs riot with your clothes, and flies away with your hat; nor is there any escape from its impertinence. The eyes inflame, the lips blister, and the moisture of the body evaporates under the ceaseless pertinacity of the persecuting wind: you become languid, nervous, irritable, and despairing.

T. Chaplin (a medical doctor), "Observations on the Climate of Jerusalem," *PEFQS* (1883) 16:

> It is when the wind blows from the south-east that it acquires the peculiarities which Europeans usually signify by the term *sirocco*. At such time the sky may be cloudless, or with some cirrus and stratus, the temperature is high, 84° to 90°, or higher, the air destitute of ozone, and extremely dry, the difference between the wet and dry bulb being often as much as 24° or even 28° or 30°. There may be calm, but sometimes the wind amounts to 1 or 1.5, and veers between east, south-east, and south. The more the wind tends to the south, the more dull and overcast is the sky, and the more disagreeable to the feelings the state of the atmosphere; the more it tends to the east, the clearer is the sky and the stronger and fresher the breeze. The worst kind of *sirocco* dries the mucous membrane of the air passages, producing a kind of inflammation resulting in catarrh and sore throat; it induces great lassitude, incapacitating for mental as well as bodily exertion, in those who walk or work in it; headache, with a sense of constriction as if a cord were tied round the temples, oppression of the chest, burning of the palms of the hands and soles of the feet, accelerated pulse, thirst, and sometimes actual fever. It dries and cracks furniture, loosening the joints of tables and chairs, curls the covers of books and pictures hung in frames, parches vegetation, sometimes withering whole fields of young corn. Its force is not usually great, but sometimes severe storms of wind and fine dust are experienced, the hot air burning like a blast from an oven, and the sand cutting the face of the traveller who has the misfortune to encounter it. This kind of air has a peculiar smell, not unlike that of the neighbourhood of a burning brick-kiln. Sometimes the most remarkable whirlwinds are produced, especially in the western plain near the hills, by the meeting of a strong east or south-east wind with a wind from the west or north. Clouds of sand fly about in all directions, now taking the traveller in front, now behind, and now on the side, and the gusts of wind are so violent as to blow weak persons from their horses, and to overturn baggage animals.

T. Chaplin, "Observations on the climate of Jerusalem," 17; Oct., early Nov.:

> November 4th, 1868. After *sirocco* had prevailed for more than thirty days, the wind suddenly changed on October 30th, by way of south to

west, a breeze sprang up bringing cumuli and loose masses of nimbus; much dew was deposited during the night, and there were a few drops of rain. Two gusty cloudy days followed, the atmosphere becoming more and more hazy from fine dust, and on the evening of November 2nd a heavy, long-continued shower of rain fell, preceded by thunder. The next day there was more rain, and by the morning of the 5th upwards of an inch had been measured. During the days preceding the rain the barometer and thermometer both fell—the former gradually, the latter more suddenly. At 9 a.m. on October 30th the temperature was 88°, at 9 a.m. on the 31st 66°, and on the 3rd November it had fallen to 53°, a difference of 35° in four days.

E. W. G. Masterman (a medical doctor), "Hygiene and Disease in Palestine in Modern and in Biblical Times," *PEFQS* (1918) 60:

The most unhealthy and disagreeable days are those when the dry, hot sirocco blows from the south-east . . . sometimes for several successive days and nights. At such times those who have good stone houses keep the windows and doors closed, and to step outside from such a house is like stepping into the neighborhood of a furnace. The wind is intensely dry and, at times, loaded with fine desert dust, producing a haze; vegetation languishes, the leaves droop, and most people—especially, perhaps, Europeans—feel varying degrees of discomfort. During and after a bout of such a wind, the increase in "fever" and other illnesses is marked. May, just after, and September and October just before the rains, are the worst months.

G. A. Smith, *The Historical Geography of the Holy Land* (reprint of 1931 ed.; London: Collins, 1966) 65-66:

The name Sherkiyeh, our Sirocco, literally "the east", is used of winds blowing from the desert—E, SE, S and even SSW. Except for one in winter off the snows of the Belka, they are hot winds. . . . They come with a mist of fine sand, veiling the sun, scorching vegetation, and bringing languor and fever to men. They are painful airs, and, if the divine economy were only for our physical benefit, inexplicable, for they neither carry rain nor help at harvest. . . . They blow chiefly in spring, and for a day at a time. The following extracts, from our diary in 1891, give some impression of what these hat sandy winds make of the atmosphere. It will be noticed how readily they pass into rain, by a slight change from SSW to full SW: *Edh-Dhaheriyah*, *Sat-*

urday, April 25 (in the Negeb, four hours south of Hebron), 8 P.M.—Night dark and clear, with moon in first quarter. Temp. 58° Fahr.; 11 P.M. 62°, moon hazy.

Sunday—8 A.M. 78°. Hot wind from south, yet called Sherkeh or Sherkiyeh, i.e. east wind, by our men. Temperature rises to 88° at 10, and 90° at 12. Sky drumly all forenoon, but the sun casts shadows. Atmosphere thickening. At 1.45 wind rises, 93°; 2.30, gale blowing, air filled with fine sand, horizon shortened to a mile, sun not visible, grey sky, but a slight shadow cast by the tents. View from tent-door of light grey limestone land under dark grey sky, misty range of hills a mile off, and one camel visible; 3.40, wind moderate, temp. 93°; 4.40, strong wind, half-gale, 83°; 5 P.M., wind SSW, temp. 78°. Wind veers a little farther W in the evening; 6 P.M., temp. 72°; sunset, 68°; 10.30 P.M., 63°. A slight shower, stormy-looking night, clouds gathering from many quarters. . . .

Monday, April 27—Rain at intervals through the night, with high SW wind endangering the tents; 5.45 A.M., temp. 58°. Distant hills under mist, with the sun breaking through. Scudding showers, grey clouds, no blue sky. . . .

Here is another Sherkiyeh (called also Khamsin) a fortnight later, in Samaria, between Sebastiyeh and Jenin:

May 11:—At Sebastiyeh at sunrise only 48° with slight west wind. Towards noon, under the same wind, 80°. Then the wind changed. A Sherkiyeh blew from SSE, and at 2 P.M., at our resting-place, Ḳubaṭiyeh, high and open, 92°. Sun veiled, afternoon dull. At 5, at Jenin, Engannim, 88°, with more sunshine. At 10, still 84°. A few hours later we were wakened by cold. The wind had changed to W, the temperature was 72°, at sunrise, 68°

W. F. Lynch, *Narrative of the United States' Expedition to the River Jordan and the Dead Sea* (Philadelphia: Lea and Blanchard, 1849) 312-16; Apr. 26, caught in a boat on the Dead Sea:

At 3.50 [P.M.] a hot, blistering hurricane struck us from the south-east, and for some moments we feared being driven out to sea. The thermometer rose immediately to 102°. The men, closing their eyes to shield them from the fiery blast, were obliged to pull with all their might to stem the rising waves, and at 4.30, physically exhausted, but with grateful hearts, we gained the shore. My own eyelids were blistered by the hot wind, being unable to protect them, from the necessity of steering the boat.

We landed on the south side of the peninsula, near Wady Humeir, the most desolate spot upon which we had yet encamped. Some went up the ravine to escape from the stifling wind; others, driven back by the glare, returned to the boats and crouched under the awnings. One mounted spectacles to protect his eyes, but the metal became so heated that he was obliged to remove them. Our arms and the buttons on our coats became almost burning to the touch; and the inner folds of our garments were cooler than those exposed to the immediate contact of the wind. . . .

Washed and bathed in one of the pools, but the relief was only momentary. In one instant after leaving the water, the moisture on the surface evaporated, and left the skin dry, parched, and stiff. Except for the minnows in the pool, there was not a living thing stirring; but the hot wind swept moaning through the branches of the withered palm-tree, and every bird and insect, if any there were, had sought shelter under the rocks.

Coming out from the ravine, the sight was a singular one. The wind had increased to a tempest; the two extremities and the western shore of the sea were curtained by a mist, on this side of a purple hue, on the other a yellow tinge; and the red and rayless sun, in the bronzed clouds, had the appearance it presents when looked upon through smoked glass. Thus may the heavens have appeared just before the Almighty in his wrath rained down fire upon the cities of the plain. Behind were the rugged crags of the mountains of Moab . . . enveloped in a cloud of dust, swept by the simoom from the great desert of Arabia. . . .

The sky grew more angry as the day declined. . . . The heat rather increased than lessened after the sun went down. At 8 P.M., the thermometer was 106° five feet from the ground. At one foot from the latter it was 104°. We threw ourselves upon the parched, cracked earth, among dry stalks and canes, which would before have seemed insupportable from the heat. Some endeavoured to make a screen of one of the boat's awnings, but the fierce wind swept it over in an instant. It was more like the blast of a furnace than living air. . . .

In the early part of the night, there was scarce a moment that some one was not at the water-breakers; but the parching thirst could not be allayed, for, although there was no perceptible perspiration, the fluid was carried off as fast as it was received into the system. At 9, the breakers were exhausted, and our last waking thought was water.

> In our disturbed and feverish slumbers, we fancied the cool beverage purling down our parched and burning throats. . . .
>
> We had spent the day in the glare of a Syrian sun, by the salt mountain of Usdum, in the hot blast of the sirocco, and were now bivouacked under the calcined cliffs of Moab. When the water was exhausted, all too weary to go for more . . . we threw ourselves upon the ground,—eyes smarting, skin burning, lips, and tongue, and throat parched and dry; and wrapped the first garment we could find around our heads to keep off the stifling blast. . . .
>
> At midnight the thermometer stood at 98°; shortly after which the wind shifted and blew lightly from the north. At 4 A.M., thermometer, 82°; comparatively cool.

There are two texts (Ps 97:4, Part V, 6; Zech 9:14, Study 4) to be discussed where on the basis of the vocabulary involved reference is made to the sirocco. In these texts mention is made of lightning and a few final remarks about the connection of lightning to the sirocco are necessary.

The meteorological literature clearly connects lightning to the rainy season. It does not occur during the rainless summer and it is a particular characteristic of the rainstorm.[13] The same literature makes clear that lightning is not characteristic of the sirocco and that situation is clearly reflected by the texts to be studied in what follows.

At the same time the literature indicates that lightning can occur without rain and in a meteorological context with the sirocco. This has already been illustrated by the first sirocco description cited from W. M. Thomson above where in a *samūm* period in the middle of April "pale lightnings played through the air like forked tongues of burnished steel," without rain, at least in the vicinity of the observer.[14] The appearance of lightning without rain in the fall is the sign that the first rains are near. Thus the Palestinian sayings: "If the world is lit up by lightning on the Feast of the Holy Cross, the rain is not far away"; or when lightning has lit up the horizon for a whole night, "The rain is near"; or "Lightning presages the rain."[15]

The truth of the sayings was experienced by Dalman in the fall of

[13] Dalman, *Arbeit und Sitte* I, 114; Ashbel, *Bio-Climatic Atlas*, 2.

[14] W. M. Thomson, *The Land and the Book* I (New York: Harper, 1880) 142-43.

[15] Dalman, *Arbeit und Sitte* I, 114.

1908. On Oct. 30 he saw the first lightning bolts; on Nov. 1 the first heavy rain fell.[16]

Dalman[17] supplies a more detailed description of the same phenomena from observations on Oct. 9, 1913:

> After a hot calm day and heavy cloud formation with a weak west wind in the evening, there arose about 4 A.M. a strong east wind. To the east there was a great cloud out of which came thunder and lightning; to the west it was clear. The temperature was 18.5° [C; 65°F] and the humidity 35%. Two hours later a storm came from the west, the heavens filled with clouds and heavy rain fell for 10 minutes accompanied by thunder and lightning. By 7 A.M., the wind had calmed once again; the temperature was 16.5° [62°F] and the humidity 60%. By 8:30 A.M. the east wind had prevailed once again; the temperature stood at 19° [66°F] with 35% humidity, similar to the previous situation. At 10:00 P.M. the temperature was 19.5° [67°F]; the humidity was only 20% without wind.

[16] Ibid.
[17] Ibid., 107.

PART II

Siroccos That Dry Up Water Sources

This study begins with a series of texts where it is a question of water sources being dried up in a storm. There is no doubt what kind of storm is meant. It can only be the sirocco since that is what the heat and extremely low humidity of that storm do. In the course of this review it will be possible to begin to isolate series of motifs and characteristic vocabulary which appear in descriptions of this type of storm and are not typical of rainstorms. These motifs and this typical vocabulary make it possible to identify other instances of sirocco storms where the motif of bodies of water being dried up is not present and to distinguish with relative clarity descriptions of siroccos from descriptions of rainstorms in the absence of this key motif.

1. Hos 13:14-15

14 Shall I deliver them from the power of Sheol?
Shall I save them from Death?
Where[a] are your Plagues, O Death?
Where[a] is your Pestilence, O Sheol?
Pity is hidden from my eyes.
15 Though he prospers (*prʾ*) among the grasses,
the East Wind (*qdym*) will come, Yahweh's wind,
rising from the desert.

It will dry up his spring;[b]
desiccate his fountain.[c]
It will loot his land[d]
of every precious thing.

a) Rd *ʾyh* with LXX. b) Rd *wĕyôbîš*. c) Rd *wĕyaḥărîb*. d) Perhaps rd *ʾrṣw* with LXX for the sake of the imagery pattern.

The verses cited appear in the probable unit 13:12-14:1[1] where the Lord is the speaker and announces the destruction of Ephraim at the hands of Assyria. The imagery of vv 14-15 presents the Lord as the supreme military commander dispatching his forces, the Assyrians. This imagery, perhaps, makes Sheol/Death the Assyrian commander; Plagues, Pestilence and the East Wind the Assyrian army. But it is probably pushing too hard to insist on such detailed correspondences. Ephraim is presented as a flock of sheep prospering (*prʾ*)[2] on the grasses of the winter rainy season. But the East Wind (*qdym*), in this case rather clearly a spring sirocco, the Lord's wind (*rwḥ Yhwh*), will come from the eastern desert (*mdbr*). It will dry up and desiccate (*ybš*, *ḥrb*) the springs and fountains (*mqwr*, *mʿyn*). It is understood that the same wind withers the grasses of the rainy season on which the flock had prospered; and both the vegetation and the waters of the springs and fountains are referred to when the text speaks of the East Wind looting[3] the land of everything precious to the flock.

Plagues and Pestilence also belong to the total picture because, as was indicated in Part I, a high incidence of diseases (malaria, dysentery, fever, etc.) is typical of periods of prolonged sirocco when men weakened by the excessive heat and low humidity were more subject to them. Whether the poet here is thinking of plagues and pestilence as affecting principally men or animals is not clear, though the former situation seems more probable.

The rainless summer is in any case a difficult period for flocks in Palestine. Modern Palestinian shepherds can milk their flocks twice a

[1] H. W. Wolff, *Dodekapropheton 1, Hosea* (BKAT 14/1; Neukirchen-Vluyn: Neukirchener Verlag, 1961) 289-90.

[2] The play on *ʾprym* (v 12) is intended. Only here does normal *prh* appear as *prʾ*; and the form is perhaps an attempt to call attention to the connection.

[3] The use of *šsh* here personifies *qdym*. Verbal forms of *šsh*/*šss* invariably have personal subjects.

day in winter and by the middle of August only once every three days.[4] The sparse grazing offered by the withered vegetation of the countryside does not offer enough food. In this particular case we are probably to think of something beyond the ordinary sirocco, a super-sirocco which besides withering the grasses dries up more or less completely the water sources without which the flock cannot survive the summer.

This imagery that compares the attack and the results of the attack of an invading army to the coming of a sirocco will be met with again in what follows. The imagery is particularly appropriate from several points of view. Both arrive on the scene with the close of the rainy season. The army does this because it must avoid the difficulties of overland travel during the rainy season[5] and at the same time must be sure of an adequate water supply on the march and be in a position to renew its food supply from the ripening or recently harvested grain when it arrives at its destination.[6] In addition, the withering effect of the sirocco upon the countryside, previously green with life from the winter rains, suggested the lifeless ruins of destroyed cities, the product of the army's work.

The text may or may not have clear and demonstrable connections with some nature myth—though it probably has, and it would be easy to hear in the text echoes of the presentation of Mot in the Baal cycle from Ugarit. At the same time it would be possible to insist that the treatment of Death/Sheol and the East Wind as persons involves simply poetic personification, and that the presentation of the effects of the Assyrian army on the Northern Kingdom as the effects of the sirocco involved simply poetic imagery. These matters are not of immediate concern here. What is of concern is the presence of the motifs, the drying up of bodies of water connected with the vocabulary *ḥrb/ybš* and disease in a clear sirocco (*qdym*) context. Both motifs are typical of descriptions of siroccos and do not occur in rainstorm contexts (Part VII, Studies 1 and 2).[7]

[4] G. Dalman, *Arbeit und Sitte in Palästina* I (Gütersloh: Evangelischer Verlag, 1928) 519-20; VI (1939) 291.

[5] For the difficulties involved in winter travel in Palestine see ibid., I, 190-91.

[6] R. de Vaux, *Ancient Israel* (New York: McGraw-Hill, 1961) 251; 2 Sam 11:1 (= 1 Chr 20:1).

[7] Though not of immediate import in the discussion, it is worth noting for future reference that the invitation to repentance (14:2-9) that immediately follows on 13:12-14:1

It has just been said that it is not necessary to see in Hos 13:14-15 any connection with nature myth. The Lord simply sends the east wind which is a figure for the Assyrian army. In the next four texts, all of which involve the east wind drying up bodies of water, the connection with nature myth is clear. In all of them Yahweh is presented as appearing in a sirocco and the storm (rather clearly in Nah 1:2-8; Isa 50:2-3; Jer 51:34-45; implicitly in Isa 19:1-7) issues from his mouth and nose. In only one of the texts is there the slightest hint that any human army is involved when the Lord goes to the attack.

2. Nah 1:2-8

ʾ 2 A jealous and avenging God is Yahweh;
an avenger is Yahweh and full of wrath (*bʿl ḥmh*).
Yahweh takes revenge on his enemies;
angry is he at his adversaries.
3 Yahweh is slow to anger but great in power
Yahweh never neglects to punish.

*

B In storm (*swph*) and tempest (*śʿrh*) was his way;
clouds (*ʿnn*) were the dust (*ʾbq*) at his feet.
G 4 He roared (*gʿr*) at the sea and dried (*ybš*) it up;
all the rivers he desiccated (*ḥrb*).
[D] Bashan and Carmel withered (*ʾml*);[a]
the bloom of Lebanon withered (*ʾml*).
H 5 Mountains were shaken by him;
the hills tottered.
W The earth cried out[b] before him—
the world and all its inhabitants.
Z 6 Before his roar (*zʿm*) who can stand?[c]
Who can stand up to the heat of his nose (*ḥrwn ʾp*)?

---

and closes out the book is also presented in terms of agricultural imagery. If Israel repents the Lord will be his dew; he will blossom like the lily; he will be like the evergreen cedar of Lebanon and olive; he will raise grain; etc. All that presumes a regular supply of winter rain and summer dew.

This contrast between the Lord as supplying the beneficent precipitation and sending the destructive sirocco is one that will be met frequently in what follows.

Ḥ His heat (*ḥmh*) was poured out like fire;
cliffs were shattered before him.

*

Ṭ 7 Good is Yahweh as a refuge
on the day of trouble.
Y He takes care of[d] those who trust in him
8 in the passing storm.
K He will make an end of his opponents;[e]
his adversaries he will pursue in darkness.

a) Because of the acrostic initial *ʾmll* is impossible; *dʾb* is, perhaps, the best conjecture, though it is otherwise not used of vegetation. b) *wtśʾ* is short for *wtśʾ qwl* as in Isa 3:7. c) Because of the acrostic rd *zʿmw my yʿmwd lpnyw* or the like. d) Because of the acrostic omit initial *w*. e) Rd *bqmyw* or perhaps better *mqwmh* without the *mappiq* (= adversity).

Nah 1:2-8 is the acrostic piece that introduces the opening section of the book (1:2-2:3).[8] Whether vv 2-8 once existed independently or not is of no concern here. The acrostic runs through only the first half of the alphabet (ʾ-*K*). Each letter of the alphabet introduces one line, save the first which opens with a line headed by *aleph* and is expanded by two additional lines.[9] Rudolph has defended this expansion of the *aleph* line as original on the grounds that this break in the pattern is an attempt to call attention from the very start to the whole point of 1:2-8 (indeed, 1:2-2:3): Yahweh may be slow to punish, but he surely does. This point is made in each of the three lines headed by *aleph*. A further argument for this view will be developed below.

In the total context of 1:2-2:3 the whole of 2-8 is aimed at solving the problem implicit in v 9:

What second thoughts[10] are you having about Yahweh?
He it is who makes an end.

[8] So, e.g., W. Rudolph, *Micha-Nahum-Habakuk-Zephanja* (KAT 13/3; Gütersloh: Gerd Mohn, 1975) 144.

[9] Ibid., 154.

[10] The translation is an attempt to render the apparent repetitive sense of the Pi. here. Cf. Ps 73:16 and E. Jenni's (*Das hebräische Piʿel* [Zürich: EVZ, 1968] 228) definition of the sense there: "Hin-und-Her-Überlegen und Nachsinnen."

That is to say, the people of Judah have no reason to doubt that the Lord will punish Assyria. He may be slow about it, but he has the power to destroy his enemies and most certainly will do so.

Vv 2-8 are readily divided into three sense paragraphs. The central piece (*B-Ḥ*) describes a tremendous sirocco or series of such storms in which the Lord appeared. Both nature and human beings were affected. All the finite tenses here are either perfects or *waw*-consecutive imperfects and the time reference is rather clearly to the past. The only exceptions are the generalizing imperfects in the rhetorical questions of the *Z* line which enunciate truths valid for all time.[11] Whether the reference is to one past sirocco theophany or to a whole series is not clear.

The opening three lines headed by *aleph* are a simple affirmation that the Lord does punish and that he has the power to do so. The one finite tense in these lines is *ynqh* (3) and in the context that is to be interpreted as oriented primarily toward the future. The whole purpose of the description of the past sirocco(s) in lines *B-Ḥ* is to prove by a description of the Lord's past activity that he still is "great in power" (*gdwl kḥ*, 3a) and still can and will act.

The final three lines (*Ṭ-K*) are an affirmation that when the Lord does act, he will protect his own from the effects of that intervention. This is a motif that will be seen again in what follows.[12] Here once again the orientation is toward the future. The only finite tenses in these lines are *yʿśh* and *ydrp*.

When vv 2-8 are viewed this way, the line-count of the sense "paragraphs" is seen to be 3+7+3. And it is to be noted further that the "paragraphs" are marked off by the occurrence of the word *Yhwh* twice in both the opening and closing line of the first paragraph and in the opening line of the third paragraph.[13] This is a further argument for viewing the two-line expansion after *aleph* as original. At least, if the expansion is secondary, it was made with clear patterns in mind.

With these details out of the way it is possible to turn to the chief point of interest, the isolation of the motifs and vocabulary in the

[11] Joüon, § 113, c. Cf. the rhetorical question in Jer 2:32 which similarly states an eternal truth.

[12] See Hab 3:2 and Joel 3:5 discussed below.

[13] *Yhwh* occurs once more in the second line of the first sense paragraph. It does not occur anywhere else in vv 2-8.

description of the storm in lines *B-Ḥ* that do not occur in descriptions of rainstorms and are characteristic of descriptions of siroccos. In the latter case it is impossible to guarantee that in every instance the appearance of the motif or vocabulary in isolation conclusively indicates that the storm involved is a sirocco. Other types of storms occur in Palestine, though the common ones are the rainstorm and the sirocco.[14] What it is necessary to do is look for the motifs and vocabulary in combinations that point infallibly in the direction of the sirocco. In the course of the discussion motifs and vocabulary that can occur in both rainstorms and siroccos are generally given little attention, unless there is a special reason for treating them. For instance, the motif of mountains being shaken by the wind (*rʿš*, v 5)[15] and the motif of the Lord roaring (*gʿr*, v 4)[16] appear in both types of storm and so are not of particular interest for this study.

The text has immediate connections with Hos 13: 14-15. Line G speaks of the drying up of the sea and its rivers (*ym*, *nhrwt*), and though the bodies of water have changed (*mqwr*, *mʿyn*, Hos 13:15), the same characteristic vocabulary (*ybš*, *ḥrb*) appears and there can be no doubt in the total context that it is the same east wind (*qdym*), that dried up the *mqwr* and *mʿyn* of Hos 13:15, that dries up *ym* and *nhrwt* here.[17]

[14] Cf. the very violent, dry and *cold* east wind of Nov. 21 and 22, 1958 described by Y. Levy-Tokatly, "Easterly Storms – November 1958," *IEJ* 10 (1960) 112-17; and the violent whirlwinds coming from the west and only partly associated with rain described by D. Nir, "Whirlwinds in Israel in the Winters 1954/55 and 1955/56," *IEJ* 7 (1957) 109-17. Storms like these are rather the exception than the rule, as is stressed by both authors. The two common storms are the sirocco and the rainstorm. This is clear from the space devoted to them by all treatments of Palestinian meteorology. If it can be shown that the storm being described is not a rainstorm, then the probabilities are the storm is a sirocco.

[15] Contrast Nah 1:5 with Ps 77:19 where the earth shakes (*rgz*) and quakes (*rʿš*) in a clear rainstorm. See p. 69.

[16] Contrast Nah 1:4 with Ps 18:16 (= 2 Sam 22:16) where the foundations of the earth are revealed at Yahweh's roar (*gʿrh*) in a tremendous rainstorm (‖ *nšmt rwḥ ʾpk*).

[17] There is a clear difference, of course. Unlike the situation presumed in Hos 13:14-15, the drying up of the sea goes beyond the possibilities of any sirocco ever experienced in Palestine. The same exaggeration is found in some of the other motifs met here. For example, no sirocco ever really shook mountains (v 5). But these exaggerations are developed out of the nature of the storm, and this development of an ordinary sirocco into a super-sirocco fits the interpretation of the storm as theophany.

In addition, the storm is designated as a *swph* and *śʿrh* (v 3). Both nouns are frequently used to designate the sirocco, but never the rainstorm (Part VII, Studies 3 and 4). The noun *ʿnn* (3), while it frequently can denote the cloud of dust raised by the sirocco, is apparently never used of a rain cloud (Study 5). Similarly flying dust (*ʾbq*, 3) is frequently met in descriptions of a sirocco; never, in a rainstorm (Study 6). V 4 speaks of the vegetation of Bashan, Carmel and Lebanon withering. The whole idea is repugnant to a rainstorm, fits easily into a sirocco context and both the motif and typical vocabulary (*ʾml* and its cognate *ʾbl*) consistently occur in this context; never in a rainstorm context (Study 7).

V 6 contains three synonyms for the Lord's "anger" as he appears in the sirocco: *zʿm*, *ḥrwn ʾp*, and *ḥmh*. The first with one possible exception and the second are used only of divine "anger"; the third, though mostly used of divine anger, can be used of human anger as well. All three frequently appear in clear sirocco contexts and are not characteristic of descriptions of a rainstorm (Studies 8, 9 and 10).

It will be argued in the Studies just referred to that all three expressions for "anger" possibly originated in the presentation of Yahweh (or ultimately some other god) as a fire-breathing being from whose mouth, and nostrils issues the sirocco. Such a presentation would clearly have its origin in nature myth. That, at least, explains the way in which the expressions tend to be limited to denoting Yahweh's anger (particularly *ḥrwn ʾp* and *zʿm*) and to be connected with siroccos. A more probable case can be made for the concrete interpretation of all three in some sirocco contexts: *zʿm* = the *roaring* sirocco; *ḥrwn ʾp* = the *hot* sirocco issuing from the Lord's nose; *ḥmh* = the *hot* sirocco. That could well be the case here:

Z 6 Before his roar (*zʿm*) who can stand (*ʿmd*)?
Who can stand up to (*qwm*) the heat of his nose
(*ḥrwn ʾp*)?
H His heat (*ḥmh*) was poured out like fire;
cliffs were shattered before him.

In the second line especially a concrete meaning for *ḥmh* is strongly suggested. It is presumably the *ḥmh* that is poured out (*ntk*) in the first colon that shatters (*nts̩*) the cliffs in the second colon.[18] Viewed in this light, the Z line could easily be understood as a reference to the sirocco blowing people away. This motif will be seen again in what follows.[19]

It is difficult to say whether this argues for a similar interpretation for *ḥmh* in *bʿl ḥmh* of v 2. The computer-like "feel" for language needed to make decisions like this can only come from having "lived" the language, not from a concordance. This is something no modern can have. The problem here is the great difficulty the modern reader has in distinguishing in a given case between the origin of a specific use of language or a use in a particular context and what overtones of this are to be heard in other texts. It is rare, indeed, that anyone hears in current English a reference to the moon in the noun "lunatic" or a reference to a muzzle-loading rifle in the now colloquial phrase "to shoot one's wad." The key is the context which will not always be sufficient. If, for example, the context has someone "shooting his wad and throwing away his rifle," it is clear that the language by exception is intended in its original sense. In the Z line we have a similar immediate context for *ḥmh*. The concrete effect of the *ḥmh* argues for a concrete understanding of *ḥmh*. Whether *bʿl ḥmh* in v 2 is to be interpreted out of the total context of vv 2-8 is less clear, though it probably is. By contrast, in Prov 15:1 *ḥmh* clearly denotes the abstract "anger." Similar problems will be met in what follows. Every attempt must be made to avoid the pitfalls involved by a careful control of the immediate context.

Behind this analysis of the language and motifs of theophany in Nah 1:2-8, which explains even minor details in terms of a verifiable meteorological phenomenon, the sirocco, lies a basic assumption and its implications ought to be spelled out from the first on the basis of this

[18] For the same verb (*nts̩*) used of cities being knocked over by the east wind in a sirocco context see Jer 4:26 which will be studied below.

[19] The *Ṭ-K* lines contain two other probable references to the sirocco. This makes the past sirocco(s) described in the *B-Ḥ* lines the model for the future sirocco in which the Lord will destroy the Assyrians. The future "day of trouble" is the day of the "passing storm (= sirocco)" (*šṭp ʿbr*) when the Lord will protect his own. The darkness: (*ḥšk*) in which the Lord pursues his enemies is the darkness caused by the dust blotting out the sun or the moon. This latter motif will be met frequently in what follows. The interpretation of *šṭp ʿbr* as "the passing storm (= sirocco)" is more problematic. The connections of nominal and verbal *šṭp* are much more clearly to flowing water and in no way are they typical sirocco vocabulary. If the interpretation of *šṭp* as the sirocco here is correct, it is an instance of vocabulary originally used of liquids being applied to the wind. Cf. *ntk* in v 6 and the use of *špk* in Joel 3:1.

example. The assumption is that the language and motifs of storm theophany are ultimately based on a mythology that is rooted in Palestinian or Syro-Palestinian geography and that the language and motifs have *generally* remained sufficiently close to actual meteorology to be patient of rational analysis on that basis.[20] This approach to the analysis of nature theophany is the one generally favored by the geographers. Dalman,[21] for instance, simply writes of Nah 1:2-8: "Nahum's description of the angry God (1, 3f.) . . . is developed on the basis of the east wind."

Rudolph's[22] approach is much more commonly employed by exegetes. He recognizes that the Lord's coming is accompanied by phenomena ultimately derived from nature. But the combination is not natural; rather it is quite arbitrary, the product of poetic imagination. Thus, the withering of the vegetation in the *D* line is the result of the sirocco; the shaking of the mountains is the *H* line is the result of an earthquake and the noise of the earth splitting in that earthquake is the cry of the earth in the *W* line; the *Ḥ* line presents the image of lava flowing forth from bursting rocks. Historical Palestine has known both the sirocco and the much less common[23] earthquake. But they are

[20] This is not true of *all* theophanies. The presentation of the theophany in Exod 19, for example, though it contains in part meteorological vocabulary, is in no way a recognizable meteorological situation like those being dealt with and to be dealt with in what follows. This is even true on the vocabulary level where it combines thunder and lightning with an *ʿnn kbd*. Hebrew *ʿnn* is not a rain cloud (Study 5). I share G. Dalman's (*Arbeit und Sitte* I, 216) view of this theophany: "Es handelt sich für die Erzähler weder um einen Vulkanausbruch noch um ein starkes Gewitter, das die Israeliten am Sinai erlebt hätten, sondern um eine Erscheinung des überweltlichen Gottes." There is a world of difference between that analysis by a geographer who makes it a practice to interpret theophanies on the basis of nature and the view of A. Weiser ("Zur Frage nach den Beziehungen der Psalmen zum Kult: Die Darstellung der Theophanie in den Psalmen und im Festkult," *Festschrift Alfred Bertholet* [ed. W. Baumgartner et al.; Tübingen: Mohr, 1950] 515): "Es ist allgemein zugestanden . . . dass die Theophaniedarstellungen traditionsgeschichtlich gesehen auf die Sinaitheophanie als ihr Urbild zurückgehen." See further p. 140 n. 6.

[21] Dalman, *Arbeit und Sitte* I, 108.

[22] Rudolph, *Nahum*, 155-56.

[23] Baly, *The Geography of the Bible* (New York: Harper, 1957) 22: "Serious earthquakes occur about once every fifty years in Palestine, though minor earth tremors are very much more frequent." For a detailed discussion see D. H. Kallner-Amiran, "A Revised Earthquake-Catalogue of Palestine," *IEJ* 1 (1950-51) 223-46; 2 (1952) 48-65.

not tied together as geographical phenomena. If they are mentioned together in Nah 1:2-8, this is due to the imagination of the poet or his source. Historical Palestine never knew an active volcano.[24] If we have volcano imagery here, that has to be borrowed from somewhere else and it is necessary to look for sources. If Rudolph is right, it is clearly going to be more difficult to rationalize the imagery in these theophanies. The geography of Palestine as observed and described by modern geographers is no reliable measuring rod with which to interpret them.

It is impossible, of course, to prove apodictically that Rudolph's approach to Nah 1:2-8 is wrong. But there are certain indications that make the Dalman approach very attractive, even more probable. In the first place it has the advantage of simplicity. Secondly, it presumes a knowledge of and respect for meteorological phenomena that might well be expected from a community whose economy was agriculturally based and who lacked the technology to resolve the problems weather's caprice might cause. Thirdly, it is quite remarkable the way almost any piece of vocabulary or motif that is described in this study as typical of the sirocco immediately evokes in the same context other vocabulary and motifs typical of the sirocco. In this regard the notes in the Studies of Part VII, "already discussed in Study x, y or z" or "already discussed in Part II, etc." are of utmost importance. The rigidity with which these motifs and this vocabulary group themselves[25] and resist rainstorm contexts calls for an explanation. That Palestinian meteorology is the controlling factor here suggests itself. This, at least, readily explains, for example, why the sea never dries up and the vegetation never withers in any rainstorm context; and why thunder and lightning are never mentioned in a context where *qš* is being driven before the wind.

Finally, there are those texts where the sirocco is played off against the rainstorm, at times in a context where the season of the year is indicated, and it is precisely a season in which these storms alternate.[26] In such texts there is little difficulty in recognizing the rainstorm and its characteristics and in interpreting them on the basis of normal

[24] F.-M. Abel, *Géographie de la Palestine* I (Paris: Gabalda, 1933) 46-50; G. Dalman, *Arbeit und Sitte* I, 216; L. Picard, "Lithological Map," *Atlas of Israel* (ed. D. H. K. Amiran et al.; Jerusalem: Ministry of Labour/Amsterdam: Elsevier, 1970) no. III, 4.

[25] The same is true when it is a question of rainstorms, though that is not the concern here.

[26] These texts will be studied in Parts V and VI. Others will be added in the Studies of Part VII.

meteorology. This is a strong argument in favor of attempting to understand the descriptions of the sirocco in the same context in terms of normal meteorology. The point to be made is that in these combined sirocco-rainstorm texts the sirocco descriptions contain precisely the same vocabulary and motifs as the descriptions of the sirocco in texts like Nah 1:2-8. That would seem to be an indication that the Dalman approach to Nah 1:2-8 is justified; or at least that it ought to be tested in a systematic way. If in the course of this testing numerous texts become clearer and genuine problems are resolved without causing new ones, that is the ultimate proof needed that Dalman is right.

What has been just said is, of course, for the most part theoretical and hypothetical. Whether this meteorological approach to this type of text is valid can only be decided after a careful review of the pertinent texts. But before returning to that review one other implication, important for the history of Syro-Palestinian religion and religious language, of the analysis of Nah 1:2-8 just presented ought also to be pointed out from the start and kept in mind during the review of similar sirocco passages that follows. The number of exegetes is not small, who presume that theophanies like Nah 1:2-8 (especially where there is reference to the effects of a storm on the sea) are simply reflexes of the theophany of the Baal-Hadad type. But all that is known of Baal relates him so inextricably to the rainstorm, that this connection almost has to be wrong. There is a clear distinction between the meteorology that leads to Yahweh sitting enthroned on subdued *Mabbûl* after a tremendous rainstorm in Ps 29:10 and the meteorology that presents the Lord drying up the sea and rivers in Nah 1:4. Presumably there is a different mythology/theology too. See the discussion of Exod 15:1-18 in Part IV.

3. Isa 19:1, 5-7

1 Behold Yahweh rides (*rkb*) on a swift cloud (*ʿb*),
advancing toward Egypt.

. . . .

5 The waters will evaporate (*nšt*) from the sea;[27]
the river will be desiccated (*ḥrb*) and dry up (*ybš*).

[27] *Ym* here is probably to be understood as the Nile. Cf. the parallelism and see A. Schwarzenbach, *Die geographische Terminologie im Hebräischen des Alten Testamentes* (Leiden: Brill, 1954) 69; and n. 36 below.

6 The streams will stink;[a]
the canals of Egypt will dwindle (*dll*) and be
desiccated (*ḥrb*).
The reeds and rushes will wither (*qml*) –
7 the bulrushes[b] along the edge of the Nile.
All the sown land of the Nile
will dry up (*ybš*), be blown away (*ndp*) and be no more.

a) Probably rd *hznyḥw*, 1QIsa[a]. b) Omit *ʿl yʾwr*, ditto.

The text presents us with a familiar picture. Bodies of water, this time the Nile, its streams and canals, are dried up (*ḥrb*, *ybš*; to which are added *nšt* and *dll*). The reeds along the Nile wither; the agricultural land is dried out (*ybš*) and blown away (*ndp*). The probable motif of fish dying and here stinking (see vv 6, 8a) as a result of the drying up of the waters is met for the first time. It occurs in other sirocco contexts; never, in a rainstorm (Part VII, Study 13).

The motif of the Lord coming in a chariot or a cloud viewed as such is met in both sirocco and rainstorm contexts (Study 14). In the present text the cloud (*ʿb*) of v 1 would at first glance seem to be the dust cloud raised by the sirocco. There are problems with that. While *ʿnn* is not a rain cloud and is typically the dust cloud (Study 5),[28] *ʿb* is typically the rain cloud[29] and its usage here to denote "dust cloud" is without parallel. It can, however, be disassociated from rain (Isa 18:4[30]) and it would be possible to argue for an exceptional usage here. But there is more against that view. The presentation of the Lord as mounted on a cloud chariot that uses verbal forms of *rkb*[31] is typical of rainstorm contexts and unparalleled in sirocco contexts (Study 14). Certainty is impossible, of course, but it is more probable that the text describes a combined rainstorm (v 1) and sirocco (vv 5-7) theophany of the type to be discussed in Parts V and VI. See the further discussion in Study 14.

It may be possible to assign this sirocco to a definite time period. In v 4 the Lord says he will put Egypt in the control of a cruel master.

[28] R. B. Y. Scott, "Meteorological Phenomena and Terminology in the Old Testament," *ZAW* 64 (1952) 24.

[29] Ibid., 25.

[30] Dalman, *Arbeit und Sitte* I, 311.

[31] Cf. the discussion of W. L. Moran, "Some Remarks on the Song of Moses," *Bib* 43 (1962) 323-24.

Though the text makes no further mention of the cruel master and everything that happens to Egypt is otherwise directly attributed to Yahweh, the cruel master is probably to be understood as the commander of an invading army.[32] The fact that such invasions generally took place in the spring and the fact that precisely April-May is the most dangerous sirocco period in Egypt[33] suggest a spring setting as in Hos 13:14-15.[34]

4. Isa 50:2-3

2b Is my hand too short to ransom[a]?
Don't I have the power to rescue?
Behold by my roar (*gʿrh*) I dry up (*ḥrb*) the sea;
I turn rivers into desert (*mdbr*).
Their fish stink (*bʾš*) for lack of water;
they die of thirst.
3 I clothe the heavens with darkness;
I make sack their covering.

a) Rd *mippĕdôt.*

The *gʿrh* with which the Lord dries up (*ḥrb*) the sea is probably here to be thought of concretely (= the *roaring* sirocco). The motif of the dying and stinking fish is identical with that just seen in Isa 19:6 (Part

[32] O. Kaiser, *Isaiah 13-39* (London: SCM, 1974) 101.

[33] Dalman, *Arbeit und Sitte* I, 320-21; F. W. Oliver, "Dust-Storms in Egypt and their Relation to the War Period, as Noted in Maryut, 1939-45," *The Geographical Journal* 106 (1945) 27-28.

[34] It is interesting to note the awareness this text betrays of the Egyptian economy and the geographical circumstances on which that economy depended. The Egyptian economy was based on the flooding of the Nile and irrigation (Deut 11:10; the Aton Hymn, *ANET*, 371, also betrays an awareness of the different sources of water for agriculture in Syria-Palestine and Egypt). Those who mourn the drying up of the Nile are the fishermen and those engaged in the manufacture of linen (vv 8-10). For obvious reasons fish were a much more important element in the Egyptian economy than in the Palestinian (*Lexikon der Ägyptologie* II, 224-28). Egypt was the country of flax in the ancient Near East. Flax grown for the manufacture of linen was a rarity in Palestine until Roman times because water was not available in sufficient quantity (S. Talmon, "The Gezer Calendar and the Seasonal Cycle of Ancient Canaan," *JAOS* 83 [1963] 179-82 and the literature cited there). In Palestine the lament would be for the loss of grain, wine, oil and grass for the flocks (Deut 11:14-15).

VII, Study 13). The motif of rivers or agricultural land being turned into a desert (*mdbr* or the like) is common in sirocco contexts; it never occurs in a rainstorm context (Study 15). The heavens can be darkened in a rainstorm, but they are also darkened by the dust of the sirocco and the motif is frequently met in this context (Study 16).

5. Jer 51:34-37, 42-45

34 "He has consumed me,[a] slurped me down[a], the king of Babylon[b];
he has left me[a] an empty vessel.
He swallowed me up[a] like the dragon (*tnyn*);
he filled his belly with my delights[c] and cast me aside.[d]
35 My torn flesh upon Babylon,"
says queen Zion.
"My blood upon the inhabitants of Chaldea,"
says Jerusalem.
36 So this is what Yahweh says:
"I will surely defend your cause;
I will take revenge for you.
I will dry up (*ḥrb*) her sea;
I will desiccate (*ybš*) her fountain.
37 Babylon will be heaps of rubble (*glym*),
a dwelling place for jackals (*tnym*),
A desert (*šmh*) to be whistled at
without an inhabitant.
. . . .
42 Though the sea go up over her,
and she be covered with its roaring waves (*glym*),
43 Her cities will become a desert (*šmh*),
a parched land (*ʾrṣ ṣyh*), a steppe land (*ʿrbh*).
No[e] one will dwell in them;
no man will pass through them.
44 I will punish Bel in Babylon;
I will make him disgorge what he swallowed (*blʿ*);
never again will there stream (*nhr*) to him nation.
Even the wall of Babylon falls—
45 depart from her, my people!
Save yourselves one and all
from the heat of the nose (*ḥrwn ʾp*) of the Lord!"

a) Rd Q. b) Omit *nbwkdr*ʾ*ṣr*; see below. c) Rd *maʿădannāy*. d) Rd *hiddîḥānî*. e) Omit ʾ*rṣ* with LXX.

The verses cited occur in the collection of oracles announcing the fall of Babylon contained in Jer 50:1-51:58. Within this larger grouping vv 34-45 belong together. In vv 34-35 the speaker cites Jerusalem's complaint and her curse directed at Babylon; in vv 36-45 he cites the Lord's answer. At first the Lord addresses Jerusalem directly (*rybk*, *nqmtk*, 36). Only with v 45 does he address the exiles in Babylon. The relation between the two quotations is emphasized by setting the identification of the speaker in vv 34-35 at the end of the first quotation (*t*ʾ*mr yšbt ṣywn*, *t*ʾ*mr yrwšlm*, v 35) where it immediately contrasts with *lkn kh* ʾ*mr Yhwh* (v 36), which introduces the second quotation of vv 36-45. That the second quotation continues through v 45 is indicated by the relation between vv 34 and 45. In v 34 Jerusalem accuses the king of Babylon, Bel, of having consumed her, slurped her down, swallowed her up (*bl*ʿ), and filled his belly with her delights like the dragon (*tnyn*). Actually in the figure it is not Jerusalem who has been eaten, but her sons and daughters. Jerusalem is still around to complain and this is the clear sense of the simile that presents Jerusalem as an empty vessel (*kly ryq*, v 34). In v 44 the Lord says he will make Bel disgorge what he has swallowed (*bela*ʿ; note how this picks up *bl*ʿ*ny* of v 34). The MT, which is reflected by the versions, of course, identifies the king of Babylon as Nebuchadnezzar (*nbwkdr*ʾ*ṣr mlk bbl*, v 34), but "Nebuchadnezzar" makes the opening colon too long, spoils the logic of the piece, and seems to be an incorrect interpretation.[35]

In announcing the destruction of Babylon the Lord says he will dry up (*ḥrb*) and desiccate (*ybš*) Babylon's *ym* and *mqwr* (v 36). The *ym* here is the Euphrates[36] upon which the existence of the city depended. The parallelism would indicate that *mqwr* is to be similarly understood. The vocabulary and the motif immediately make the connection

[35] It is characteristic of the form of the text of Jer represented by the MT as contrasted with the LXX version and its Hebrew *Vorlage* as represented by 4QJer[b] to fill in *nbwkdr*ʾ*ṣr* before *mlk bbl*. This same tendency toward expansion is already in evidence in the stage of the text represented by the LXX. See J. G. Janzen, *Studies in the Text of Jeremiah* (HSM 6; Cambridge: Harvard, 1973) 70 and 131-34.

[36] See Isa 19:5 which was just discussed. All of the texts where *ym* denotes a river (Isa 19:5; Jer 51:36; Ezek 32:2; Nah 3:8?; Job 41:23) have clear connections with myth. It may be that the equation *ym* = "river" was forged because the myth (more probably myths) originally concerned the sea or a sea monster.

with the sirocco passages already examined. A good deal of the imagery that follows is also explainable on this basis.

The wall of the city will be knocked over by the force of the storm (v 44). Babylon will become heaps of rubble (*glym*, v 37). The contrast with the protecting (see below) waves (*glym*, v 42) that cover Babylon is probably intended. The once prosperous city, now waterless, will become a desert (*šmh*, vv 37, 41, 43; *ʾrṣ ṣyh*, v 43; *ʿrbh*, v 43).[37] The motif is common in sirocco contexts; it does not occur in rainstorm contexts (Part VII, Study 15). No human being will be able to dwell there (*mʾyn ywšb*, v 37; *lʾ yšb bhn kl ʾyš*, v 43). It will be only a lair for jackals (*mʿwn tnym*, v 37). The contrast with the simile that compared Bel to the dragon (*tnyn*, v 34) is probably intended. Bel swallowed Jerusalem like *tnyn*. But the monster Bel will end up dead in a desert inhabited by *tnym* (v 37; see below). This motif with the added mention of other desert beasts and demons (cf. English "ghost town") frequently occurs in sirocco contexts; it is never associated with rainstorm contexts (Study 15).

Because of the lack of water and the presence of the beasts and demons no man will ever pass through Babylonia (v 43). If someone were to pass through, he would have to use apotropaic whistling to prevent the fate that befell Babylonia from befalling him. Babylon will be a desert to be whistled at (*šmh wšrqh*, v 37).[38] The scorching sirocco will make the Babylonians thirsty (*bḥmm*, v 39) and the Lord will give them an intoxicating drink that will kill them. Against the background of this general picture the *ḥrwn ʾp Yhwh* of v 45 from which the exiles are told to flee is conceivably to be interpreted concretely: the heat of

[37] The full force of this disaster easily escapes the modern reader. The desert for the OT farmer was the negation of civilization that made life possible and worth living. See S. Talmon, "The 'Desert Motif' in the Bible and in Qumran Literature," *Biblical Motifs* (ed. A. Altmann; Cambridge: Harvard, 1966) 31-63 and the literature cited there.

[38] See H. Wildberger's (*Jesaja* [BKAT 10/1-3; Neukirchen-Vluyn: Neukirchener Verlag, 1965-] 522-24) commentary on the similar Isa 13:20-22 and the literature cited there. For East-Semitic parallels see *CAD*, Z, 58-60, s.v. *zaqīqu*, and especially the discussion at the end. The sense of the whistling is indicated by 1 Kgs 9:6-8 (= 2 Chr 7:19-21). There is no question there of malicious pleasure or mourning. Those passing by are scared stiff. Cf. further Jer 18:16; 19:8; 49:17; 50:13. See L. Köhler's treatment of *šĕrēqâ* in "Zum hebräischen Wörterbuch des Alten Testamentes," *Studien zur semitischen Philologie und Religionsgeschichte, Festschrift Julius Wellhausen* (BZAW 27; ed. K. Marti; Giessen: Töpelmann, 1914) 254; and H. Jahnow, *Das hebräische Leichenlied* (BZAW 36; Giessen: Töpelmann, 1923) 44.

the nose of Yahweh. The phrase is characteristic of sirocco contexts and never occurs in a rainstorm (Study 9).

The interpretation given to vv 42-43 in the translation above (on p. 38) is quite unusual:

42 *ʿlh ʿl bbl hym*
bhmwn glyw nksth
43 *hyw ʿryh lšmh*
ʾrṣ ṣyh wʿrbh
Though the sea go up over her,
and she be covered with its roaring waves,
Her cities will become a desert,
a parched land, a steppe land.

Generally v 42 is understood as describing the sea, i.e. the Euphrates, washing away lady Babylon's cities, Babylon itself included. This, of course, would introduce another nature force into the imagery pattern.[39] But that makes the connection with v 43 awkward. How can a flooding Euphrates be thought of as turning Babylonia into a *šmh*, an *ʾrṣ ṣyh*, an *ʿrbh*? And the text does seem to indicate that the effect is immediate. For this reason it seems best to understand v 42 as containing two concessive clauses which set the circumstances in which the action described in v 43 takes place.[40]

This understanding of v 42 gives a completely rational picture of the fate of Babylonia, Babylon and the monster Bel in vv 12-45. Though Babylon is protected on all sides and in part covered by the waters of the Euphrates (see below) (v 42), the Lord's sirocco will come, dry up the Euphrates and turn Babylon and all of Babylonia into an uninhabited desert (v 43). The Lord will grab hold of the dying monster, Bel, make him disgorge what he has swallowed (first and foremost Jerusa-

[39] Cf. the imagery in Isa 8:7-8; Jer 47:2.

[40] Cf. "Man proposes; God disposes." Among the examples cited by H. Ewald, Ausführliches Lehrbuch der hebräischen Sprache (8th ed.; Göttingen: Dieterich, 1870) § 354, q, Ps 119:51, 61 are exact parallels for the situation in Jer 51:42-43. See also Gen 44:4; 50:20; Jer 50:33-34; Ps 46:7; Ps 118:10-12. Jer 51:55 could well serve as the needed commentary on 51:42-43:

For the Lord will lay waste Babylon,
and still her loud cry,
Though her waves (rd *glyh*) roar like the mighty waters,
and raise their loud din.

lem's sons and daughters mentioned in v 34). No longer will the nations stream (v 44, *nhr*; the verb is particularly appropriate) to him, because the Euphrates is no more and Bel is dead.

The text clearly reflects an awareness of the significance of the Euphrates for the life of Babylonia. In other ways too it seems to reflect first-hand knowledge of the city. The Babylon of Nebuchadnezzar II, both the old city on the east bank and the new city on the west bank, was surrounded by a moat made up of canals flowing from the Euphrates which ran between both cities. In addition there were canals that ran through the city itself.[41] This situation may be the inspiration for the poet's description of Babylon in v 42 as covered by the protecting waves of the Euphrates. Furthermore, the text shows an awareness of the fact that the dragon was Marduk's animal and along with the spade his symbol.[42] Representations like *ANEP*, 523, could easily be the source for the presentation of Bel, the dragon, in Jer 51:34-45. There Marduk stands in water (the Euphrates?) that covers his feet. At his side his dragon crouches in the water. The interpretation of the water as the Euphrates could well be a possibility, though not to the exclusion of other interpretations, if, as has been suspected,[43] the image of Marduk in *ANEP*, 523, is modeled on the great statue that stood in the Esagila temple in Babylon right on the east bank of the Euphrates.

What the poet has apparently done is take the mythological material familiar from the OT which presents the Lord as drying up the sea or killing a dragon in it; and on the basis of the fact that Marduk's symbol was the dragon, used that material to describe what the Lord intends to do to Babylon. What precisely the poet meant by using this mythology, how exactly he understood it, what he really expected to happen, it is not possible to say on the basis of this text alone. The same problem must be faced in the clearly myth-based presentations already looked at in Nah 1:2-8; Isa 19:1, 5-7; and Isa 50:2-3 where what the Lord is expected to do to Assyria, Egypt and Babylon is presented

[41] See the map (Tafel 57) in E. Unger, *Babylon* (reprint of 2nd ed., 1931; Berlin: de Gruyter, 1970) after p. 382; and pp. 93-107; or F. M. Th. Böhl, "Babylon, de heilige Stad," *JEOL* 3 (1944-48) 499.

[42] See *WdM*, 97 and the literature cited there; especially E. D. Van Buren, *Symbols of the Gods in Mesopotamian Art* (AnOr 23; Rome: Pontificium Institutum Biblicum, 1945) 14-20.

[43] Unger, *Babylon*, 209-10.

in a similar way. Attention is simply called to this problem here. It will be faced in the discussion of Lamentations 2, which suggests a solution.[44]

It is also worth noting that the comparison of Marduk to the dragon (*tnyn*, v 34) has been used to connect Yahweh's attack on Marduk with Anat's bringing *tnn* (apparently pronounced *tunnanu/tunnānu*[45]) under control in one way or another as part of Anat's and Baal's difficulties with Yamm at Ugarit. Whether the meteorology of the piece allows this is again problematical. It is further interesting to note that the Lord's problems with *tnyn* are elsewhere presented in terms of the sirocco rather than the rainstorm (Part VII, Study 17).

[44] Pp. 59-65 below.
[45] *Ugaritica* V, 241, 1.8'.

PART III

Siroccos without Direct Mention of Water Sources Drying Up

All the examples of the sirocco looked at to this point have contained a direct mention of the motif of water sources drying up. The motif was important at first for it is an almost infallible indicator of the nature of the storm involved. But enough of the motifs and vocabulary characteristic of these storms as opposed to rainstorms has been isolated to identify the storm even in the absence of this motif.

1. Isa 13:2-22

The poem is an oracle against Babylon that describes the fate of the city that is soon to come. Unlike the last four examples just examined (Nah 1:2-8; Isa 19:1, 5-7; Isa 50:2-3; Jer 51:34-37, 42-45) where there is hardly a hint that a human army is involved, here attention is given to the role of the Medes (vv 14-18) and their allies (vv 2-4). But there is clearly more involved. The effects of the attack go beyond the possibilities of a human army.

The end of the poem, vv 19-22, describes the results of the attack on Babylon. Babylon will become a desert (cf. *šmh*, v 9) like Sodom and Gomorrah (v 19), never to be inhabited (*lnṣḥ*), not even by nomads (v 20). Only the desert beasts and demons will dwell there (vv 21-22).[1]

[1] Unfortunately it is impossible to identify with precision all the animals and demons involved. See H. Wildberger, *Jesaja* (BKAT 10/1-3 Neukirchen-Vluyn: Neukirchener

Whether we are to think of the Euphrates, the one thing that kept Babylon from being a desert land, as being dried up permanently or not is not completely certain. But that is probably implied. It would be the ready explanation for Babylon's never being inhabited again. In any case the motif of land being turned into a desert and the abode of desert beasts and demons belongs to sirocco theophanies (Part VII, Study 15). The comparison of the destruction of Babylon to that of Sodom and Gomorrah has the same pedigree (Study 18).

The attack will also affect nature in other ways. The stars, sun and moon will be blotted out (v 10). The heavens and the earth will quake and shake (v 13) at the *ʿbrh* of the Lord, on the day of his *ḥrwn ʾp*. The latter term, as has already been seen, is typical of sirocco contexts; it never occurs in rainstorm theophanies (Study 9). Once again it is conceivably to be interpreted concretely, "the heat of his nose," i.e. the hot sirocco. The other term, *ʿbrh*, is seen here for the first time. The noun has much the same character as *ḥrwn ʾp* insofar as it appears in sirocco contexts and avoids rainstorm contexts. In some cases at least, and plausibly here, it is to be interpreted concretely, the Lord's "outburst/blast," the sirocco *rushing* forth from his nostrils (Study 19). Thus the *ʿbrh* and the *ḥrwn ʾp* are the sirocco that shakes the mountains and blots out with dust the luminaries in the sky.

In v 9 there is another arguable instance of the concrete sense of *ʿbrh* and *ḥrwn ʾp*:

> Behold the day of Yahweh (*ywm Yhwh*) comes—
> cruel, a blast (*ʿbrh*) and heat of the nose (*ḥrwn ʾp*)—
> To turn their land into a desert (*šmh*),
> and eliminate sinners from it.

The concrete effect on *ʾrṣ* in the second line, which is spelled out in detail in vv 19-22, argues for the concrete sense of *ʿbrh* and *ḥrwn ʾp* here. In this verse as well as in v 6 the day on which the Lord punishes Babylon is called the *ywm Yhwh*. This phrase too identifies the storm. It consistently occurs in sirocco and never in rainstorm contexts (Study 20) and is to be equated here with the *ywm ḥrwn ʾp* of v 13.

In vv 2-4 the speaker reports to his audience a vision in which he

---

Verlag, 1965-) 522-24. For present purposes the *ṣyym*, the inhabitants of *ṣyh*, are most significant.

heard the Lord issuing orders for his army to assemble (2-3), saw and heard the assembling army, and saw the Lord inspecting his troops (4). In v 5 he reports the vision of the Lord setting out:

> There comes from a distant land,
> from the end of the heavens,
> Yahweh and the *kly zʿmw*
> to destroy the land.

Since the common noun *kly* always denotes a thing, it probably cannot refer to the army of vv 2-4.[2] Possibly it refers to the equipment of the army, siege towers etc., or the Lord's sword or the like. But there is another possibility. The noun *zʿm* consistently appears in sirocco contexts, not in rainstorms (Study 8). Sometimes a concrete interpretation, "the *roaring* sirocco," seems called for, and *zʿm* in Nah 1:6 has already been interpreted that way. That would be a possibility here: "Yahweh and his roaring weapons," i.e. the blasts of the sirocco. Thus, v 5b describes only Yahweh who leads the army of vv 2-4 against Babylon. The phrase *kly zʿm* is once more attested in Jer 50:25 where the Lord takes forth from his armory (*ʾwṣr*) his *kly zʿm* because he has work to do in the land of Chaldea. This is in a context where Babylon is being turned into a *šmmh klh* (v 13), a *šmh* (v 23), etc.[3] Here too the *kly zʿmw* could well be the blasts of the sirocco, and the *ʾwṣr*, the armory of the Lord's winds,[4] though it is also clear from the general context that a human army participates in this destruction.

2. Jer 4:5-31

In Isa 13:2-22 the role of the human army in the Lord's attack on Babylon was given prominence. Both the Lord and a human army attack

[2] "He is the *instrument* (*kly*) of my . . . ," while possible in English, is not OT Hebrew idiom – at least, it is unparalleled.

[3] From the complex of oracles against Babylon in Jer 50:1-51:58, Jer 51:34-37, 42-45 has already been dealt with. Actually the whole of the complex is filled with vocabulary and motifs characteristic of the presentation of the Lord coming in a sirocco to destroy his enemies. The only mention of rain in the complex is in Jer 51:15-19 (= Jer 10:12-16). The rainstorm here is not used against Babylon. Its function in the complex will be discussed in conjunction with the combined sirocco-rainstorm description in Jer 10:10-13. See pp. 126-28.

[4] See Deut 28:12; Jer 10:13 (= Jer 51:16); Ps 135:7; Job 38:22.

Babylon. This contrasted with the texts already studied (Nah 1:2-8; Isa 19:1, 5-7; Isa 50:2-3; Jer 51:34-37, 42-45) where the Lord alone attacks his enemies, with only the slightest hint in Isa 19:4 that a human army is involved. There is a difficult situation in Jer 4:5-31. In this piece the Lord sends the Babylonian army and this army is presented as the sirocco. The situation is similar to that in Hos 13:14-15, the first text examined.

Within the larger complex, Jer 4:5-6:30, Jer 4:5-31 is a unit unto itself. It traces an invasion of Judah from the Lord's decision to send the Babylonians (v 6), to the setting out of the army (7), to the devastation of Dan and Ephraim (v 15) and Judah (v 16), to the dying gasp of queen Jerusalem (v 31). The abruptness of some of the transitions probably indicates that the unit is editorial.[5] There are not a few problems in the piece and the problem of address is particularly difficult. These matters cannot be dealt with here. The concern is with the consistent imagery pattern throughout that presents the Babylonian army principally in terms of the sirocco.

The army comes along the traditional invasion route from the north (v 6), behind which possibly there is to be heard an echo of the foe-from-the-north motif. But in vv 11-12 the army is a (veritable) east wind:

> A hot wind (*rwḥ ṣḥ*) on the bare heights in the desert
> right at the daughter[6] of my people—
> Not to winnow, not to cleanse
> does the wind come from there[7] at my command.

The same imagery is found in v 13 where the dust raised by the approaching army and its chariots is presented as a sirocco and the clouds it raises:

> Behold like clouds (*ʿnnym*) it advances;
> like a storm (*swph*) are its chariots.

[5] J. Bright, *Jeremiah* (AB 21; Garden City: Doubleday, 1965) 33-34; W. Rudolph, *Jeremia* (HAT 12; 3rd ed.; Tübingen: Mohr, 1968) 32.

[6] For *bt* as a title for capital cities (here Jerusalem) see A. Fitzgerald, "*BTWLT* and *BT* as Titles for Capital Cities," *CBQ* 37 (1975) 167-83.

[7] Omit *mlʾ*, ditto. There are other ways of handling this overloaded colon. See Bright, *Jeremiah*, 29; Rudolph, *Jeremia*, 34. The translation supposes *ʾlh* refers back to *špyym*.

Both *ʿnn* and *swph* are frequently connected with the sirocco; never with a rainstorm (Part VII, Studies 5 and 3).

Vv 23-26 describe the prophet's vision of the results of the invasion. The land becomes a desert (*bhw*, v 23);[8] the orchards and vineyards (*hkrml*) become steppe land (*mdbr*, v 26; see *šmh*, v 7; *šmmh*, v 27). The mountains shake (*rʿš*); the hills bounce around (*qll*, v 24). There is no man left in the land (v 25; see vv 7 and 29); even the birds flee (v 25). The cities are knocked down (v 26; see v 7). The dust raised by the army as it ranges through the land like a sirocco darkens the luminaries of the sky (v 23). And all this happens:

> Before the Lord,
> before the *ḥrwn ʾpw* (v 26).

See *ḥrwn ʾp Yhwh* in v 8. V 28 presents the withered (*ʾbl*) land as mourning (*ʾbl*) and the heavens darkened (*qdr*) by the dust of the sirocco as a mourner (*qdr*)[9] grieving over what has taken place.

There can be little doubt where this language is coming from. The vocabulary and motifs met here have been met in the descriptions of the Lord appearing in a sirocco to destroy his enemies. The language has come out of the myth-based presentation of Yahweh as the Lord of the east wind, only here the language has become a figure for the Babylonian army.[10] All this is clear if *ḥrwn ʾp* in v 26 (see v 8) is to be interpreted concretely as the "heat of the Lord's nose"; i.e., the Babylonian army is (destructive like) the sirocco that comes from the Lord's nose. If it is to be understood abstractly as "the Lord's burning anger" and the army is to be thought of as the manifestation of that anger, at least the poet-editor understood the connection of *ḥrwn ʾp* with the sirocco (Study 9). The strongest argument, however, for viewing the imagery of vv 23-26 and its parallels in the rest of vv 5-31 as ultimately derived

[8] Omit *thw w* with LXX, though the expansion fits the general context. For *bhw* see A. Schwarzenbach, *Die geographische Terminologie im Hebräischen des Alten Testamentes* (Leiden: Brill, 1954) 105-7.

[9] The verbs *ʾbl* (to wither, to mourn) and *qdr* (to be dark, to mourn) are probably to be understood in both senses here.

[10] The piece is probably an editorial unit. Parts of it removed from the present context and restored to their original context might get the human army out of the picture or give us a human army and Yahweh acting directly together against his enemies. See especially v 26 which could easily be interpreted to mean the Lord himself leads the attack. For present purposes that is of no significance. The edited piece as a whole reflects the point of view indicated.

from the mythological presentation of Yahweh as the Lord of the east wind is that the imagery does not really fit an invasion.

The lifeless ruins of a destroyed city might well suggest agricultural land being turned into a desert. The dust raised by an army on the march might well suggest the approach of a destructive sirocco. But there is nothing in the course of a mere military invasion, no matter how destructive, that might suggest the motif of birds fleeing[11] or mountains and hills shaking. The plausible explanation is to view the language here as borrowed from the myth-connected presentation of the Lord coming in the east wind to destroy his enemies. All these motifs are readily understandable in that context, though in part they go beyond the bounds of any sirocco ever actually experienced. This simply fits the storm interpreted as theophany and become super-sirocco. What the poet has done is take this language out of its original context, use it figuratively of the Babylonian army and in this way he directly attributes all that the army does to the intervention of the Lord—a point of view otherwise clear from the general context. The appearance of sirocco imagery in Hos 13:14-15 is probably to be explained in the same way. All this has obvious implications for the understanding of this myth-based material in Israelite circles. The point will be returned to in the treatment of Lamentations 2.

In the whole of the complex Jer 4:5-31 there are only three other figures for the Babylonian army that seem to break out of this imagery pattern based on the sirocco. In v 17 the soldiers are compared with grim irony to "guardians of a field" (*kšmry śdy*). Those who might be expected to guard the crops ripening in the field will eventually turn the field into the likes of a field devastated by the east wind. The other two figures compare the chariot horses to eagles (*nšrym*, v 13) and the army itself to a lion (*ʾryh*, v 7). In the immediate contexts of the last two images there is sirocco language:

7 The lion has come up from his thicket;
  the destroyer (*mšḥyt*) of nations has set out;
  he has left his place,
To make your land a desert (*šmh*)
  with your cities uninhabited ruins.

[11] W. M. Thomson, *The Land and the Book* I (New York: Harper, 1880) 142, makes specific mention of the birds along with all other living creatures seeking shelter and disappearing in a sirocco period.

8 So put on sack!
Mourn and wail!
For there has not turned from us
the *ḥrwn ʾp Yhwh*.[12]

The motif of the land becoming desert (*šmh*) with its cities in ruins can have sirocco connections. The noun *mšḥyt* could call to mind the *rwḥ mšḥyt* of Jer 51:1, which in the total context of Jeremiah 50-51 would seem to be the sirocco.[13] All the connections of *ḥrwn ʾp Yhwh* (v 8) are with the sirocco (Part VII, Study 9).

V 13 reads:

Behold like clouds (*ʿnnym*) it advances;
like a storm (*swph*) are its chariots.
Its steeds are swifter than eagles (*nšrym*).
Woe to us! We are ruined!

Here the occurrence of *ʿnnym* and *swph* (Part VII, Studies 5 and 3, respectively) in the total context of vv 5-31 clearly points to the sirocco character of the storm figure.

Is it possible that the figure of the lion and eagle or the lion-eagle (griffin) is part of the background for this east-wind imagery of the whole unit? *ANEP*, 689 is an Akkad-period representation of a lion-headed eagle pulling the chariot of a rainstorm god.[14] On the monster there is a nude goddess holding lightning bolts or more probably streams of rain in her hands. This could be connected with the literary presentation of the Mesopotamian weather gods as riding (*rakābu*) on winds, storms and the like as in Atra-hasīs; *Adad ina šār erbetti*

[12] Rd *ky lʾ šb* as the first colon.

[13] Cf. n. 3.

[14] For the interpretation and parallels see E. Porada, *Corpus of Ancient Sear Eastern Seals in North American Collections: I, The Collection of the Pierpont Morgan Library* (Bollingen Series 14; New York: Pantheon, 1948) 28; E. D. Van Buren, "The Dragon in Ancient Mesopotamia," *Or* 15 (1946) 11-12. The more common representation has the weather god standing on the back of such monsters. See E. D. Van Buren, "A Further Note on the Dragon in Ancient Mesopotamia," *Or* 16 (1947) 251-53 and pl. IX, fig. 1; and the remarks of Porada, ibid. The example, of course, involves a rain god. What is being suggested here is the possibility of a parallel, *mutatis mutandis*, presentation for a god connected with a sirocco. See also W. L. Moran, "Some Remarks on the Song of Moses," *Bib* 43 (1962) 323-24 and the literature cited in p. 324, n. 1.

irtakab parê[-šu], Adad rode on the four winds, his asses.[15] The precise example just cited is much too old to be directly relevant for the present text. But the griffin is represented in art from all over the Middle East and the eastern Mediterranean more generally from the earliest period right into the Christian era.[16] More significantly Dan 7:4 knows the creature and uses it fittingly as a symbol of the Babylonian empire. It is clear that the OT preserves traces of this or a related iconography. In Hos 4:19 the wind has ***knpym*** like the ***kappu*** of Šūtu. In 2 Sam 22:11 (= Ps 18:11) and Ps 104:3, while it is not the easiest thing to draw a picture of what precisely is being described, it does seem that Yahweh rides a chariot drawn by winged cherubs, i.e. the wind (*ʿl knpy rwḥ*), or directly on the back of these mythical creatures.[17] From the lion side of the picture, Amos 1:2 (discussed below) presents the Lord roaring (*šʾg*; like a lion?) and the meadows and peak of Carmel withering (*ʾbl, ybš*). The results of the Lord's roaring (here the "roar" of the sirocco) indicate rather clearly that the sirocco is involved. In the oracle against

[15] W. G. Lambert and A. R. Millard, *Atra-ḫasīs, The Babylonian Story of the Flood* (Oxford: Clarendon, 1969) 122, rev. 5. For parallels see *AHW*, 945. In the Adapa myth the hero breaks the wing (***kappu***) of Šūtu, the South Wind (*WdM*, 39) who is a bird.

T. Jacobsen's (*The Treasures of Darkness* [New Haven: Yale, 1976] 128-29) interpretation of Sumerian *AN.IM.DUGUD.MUŠEN* as ^{d} *IM.DUGUD* ^{mušen} a griffin-like rainstorm god conceived of as an eagle (because rain clouds fly) with a lion's head (because thunder, the lion's roar, comes with the storm) would be helpful here (see also *WdM*, 80-81, 138-39). But the whole picture has been made suspect by B. Landsberger ("Einige unerkannt gebliebene oder verkannte Nomina des Akkadischen," *WZKM* 57 [1961] 1-21) who reads *ANZU(D)* ^{mušen} undermining Jacobsen's interpretation of the name, and rejects rainstorm connections for this eagle. See *CAD* A/2, 155; G. Pettinato, "Die Lesung von AN.IM.DUGUD.MUŠEN nach einem Ebla-Text," *JCS* 31 (1979) 116-17; B. Hruška, *Der Mythenadler Anzu in Literatur und Vorstellung des alten Mesopotamien* (Assyriologia 2; Budapest: Eötvös-Loránd-Universität, 1975). In the Akkadian Anzu myth this eagle apparently does have rainstorm connections. See W. W. Hallo and W. L. Moran, "The First Tablet of the SB Recension of the Anzu-Myth," *JCS* 31 (1979) 93.

[16] For summaries and literature see E. R. Goodenough, *Jewish Symbols in the Greco-Roman Period* VII (Bollingen Series 37; New York: Pantheon, 1958) 29-86; VIII, 121-46; R. D. Barnett, *A Catalogue of the Nimrud Ivories* (2nd ed.; London: British Museum, 1975) 70-77.

[17] See the discussion of 2 Sam 22:11 (= Ps 18:11) in M. Dahood, *Psalms* I (AB 16; Garden City: Doubleday, 1966) 107-8; and G. Schmuttermayr, *Psalm 18 und 2 Samuel 22* (SANT 25; München: Kösel, 1971) 64-69. It is possible to wonder whether behind texts like Exod 19:4, Deut 32:11, Isa 31:5, and Ps 91:4 are to be heard faint echoes of a related iconography.

Edom, Jer 49:7-22, Edom becomes an uninhabited desert (vv 13, 17-18, 20) like Sodom and Gomorrah (v 18). The vocabulary and motifs are typical of sirocco contexts (Part VII, Studies 15 and 18). In v 19 the Lord comes up from the thicket of the Jordan like a lion; in v 22 he flies over Bozrah like an eagle. And with these texts can be compared the lion imagery in Jer 25:38 which will be treated next and which in some ways is even more suggestive.[18]

Much of what has just been said is conjectural, but some sort of concrete picture or pictures presumably lies behind the imagery involved in this language. Unfortunately the possibilities open to the modern reader for analysis are too limited. What is ultimately being suggested here is that the sirocco, lion and eagle images of the piece perhaps present a more unified pattern than would appear at first glance.

3. Jer 25:30-38

30 Yahweh bellows (*šʾg*) from on high;
from his holy dwelling his voice resounds (*ntn qwl*).
He bellows (*šʾg*) over his own meadow (*nwh*);
a roar like vintagers he utters.
Against all the inhabitants of the earth
31 the din (*šʾwn*) presses on to the ends of the earth.
Yes, Yahweh has a grievance against the nations;
he has judged all flesh.
The wicked he has condemned to the sword—
word of Yahweh.
32 Thus says Yahweh of hosts:
Behold disaster goes forth
from nation to nation!
A great storm (*sʿr*) is unleashed
from the ends of the earth.
33 . . . .[a]
34 Howl, you shepherds, and cry out!
Roll in the dust, you leaders of the flock!
Yes, the time for your slaughter is come;[b]
you will fall like handsome rams.[c]

[18] This discussion is not meant to deny that imagery based on more normal lions exists in the Bible. See Jer 5:6 and Judg 14:5 where *šʾg* is used of a real lion.

35 There will be no refuge for the shepherds,
or sanctuary for the leaders of the flock.
36 Listen! The cry of the shepherds!
The howl of the leaders of the flock!
Yes, Yahweh lays waste (*šdd*) their pasture (*mr*ʿ*yt*);
37 desolate (*dmm*) are the pleasant meadows (*n*ʾ*wt*)
because of the heat of Yahweh's nose (*ḥrwn* ʾ*p Yhwh*).
38 The lion[d] has left his lair;
their lands[19] have become a desert (*šmh*),
Because of the cruel[e] sword,
because of the heat of his nose (*ḥrwn* ʾ*p*).

a) Omit 33 as a prose plus. b) Omit the unintelligible *wtpwṣwtykm*. c) Rd with LXX *k*ʾ*yly*. d) Omit *k* as ditto. See 4:7. e) Rd with LXX, Jer 46:16 and 50:16 *ḥrb*.

Jer 25:30-38 may be an editorial unit. The *kh* ʾ*mr Yhwh ṣb*ʾ*wt* of v 32 might well indicate a seam. The prose insert (v 33) severs the connection between the poetry of vv 32 and 34 and that could likewise indicate another seam. At the same time it would be possible to eliminate both of these and come up with a unit that could easily be read as one poem. Whether that is the correct approach to the piece or not cannot be proved. One thing is clear. Both the MT (see below) and the LXX[20] read it as a unit (even 33 and the *kh* ʾ*mr Yhwh ṣb*ʾ*wt* of 32 do not disturb this); and for present purposes, where the issue is the consistent use of imagery throughout, that is sufficient.

The subject matter of the whole is the Lord's judgment of the nations, Judah included. In addition there is a unity of address from beginning to end. The speaker refers to Yahweh throughout in the third person, despite the *n*ʾ*m Yhwh* of v 31 and the *kh* ʾ*mr Yhwh ṣb*ʾ*wt* of v 32. Who exactly the addressees of vv 30-38 are, is not all that clear. In their present position in the MT vv 30-38 are hung on the end of the piece about the cup of the Lord's judgment being distributed to the nations and are a comment on v 29 where the Lord says that though he

[19] "Earth" would do here. See vv 30, 31, 32, 33, 33; but the immediate context makes "their lands" preferable. The construction is the familiar *r*ʾ*šm* = "(their) heads." For the same construction with ʾ*rṣm* see: 2 Kgs 18:35 (= Isa 36:20; contrast the construction in 2 Kgs 18:33 = Isa 36:18); 2 Kgs 19:17 (= Isa 37:18); Jos 10:42; 23:5.

[20] In the LXX, MT 25:15-38 follows the prophecies against the nations (in a different order) and precedes MT 26 which contains different material.

intends to destroy Jerusalem, he will also destroy the other nations.[21] The prose introduction to vv 30-38 in the first part of v 30 identifies the other nations as the addressees of the unit.[22] But the problem is that these nations throughout are also spoken of in the third person. The one exception to that is v 34 where the speaker apparently breaks the pattern of address to shout directly to the foreign nations to tell them to begin a mourning ceremony over what is about to befall them. This suggests that the real addressees of the whole are an Israelite audience.

The use of the tenses throughout indicates that the disasters impending for both Judah and the nations are future disasters. To some extent, though, the speaker slips into the description of a vision where he sees what he is describing as already happening (see especially vv 32 and 36) and in v 38 he describes the destruction of the nations as already accomplished in vision.

The imagery of the piece clearly attributes the devastation of both Judah (v 30) and the nations to Yahweh alone. No other destroyer is mentioned. V 31 says that the Lord has condemned the nations to the sword (*ḥrb*) and the prose insert speaks of the slain as *ḥlly Yhwh* (v 33). This connects with v 34 which speaks of the slaughter of the shepherds (= kings).[23] It also connects with the imagery of v 30 where the Lord is described as uttering (*ʿnh*) a roar (*hydd*) like those treading grapes. The things directly compared are the Lord's and grape-treader's shout, but the image indirectly suggests the warrior with his garments covered with the blood of his enemies like the purpled garments of the treader.[24]

For the rest the Lord is described as roaring (*yšʾg*, v 30; *ytn qwl*, v 30; *hydd . . . yʿnh*, v 30; *šʾwn*, v 31). He is presented as a lion (v 38) and his coming to destroy is presented as a great storm (*sʿr gdwl*, v 32). Is this a collection of unconnected images or a unified imagery pattern? The solution to that problem may lie partially in the imagery used to present the Lord's enemies. It is all pastoral. Judah which the Lord roars at is the Lord's meadow (*nwh*, v 30). The kings of the foreign nations are *rʿym* and *ʾdyry hṣʾn* (vv 34, 35). The Lord lays waste (*šdd*) their

[21] Rudolph, *Jeremia*, 167.

[22] The LXX lacks *ʾlhym*.

[23] This is the first text examined where a weapon of a human warrior is put in the hand of Yahweh; though perhaps, this was also implied in Isa 50:2.

[24] See Isa 63:1-2; also Lam 1:15; Joel 4:13.

pasture (*mrʿyt*, v 36); and their (once) pleasant meadows (*nʾwt hšlwm*) end up desolate (*dmm*, v 37). This picture could easily call to mind the first text studied, Hos 13:14-15, where the Lord sends the Assyrian army under the figure of the east wind which dries up the water sources and the grasses of winter that made the flock, Ephraim, prosper.

That there is storm imagery involved is clear from v 32 where the coming destruction of the nations is attributed to a *sʿr gdwl* that comes from the ends of the earth. The *sʿr*, while it is never a rainstorm, is frequently the sirocco (Part VII, Study 4). Vv 36b-37 read:

> Yes, Yahweh lays waste (*šdd*) their pasture (*mrʿyt*);
> desolate (*dmm*) are the pleasant meadows (*nʾwt šlwm*),
> because of the *ḥrwn ʾp Yhwh*.

The pastures and meadows could be described as laid waste (*šdd*) and desolate (*dmm*) because the Lord has come with his sword and killed the shepherds and the sheep. The pasture and the meadows are then laid waste and desolate in the sense that there is no life present and so the *mrʿyt* and the *nʾwt šlwm* are now lifeless and quiet (*dmm*). But the text itself might well suggest a more direct harm to the *mrʿyt* and the *nʾwt šlwm*; and the presence of *ḥrwn ʾp Yhwh* (here possibly concretely, the sirocco) in the light of what has already been said and Study 9 makes the sirocco the possible cause. The verb *šdd* does fit this context.[25]

V 38 could easily be understood in a similar way:

> The lion has left his lair;
> their lands have become a desert (*šmh*),
> Because of the cruel sword,
> because of the heat of his nose (*ḥrwn ʾp*).

[25] See *šdd* used of *śdh* and *dgn* in Joel 1:10 in a context where *ʾdmh* dries out (*ʾbl*), (the vines that produce) must (*tyrwš*) and (the olive trees that produce) new oil (*yṣhr*) wither (*ʾml, ybš*). In Joel 1:10 the devastation of the *śdh* and the *dgn* may be simply due to the lack of rain or a spring heat-wave, but for present purposes that is the same thing. This text will be discussed in Part VI. See p. 112, n. 9; G. Dalman, *Arbeit und Sitte in Palästina* I (Gütersloh: Evangelischer Verlag, 1928) 322. For *dmh* (= *dmm*) in a similar setting see Isa 15:1 where Moab is devastated (*šdd*) and becomes desolate (*dmh*) in a context where the waters of Nimrim become a desert (*mšmwt*), the grass (*ḥṣyr*) withers (*ybš*), and the fresh grass (*dšʾ*) and everything green (*yrq*) disappear (v 6).

The motif of agricultural land becoming a desert is typical of sirocco contexts (Part VII, Study 15). The same is true of *ḥrwn ʾp* (Study 9). It also worth noting that in the prose of v 33 the LXX reflects *bywm Yhwh* rather than MT *bywm hhwʾ*. The *ywm Yhwh* is typically a day of sirocco (Study 20). When the text is viewed this way, the imagery used to present the Lord coming to destroy his enemies becomes a tidy package. Yahweh is a roaring (vv 30, 31) lion (v 38) whose roar is the sirocco (v 32). The presentation has at the same time become more personal insofar as the Lord also fights with a sword. Poets not only can present human enemies in the language of sirocco theophany; they can also present the Lord coming in the sirocco with the weapons of human warriors. The last line of the unit sums up the whole with its mention of the two instruments used in the onslaught, the sword (*ḥrb*) and the sirocco (*ḥrwn ʾp*).

There is still another way to approach the problem of the imagery here. The language of Jer 25:30-38 clearly echoes that of other texts. It is possible to attribute this to the traditional character of the language or to borrowing on the basis of memory. Direct borrowing is ruled out by the nature of the variants. The clearest parallels are: a) Jer 6:22 = Jer 25:32; b) Amos 1:2 and Joel 4:16 = Jer 25:30; c) Jer 4:7 = Jer 25:38.

The last of these texts (c) has just been studied and a case was made for the sirocco character of the imagery. That imagery is clear in (b) Joel 4:16 which will be studied in Part VI. It is also clear in Amos 1:2:

> Yahweh bellows (*šʾg*) from Zion;
> from Jerusalem his voice resounds (*ntn qwl*).
> The meadows (*nʾwt*) of the shepherds wither (*ʾbl*);
> the peak of Carmel is desiccated (*ybš*).

The concrete effect of vegetation withering with the typical vocabulary (*ʾbl*, *ybš*) is a clear indication of the nature of the Lord's roaring. It can only be the sirocco (Study 7). And if what has been said about the lion imagery in Jer 4:7 and 25:38 has any base in fact, that could be implied in Amos 1:2 also.

4. Deut 32:21-25

21 They provoked me with a no-god;
they angered me with their nonentities.

I will provoke them with a no-people;
with a nation of no consequence I will anger them.

*

22 Yes a fire (*ʾš*) is kindled (*qdḥ*) in my nose (*ʾp*);
it burns to the depths of Sheol.
It will consume (*ʾkl*) the earth and its yield;
it will burn up (*lhṭ*) the foundations of the mountains.
23 I will send disasters sweeping (*sph*) over them;
I will use up my arrows (*ḥṣ*) on them.

*

24 Exhausted by hunger,
consumed by disease and bitter pestilence—
I will send the teeth of wild beasts among them,
and the venom of those who slither in the dust.

*

25 Outside the sword will bereave;
inside, terror—
Both young man and maiden,
the baby and hoary old man.

The Lord's announcement of what he intends to do to Israel is governed by an inner logic which apparently has not been noticed. In v 21 he announces that he will send a no-people, a nation of no consequence, to attack Israel. Since the Lord is on that nation's side, one warrior among them will be able to put a thousand Israelites to flight (v 30). But the description of the attack by the nation of no consequence does not begin till v 25. The Lord first softens up Israel for the attack. He comes in a sirocco (vv 22-23) which has disastrous effects. Then, he sends against them in their weakened condition both wild beasts (2 Kgs 17:25) and poisonous snakes with further disastrous effects (v 24). Only then comes the attack of the nation of no consequence. The "paragraphing" this analysis presumes is in line with that of the whole of Deut 32:1-43 which is written in sense units of 2 and 3 lines.[26]

[26] P. W. Skehan, "The Structure of the Song of Moses in Deuteronomy (Deut. 32:1-43)," *CBQ* 13 (1951) 153-63 (= *CBQMS* 1 [1971] 67-77).

What is of prime concern here is the description of the sirocco in vv 22-23. The effect of the Lord's intervention, the destruction of the crops through withering, is precisely what the sirocco does. The noun *ʾš* is used to denote the hot sirocco (Part VII, Study 12). The combination *ʾš* + *ʾkl* is frequently used of the sirocco and its effects; it is never used of lightning (Study 12). The noun *ʾp* is probably to be understood concretely. The picture of the Lord with the hot nose (*ʾš qdḥh bʾpy*) from which issues forth the hot wind is characteristic of sirocco contexts; it does not appear in rainstorm contexts (Study 9). The verb *lhṭ* is frequently used of a hot sirocco; it never occurs in a rainstorm context (Study 22).[27] Note how this understanding of vv 22-23 explains both the writing and the pointing of *ʾaspeh* which is to be connected with *sph* (= to sweep) and is probably used of the wind elsewhere.[28] The noun *rʿwt* fits this context too. Note how Jer 25:32, which has been looked at already, the *rʿh* that goes forth is a *sʿr gdwl.* The first colon of v 23 should possibly be glossed: I will cause evil blasts to sweep over them.

The destruction of the harvest explains the hunger of v 24. The motif of disease and pestilence is typical of sirocco contexts; it does not occur in rainstorm contexts (Study 2). What precisely is to be made of the arrows (*ḥṣy*) which the Lord shoots in v 23 is not absolutely clear. Probably, though, they are to be understood as the (pangs) of hunger, the disease and pestilence of v 24.[29]

The temporal setting for the events described in vv 21-25 is probably the spring. The previous year's harvest had been exhausted. A spring super-sirocco destroys the maturing grain, the grape vines and the

[27] *Tg. Onq.* understood v 22 this way. It renders *ky ʾš qdḥh bʾpy*: There came out from before me a mighty east wind like fire (*qdwm tqyp kʾšʾ*). *Tg. Jon.* uses the same phrase for the sirocco in Joel 1:20. See p. 113, n. 13.

[28] KB, BDB, GB, s.v. *sph*, read *ʾōsīpâ* (*ysp*) here. F. Zorell, *Lexicon hebraicum et aramaicum Veteris Testamenti* (Roma: Pontificium Institutum Biblicum, 1963) lists this case under *sph*^{2} = *ysp*. The form is, perhaps, best left alone and interpreted as indicated. For *sph* probably used of the wind see Gen 19:15, 17; Deut 29:18. It should be noted too that the construction, add/increase + acc. + *ʿl* (= against) + a person, is uncommon and late. It is attested in Neh 13:18 and Ezek 5:16. The second instance is missing in the LXX and probably is a late plus (W. Zimmerli, *Ezechiel* [BKAT 13/1-2; Neukirchen-Vluyn: Neukirchener Verlag, 1955-69] 99). The preposition *ʿl* after *ysp* regularly introduces the thing added to (1 Kgs 12:11, 14; etc.). With *sph* should probably be connected *sûpâ.*

[29] Cf. the similar figure in Ps 38:3; Job 6:4; and especially Ps 91:5-6 where *ḥṣ* appears in the same context with *dbr* and *qṭb.*

olive trees. Then the enemy comes.[30] The date for the poem is controverted and the problem cannot be adequately resolved. Eissfeldt's arguments for a date in the period of the Judges, however, seem strong.[31] To them could be added the fact that the poem does not speak of an attack on an Israelite capital city, which also fits that period. Arguments against an early date based on theories concerning the development of Israelite religious thought are hardly probative. Not enough is known to write a history of this development in the detail necessary to make this judgment; and such arguments do not leave room for the possibility that an individual poet had points of view different from his contemporaries. If Eissfeldt is correct, this poem is the earliest instance of Yahweh as the Lord of the sirocco seen to this point.

It is worth noting too that vv 13-14 present the Lord as supplying his people with all the products of the field and flock. In Palestine that means he sent the rains. Thus the poem presents Yahweh as in control of the beneficent rains and the destructive sirocco. This point of view has been seen already[32] and will be seen frequently in what follows. In vv 41-42 the Lord describes himself as a warrior with a sword coming to fight for his people. Whether any of this is to be read back into vv 21-25 or vice versa is completely uncertain; but see the previous discussion of Jer 25:30-38 where the Lord fights with both sword and sirocco. Other instances of this combination will be seen below.

5. Lamentations 2

Lamentations 2 is a peculiar piece in the sense that the poet, despite the fact that he knew precisely what really happened to Jerusalem in 587 and knew it in detail,[33] attributes the destruction almost exclusively to

[30] For the same sequence of events in the visions of Amos see p. 114, n. 17.

[31] O. Eissfeldt, *Das Lied Moses Deuteronomium 32:1-43 und das Lehrgedicht Asaphs Psalm 78 samt einer Analyse der Umgebung des Mose-Liedes* (Berlin: Akademie, 1958) 15-25; *The Old Testament: An Introduction* (Oxford: Blackwell, 1965) 226-27; for the linguistic evidence see D. A. Robertson, *Linguistic Evidence in Dating Early Hebrew Poetry* (SBLDS 3; Missoula: SBL, 1972) 147-56.

[32] See pp. 26-27.

[33] The poem in all probability was written shortly after 587 and before Cyrus (W. Rudolph, *Das Buch Ruth. Das Hohe Lied. Die Klagelieder* [KAT 17/1-3; Gütersloh: Gerd Mohn, 1962] 193). Even if it were written later, this is a fully historical period and the poet still knew what really happened.

the direct action of the Lord. Rudolph appropriately entitles the poem "Yahweh hat's getan,"[34] and Hillers' title is similar: "The Lord became like an enemy."[35]

The first speaker in this dramatic poem is probably to be understood as a figure like Job's *mnḥym* (Job 16:2). During a mourning ceremony at which Jerusalem is the chief mourner, he first describes what happened to mourning Jerusalem and why (vv 1-12), assesses her present situation and advises her to pray (vv 13-19). In vv 20-22 Jerusalem takes this advice. In the first part of the poem the speaker describes the attack on Judah (vv 2-5) and finally Jerusalem (vv 6-9).[36] It is this part of the poem that is of concern here.

The Lord who comes to destroy Jerusalem is clearly Yahweh the warrior who fights with human weapons (*drk qštw*, v 4a). Is this all there is to the imagery used to present the Lord? The Lord destroys in anger (*ʿbrh*) the fortresses of Judah (v 2b). He breaks in fiery wrath (*ḥry ʾp*) the horn of Israel (v 3a). He rejects in angry wrath (*zʿm ʾp*) king and priest (v 6b). This is vocabulary that has been seen already hovering around sirocco contexts, though there is no indication here that a concrete interpretation is called for (Studies 19, 9, 8). The same is true of *ḥmh* and the combination *špk ḥmh* in v 4c (see *špk* + *ḥmh* in Nah 1:6 and Study 10). Though not seen yet, the presentation of the Lord blazing (*bʿr*) against Jacob like a flame of fire that consumes (*ʾš lhbh ʾklh*, v 3c) is likewise typical of sirocco contexts (Studies 21 and 12).

None of this, of course, proves that there is sirocco imagery in the piece. V 6a, however, does point in that direction:

> *wyḥms kgn śkw*
> *šḥt mwʿdw*
> He has demolished his hut like the garden;
> he destroyed his assembly place.

Of the first colon Rudolph writes: "The comparison with a garden is incomprehensible."[37] But the comparison becomes completely under-

[34] Ibid., 216.

[35] D. R. Hillers, *Lamentations* (AB 7a; Garden City: Doubleday, 1972) 31.

[36] Rudolph, *Klagelieder*, 221-24.

[37] Ibid., 219. Similar are the views of Hillers, *Lamentations*, 37; and H.-J. Kraus, *Klagelieder* (BKAT 20; 3rd ed.; Neukirchen-Vluyn: Neukirchener Verlag, 1968) 37-38.

standable if the garden is Judah and Jerusalem is the *śk*; and if the imagery pattern here involves Yahweh the warrior coming in a sirocco.[38] For Judah as garden land see: Joel 2:3 (note the sirocco context; this text will be discussed in Part VI); Isa 51:3; Ezek 36:35. And for Jerusalem as a hut (*skh*) in a vineyard or melon patch see Isa 1:8. This immediately connects with the destruction (*blʿ*) of the *nʾwt yʿqb* in v 2a, though 2a and 6a emphasize different aspects of the agriculture. The numerous parallels in the texts already examined come immediately to mind.

There is probably another reference to the sirocco in the first colon of v 13b: For great like the sea's is your destruction (*ky gdwl kym šbrk*).[39] We have already seen two texts (Isa 19:1, 5-7; Jer 51:34-37, 42-45) where the Lord comes in a sirocco to destroy Egypt and Babylon and in the course of that destruction destroys *ym* (= the Nile and the Euphrates) as well as the agricultural land which depended on them. It was also suggested that in these texts *ym* was used with the denotation "river" under the influence of the mythology concerned with Yahweh's drying out *ym* with a sirocco.[40] There the drying up of the Nile and the Euphrates had to be mentioned directly because of the significance of the rivers for Egypt and Babylon. Here the comparison with the sea comes in because it was Yahweh coming in a sirocco who had destroyed the sea (Isa 50:2) and now destroys both Judah and Jerusalem. No river was of crucial import to the agricultural economy of Judah which depended on rain; so direct reference to the drying up of *ym* was inappropriate. The way the imagery in 6a and 13b immedi-

38 The verb *ḥms* does have limited agricultural connections. See Job 15:33 where under the figure of a withering vine a wicked man is described as "dropping (doing harm to, *ḥms*) its unripe grapes." Cf. the discussion of P. Dhorme, *Le livre de Job* (Paris: Lecoffre, 1926) 204-5.

39 The comparison is usually understood as involving the immeasurable character of the sea and the destruction of Jerusalem. But note that these are immeasurable in different senses: the broadness or depth of the sea; the degree of the destruction of Jerusalem that approaches completeness. Besides, the destruction of Jerusalem is not really immeasurable. It is there for all to see; it is complete or almost so. The interpretation suggested here supposes this completeness of the destruction is the *tertium comparationis*. Contrast the treatment of Rudolph, *Klagelieder*, 225; Kraus, *Klagelieder*, 46; Hillers, *Lamentations*, 46. For *kym*, "like (the destruction) of the sea," see Ps 18:34 where *kʾylwt* means "like (the feet) of hinds"; Isa 29:4; 63:2; etc.

40 See p. 39, n. 36.

ately falls into place once the sirocco is brought into consideration is a good argument for regarding it as part of the overall picture in Lam 2. This understanding of Lam 2:13b can also be related to Isa 51:9-10 where the Lord is called upon to assist his people against Babylon and the model offered for this intervention is the Lord's past drying up of the sea, probably with the sirocco. This text will be discussed in Part IV.

Several times already the problem of how this sirocco imagery was understood in Israel has been alluded to and was postponed to this point. The remarks to be made here are not intended as a full discussion of myth in the OT or even nature myth, which is the type of myth to which the imagery being discussed is directly related. An extended discussion is inappropriate in the present context and in any case the writer is not sufficiently competent to resolve the thorny problems involved in this difficult question. The intent is only to pull together a few concrete indications of the Israelite attitude toward this imagery from the texts studied to this point, indications which will find further parallels in the texts still to be studied. The principal purpose is to avoid any misunderstanding of what is intended by the interpretation offered here of sirocco theophany descriptions. The intention is certainly not to present Yahweh as a sirocco god in any way defined by or tied to this meteorological phenomenon. He is not an Anu (Sky/sky) or a Šamaš (Sun/sun) or a Dagan (Grain/grain) or a Baal-Hadad who comes in a rainstorm, though it is clear that what can be said of these at base nature gods can be predicated of Yahweh (Psalm 29).

It was noted in the Introduction that the texts studied in Parts V and VI where siroccos are played off against rainstorms generally reflect the meteorology of the fall interchange period which opens around the middle of Tishri. Other texts of this type are isolated in the Studies of Part VII. The stereotyped language in which these storms are presented suggests a common *Sitz* for the language and it was suggested that the liturgy of Sukkoth presents itself as the probable *Sitz*. The whole question needs to be studied on its own and from a broader base, but I think that understanding probable. Thus this meteorological mythology was in significant part at least originally meant to explain why and how the east wind and the west wind blow in the fall and why and how the dry season is replaced by the rainy season and the agricultural cycle is renewed—an item of utmost import for the Palestinian farmer. The fact that the OT can use this material in the correct meteorological setting and tie it to the feast of Sukkoth and the fall interchange period indicates that the fundamental intent of the material was still correctly understood. In a monotheistic system both storms are tied to Yahweh, and in a more complicated world where salvation and the good order of the universe depend not only on the renewal of the agricultural cycle but on the annihilation of hostile political forces and the like, the Lord comes in these storms not only to renew the agriculture but to destroy his people's enemies.

But at this point tensions arise, at least for the modern mind. Language originally fashioned to describe deified nature immanent in this world and eventually personified is now used to describe the transcendent Yahweh who is not part of nature but rather the Lord of all nature. New things are being said in old forms. The problem is not exclusively Israelite in the ancient world, but the question must be asked: how was this language understood in Israel?

A text like Nah 1:2-8 which speaks of the Lord's past coming in a sirocco and its effects on nature and human beings and turns this into a model for what the Lord intends to do in the future when he comes to save his people, is of little use in determining how the poet or his audience understood this imagery. The past sirocco (or siroccos) in which the Lord came was probably or at least conceivably not something they had personally experienced. It is possible to think they really thought it happened that way back then; or, so far as the future intervention of the Lord to save his people is concerned, since that is in the future, it is not possible to say what was really expected to happen. The same is true, e.g., of a text like Jer 51:37-45 where the Lord promises to come in a sirocco to destroy Bel and Babylon.

But Lamentations 2 is a completely different situation. The text in all probability dates from a period very close to the historical events it purports to describe.[41] And even if the text were very late, these events date from a fully historical period. The poet and his intended audience certainly knew what had happened. Still the Babylonians are hardly allowed to contribute anything to the destruction of Jerusalem. Everything for all practical purposes is attributed to the action of Yahweh, the warrior, coming in a sirocco. For this poet, at least, nature mythology has become what a modern would probably characterize as pure and simple imagery, though to some extent, at least, that is probably projecting new ideas into an old text. The poet could have said things "more soberly"; but the mythology gets in because this is poetry and

[41] See p. 59, n. 33.

the imagery allows the audience to "feel" the Lord's power in the terrible storm. In addition the mythology which had remained to some extent the *language* of theology was a convenient way to say: the Lord alone, not Babylon, was responsible.[42] It is worth noting too that Jerusalem fell in August of 587. Sirocco imagery can be used within a time frame in which the sirocco is meteorologically impossible.

About the basic historical events of the fall of Jerusalem and their theological interpretation, I do not think there is any essential difference between Lamentations 2 and texts like 2 Chr 36:11-21: Israel provoked the Lord and he sent the Babylonians to destroy the city. This fact raises obvious questions about texts like Nah 1:2-8 which treats of the Lord's past coming in a sirocco to destroy his enemies (unspecified) and Jer 51:37-45 which treats of the Lord coming in a future sirocco to destroy Babylon. In both cases the language is capable of a symbolic interpretation, and I suppose the poet of Jer 51:37-45 still regards Cyrus' peaceful entry into Babylon as the fulfillment of his prophecy. This is, perhaps, to turn the poet of Jer 51:37-45 into a 20th century rationalist and I am sure he would not have felt the problem in exactly the same way as a modern does, but he certainly understood the point of view of the poet of Lamentations 2.

To what extent the attitude of the poet of Lamentations 2 toward sirocco mythology can be used to interpret what other individual poets and their audiences thought of this language in other poems examined is nonetheless not completely clear.[43] But there are, some keys that indicate the attitude was similar. Note how in Jer 4:5-31 it is the Babylonian army that comes in the trappings of a sirocco theophany. That is once again a way to say: what the Babylonians will do is the Lord's work. It is hardly thinkable that a peculiar characteristic of divinity would be used to present the work of a mere human army, if the sirocco was conceived of as having a connection to divinity more intimate than simple control. It may be suspected that the situation in

[42] Too much ought not to be made of this development in Israelite religious language. The third millennium "Lament for Ur" (*ANET*, 445-63) presents the destruction of Ur as principally the work of Enlil coming in a storm despite the fact that the poet knew it was the work of marauders from the East. See the remarks of Jacobsen, *Treasures*, 88.

[43] The difficult 1 Kgs 19:11-12 has been understood to indicate that some in Israel had a more naturalistic notion of Yahweh. See the discussion in J. Jeremias, *Theophanie* (WMANT 10; Neukirchen-Vluyn: Neukirchener Verlag, 1965) 112-15.

Isaiah 13 is much the same. The Medes are present (v 17) and that is the rational explanation of what is expected to happen. But the Lord in a sirocco will lead the attack and that is the religious understanding of what is expected to happen.

There is still another angle from which this problem can be approached. The texts being examined here are all concerned with the east wind. Most of them have been sirocco theophanies which present Yahweh as the Lord of this natural phenomenon. But it is also evident, even from texts already examined (Hos 13:14-15 vs 14:2-9; Deut 32:21-25 vs 13-14), that Yahweh is Lord of the rain-bringing west wind; and from other texts Lord of all nature. That this was so even from the earliest period is clear from Deut 32 and the next text to be examined, Exod 15:1-18 + 21. That means he is no nature force or nature god limited to or defined by any particular set of natural phenomena.[44] That is clearly recognized on all sides and needs no special discussion. The present study, perhaps, sharpens the total evidence by drawing attention to the contrast between Yahweh as Lord of such opposed phenomena as the sirocco and the rainstorm.

Having said that, I must confess to the suspicion that the whole problem discussed here is a modern one occasioned by the culture-shock the western mind experiences in being transported back into a world of religious experience that is and is not its own expressed in language rooted in a mythological world view it does not share and cannot even sympathize with. How Jeremiah, for example, would react to what has just been said, I do not know. In this regard I can do no better than cite the words of Goodenough in discussing the use of pagan symbols by both Jews and Christians: "We who have been educated in the literalism of theology find it hard to put ourselves into the spirit of those who thought still in poetic fancy. . . . Again may I point out that it was precisely this elasticity which made it possible for Jews and Christians to use such figures without feeling they had betrayed their own faith."[45] It was this same "elasticity" that allowed the Christian poet and artist to turn Jesus into the *Sol Invictus* and put *Tychē*'s walled crown on the head of the Blessed Virgin.

[44] Too much cannot be made of this either. *Enuma Elish*, for example, had long since done the same thing for Marduk.

[45] Goodenough, *Jewish Symbols* VIII, 121.

PART IV

The Miracle at the Sea: Exod 15:1b-18 + 21b[1]

This text contains sirocco imagery without reference to the motif of drying up bodies of water much like the texts treated in Part III. The poem is given a separate treatment, however, because of the parallel frequently drawn between the OT versions of the miracle at the sea and Baal's struggle with Yamm at Ugarit. The analysis of the meteorology of the piece does not support that view.

The theme of this hymn is the heroic deeds of Yahweh who defeated the Egyptians and settled his people in Palestine. The Lord is presented as a warrior (*ʾyš mlḥmh*, v 3) who smashes his enemies with his right hand (v 6). That the Lord comes in some sort of storm which seems to issue from his mouth and nose is indicated by v 10:

> You blew (*nšpt*) with your wind (*rwḥ*);
> the sea covered them.

This suggests a concrete interpretation of *ʾpyk* in v 8:

> At the wind of your nose (*brwḥ ʾpyk*)
> the waters piled up.

[1] An extensive treatment of the poem is S. I. L. Norin, *Er spaltete das Meer* (ConB, OT Series 9; Lund: Gleerup, 1977) 77-107. An important treatment is D. N. Freedman, "Strophe and Meter in Exodus 15," *A Light unto my Path, Old Testament Studies in Honor of Jacob N. Myers* (ed. H. N. Bream et al.; Philadelphia: Temple, 1974) 163-203. Both gather the important older bibliography. Freedman has made a case for the analysis of the whole of 1b-18 + 21b as a highly structured unit in which the original unit, vv 3-18, was expanded by vv 1-2 and 21 when the poem was adapted for liturgical usage.

It is presumably this wind that heaves (*rmh*, vv 1, 21; *yrh*, v 4) the Egyptians into the sea. But what kind of storm is involved, a rainstorm or a sirocco? There is no mention of rain, thunder or lightning. But by the same token neither is there mention, inappropriate in the context, of the withering of vegetation or the drying up of water sources. V 7b would, however, point in the direction of the sirocco:

> You sent forth (*šlḥ*) your wrath (*ḥrn*);
> it consumed (*ʾkl*) them like stubble (*qš*).

The noun *ḥrn* is typical sirocco-context vocabulary; it never occurs in a rainstorm (Study 9).[2] The same is true of the *qš* simile. Like its synonyms *mṣ* and *glgl* it is a product of the summer heat and especially the heat of the spring siroccos.[3] It consistently appears in sirocco contexts; never in rainstorm contexts (Study 11). The combination *ʾkl* + *qš* where the picture is either a real fire burning off *qš* or a super-hot sirocco doing the same thing has the same connections (Study 11). The other possibility would be: just as the sirocco "wilts" (*ʾkl*) grass and turns it into flying *qš*, so the Lord's wind "wilts" (*ʾkl*) the Egyptians and blows them away. The typical setting for the simile is that of Jer 13:24.

> I will scatter them like flying stubble (*qš*)
> before the desert wind (*rwḥ mdbr*).

This too would indicate that the storm involved here is rather the sirocco than the rainstorm.[4]

That immediately hooks in with Exod 14:21, though it is clear here that the east wind is only a tool of Yahweh, not his breath:

> *Then Moses stretched out his hand over the sea* and the Lord drove the sea with a strong east wind (*rwḥ qdym ʿzh*) throughout the night. He turned the sea into dry land *and the waters were split* (*bqʿ*).

[2] In the light of v 10 this verse is just about the best argument for the concrete interpretation of *ḥrwn* = "the *hot* sirocco" that exists. But the case is clearly not open and shut. "Wrath" = "the sirocco" is also possible (see Study 9, pp. 150-59 below).

[3] G. Dalman, *Arbeit und Sitte in Palästina* I (Gütersloh: Evangelischer Verlag, 1928) 323-25.

[4] It is worth noting how the temporal setting of the miracle at the sea in Exodus 14-15 in the period after passover fits into the spring sirocco period.

The sources involved in the verse are probably J and P; and P has been indicated by the italics.[5] The connection of the miracle at the sea with the east wind is, then, only in J and the combined sources. What about the other reminiscences of this miracle in the rest of the OT?[6] For the most part meteorology plays only a limited role.

There is a whole series of texts that presume or explicitly refer to the drying up of the sea, at times with what is typical sirocco vocabulary (e.g., *ybš*, Jos 2:10; *ḥrb*, Isa 51:10). But it is not always clear whether this is done by a storm or not. See, e.g., Isa 44:27 where the Lord dries up the sea with his word. For present purposes the only point to be emphasized is that none of these texts can have anything to do with a rainstorm. The context of Isa 51:10, however, probably favors something more physical than the mere issuing of a command. V 9a speaks of the Lord's arm. V 9b speaks of killing sea monsters. V 12 compares Israel's oppressors to grass which can be withered by the east wind (Isa 40:6-8). In 50:2-3, studied in Part II, there is clear sirocco imagery in a very similar setting. In 51:19-20 the effect of the attack of the Babylonians on Jerusalem's sons is described as in Lamentations 2, studied in Part III, in terms of the hot sirocco. Jerusalem's sons fainted (*ʿlp*) just as Jonah grew faint (*ʿlp*, Jonah 4:8) when the hot sun beat on his head. These sons got their fill of the *ḥmt Yhwh* and the *gʿrt ʾlhyk*. The Lord's roar is presumably the same as the *gʿrh* that dries up the sea in 50:2 studied in Part II; and *ḥmh* is typically a designation for the sirocco (Study 10).[7]

Ps 106:9 presents the sea drying up (*ḥrb*) in a context where the Lord "rebukes/roars at" (*gʿr*) the sea. The text clearly reflects some myth concerned with an antagonism between Yahweh and the sea. If a storm is involved, in view of *ḥrb* it has to be the sirocco. Ps 114:3, 5 presents

[5] B. S. Childs, *The Book of Exodus* (Philadelphia: Westminster, 1974) 218-21.

[6] The texts have been collected and studied by A. Lauha, "Das Schilfmeermotiv im Alten Testament," *Congress Volume, Bonn 1962* (VTSup 9; ed. G. W. Anderson et al.; Leiden: Brill, 1963) 32-46. See also G. W. Coats, "The Traditio-historical Character of the Sea Motif," *VT* 17 (1967) 253-65; B. S. Childs, "A Traditio-historical Study of the Reed Sea Tradition," *VT* 20 (1970) 406-18.

[7] Through the whole of Isaiah 40-55 there unfolds an imagery pattern based on the alternating siroccos and rainstorms of the fall interchange period. The topic needs a separate and lengthy discussion and cannot be pursued here. Other tests with this pattern are discussed in Parts V and VI. See in particular the discussion of Isa 42:10-17 on pp. 105-6, n. 79.

the sea fleeing in a context where the mountains "dance" (*rqd*, v 4). The text probably reflects a storm, but what kind is not clear.[8] Other texts follow P's splitting version (Isa 63:12; Ps 78:13; Neh 9:11).

There is one text, however, Ps 77:17-20 which clearly connects the events at the sea with a rainstorm theophany:[9]

16 With your arm you redeemed your people,
the sons of Jacob and Joseph.
17 The waters saw you, O God;
the waters saw you and shuddered;
the depths also trembled.
18 The clouds (*ʿbwt*) poured down water;
the thunderhead resounded;
your arrows zigzagged abroad.
19 The noise of your thunder in the chariot—[10]
your lightning bolts lit up the world;
the earth trembled and shook.
20 Your way was through the sea;
your path through the vast waters,
though your footsteps were not seen.
21 You led your people like a flock
under the direction of Moses and Aaron.

The text is usually understood as a reference to the miracle at the sea,[11] though it is not at all clear how the text interpreted that miracle. This clearly cannot be the version of Exod 14:21 or the J version or that of Exod 15:1-21 where the sirocco is involved. And there especially can be no question here of the sea drying up as, e.g., in Exod 14:21; Jos 2:10; Isa 51:10. Rainstorms do not do that.

[8] The motif of shaking mountains goes with both the rainstorm and the sirocco. See p. 30, n. 15.

[9] The looseness with which vv 17-20 fit into the total context of Ps 77 has frequently been noted. These verses are consistently tricola. This contrasts with the pattern throughout the rest of the psalm. Note the *slh* at the end of v 16. In addition note how with vv 17-20 omitted v 16 reads directly into v 21. See M. Dahood, *Psalms* II (AB 17; Garden City: Doubleday, 1968) 224; J. Jeremias, *Theophanie* (WMANT 10; Neukirchen-Vluyn: Neukirchener Verlag, 1965) 4; H.-J. Kraus, *Psalmen* (BKAT 15/1-2; 2nd ed.; Neukirchen: Neukirchener Verlag, 1961) 530.

[10] Possibly by synecdoche "wheel" for "chariot." See Jeremias, *Theophanie*, 26.

[11] Lauha, "Das Schilfmeermotiv," 41; Coats, "The Reed Sea Motif," 260; Childs, "Reed Sea Tradition," 410-13.

What precisely is to be made of this is not clear.[12] But it does seem obvious that, insofar as the miracle at the sea is recounted in terms of nature myth, a distinction ought to be made between the myths that involve the east wind and the rain-bringing west wind. What is being said here, of course, runs counter to the view that understands the miracle at the sea as a general reflex of Baal vs Yamm at Ugarit.[13] Whether Baal's connections with the sirocco allow that is open to doubt.

Two other remarks are worth making about Exod 15:1-21 in the context of this discussion. Not only does the text make Yahweh the Lord of the sirocco; it also presents him as the farmer who plants (*nṭ*ᶜ, v 17) Israel in Palestine. The imagery presumes he sends the rain too. It is, of course, notoriously difficult to date a text like Exod 15:1-21. But the concentration of linguistic archaisms in the piece indicates that Exod 15:1-21 is very old—possibly pre-monarchic.[14] Thus, the presentation of Yahweh as the Lord of the east wind and the beneficent bestower of rain is a picture of Yahweh as ancient as any preserved in the OT. It has already been argued that this was indicated by Deuteronomy 32,[15] though the evidence for early dating is clearer here in Exodus 15.

[12] So loosely does the rainstorm theophany fit into the psalm and so unique is the rainstorm's connection with the miracle at the sea that it is possible to wonder whether the combination here is a late mistake.

[13] The influential study here was O. Eissfeldt, *Baal Zaphon, Zeus Kasios und der Durchzug der Israeliten durchs Meer* (Halle: Niemeyer, 1932) esp. 66-71. See M. S. Smith, *The Ugaritic Baal Cycle: Volume I. Introduction with Text, Translation and Commentary of KTU 1.1-1.2* (VTSup 55; Leiden: Brill, 1994) 98, 352-53.

[14] See especially D. N. Freedman, "Strophe and Meter in Exodus 15," 201-2; D. A. Robertson, *Linguistic Evidence in Dating Early Hebrew Poetry* (SBLDS 3; Missoula: SBL, 1972) 147-56. A late dating of the hymn (e.g. A. Lauha, "Das Schilfmeermotiv," 21) on the basis of its "deuteronomic atmosphere" ignores the linguistic evidence and presumes more is known about the history of Israelite religion than actually is. At the same time it is impossible to reject Childs' 9th century date (B. S. Childs, "Reed Sea Tradition," 411). The linguistic evidence is not that easy to control either (see Robertson).

[15] See p. 59, n. 31.

PART V

Combined Siroccos and Rainstorms

The next group of texts to be examined is one where a rainstorm and a sirocco appear in the same immediate context. This group of texts is important for what is being attempted here. First of all, the rainstorms are quite easy to analyze from a meteorological point of view and the meteorology is relatively normal, though embellished with poetic hyperbole. Secondly, the texts generally indicate the time of the year in which the rain occurs. For the most part the reference is to the first rains in the period after Sukkoth. This is precisely the fall interchange period when the coming of the fall siroccos announces the coming of the first rains and when in fact, as was seen in Part I, siroccos and rainstorms alternate. Granted this setting and a knowledge of the effects of the sirocco, it becomes possible to identify and analyze these storms even when presented in the extravagant language of the poet. The thing to notice in these texts is the way in which the language and motifs that have been to this point described as characteristic of descriptions of siroccos recur. This helps guarantee that the identification of the sirocco in isolation in the texts already discussed is correct and that the analysis of these descriptions on the basis of normal Palestinian meteorology is a valid procedure.

The first text studied in this section is the finale of I Isaiah, Isaiah 34-

35. The text has been interpreted eschatologically, e.g., by O. Kaiser and G. Fohrer.[1] It deals with the destruction by the Lord coming in a fall sirocco of the nations (34:2-3), particularly Edom (34:5-17), who might in the future disturb Israel's peace and with the return of the diaspora. The diaspora returns crowned with *eternal* joy (35:10) through the desert rained upon by the first fall rains to well watered Jerusalem (chap. 35). I share the view of Kaiser and Fohrer that, at least in its present context in the Isaiah book, the text is to be interpreted eschatologically. The arguments for that have to do principally with the ordering of the materials in chaps. 13-35 which cannot be gone into here. Consequently I will treat Isaiah 34-35 as an instance of an eschatological, agricultural new year. By that is meant that the arrival of the new age is described with imagery derived from the contrasting storms that open the agricultural year. The eschatological character of the text does not have to be insisted on for the purposes of the present argument. If the text simply looks forward to a period of prosperity for Israel in the normal unfolding of history and describes in extravagant language the arrival of that prosperity with imagery derived from the contrasting storms of the fall interchange period, the continuity of the argument is not undermined. The point of the present discussion is simply to call attention to the potential of this language to become the language of eschatology. That this development has in fact taken place will be made perfectly clear by Joel 3:1–4:21. This text will be discussed in Part VI.

Further texts combining the sirocco and the rainstorm in the fall interchange period are treated in Part VI and in the Studies of Part VII. The pattern, as will be seen, is common and the texts discussed in which it is reflected are gathered in n. 6 of the conclusion (p. 206).

1. Isaiah 34-35

These two chapters, which clearly are intended to be read together whether they come from the same hand as an original unit or not, will serve as the first instance of rainstorm and sirocco imagery in combi-

[1] O. Kaiser, *Isaiah 13-39* (London: SCM, 1974) 351-66; G. Fohrer, *Das Buch Jesaja* II (Zürich/Stuttgart: Zwingli, 1962) 138-50. H. Wildberger, *Jesaja* (BKAT 10/1-3; Neukirchen-Vluyn: Neukirchener Verlag, 1965-) 1330-33, denies that Isaiah 34-35 are eschatological.

nation. Chap. 35 describes the Lord coming to save his people. The glory and splendor of the Lord (*kbwd Yhwh*, *hdr ʾlhynw*, v 2) will be seen when he comes:

> Behold your God with vindication—
> he comes with divine recompense;
> he comes to save you. (v 4)

Two effects of this coming are of concern here. In the first place it will rain in Judah and even those areas not usually blessed with abundant rain[2] will receive plenty:

> The steppe (*mdbr*) and the parched land (*ṣyh*) will exult;[3]
> the desert (*ʿrbh*) will rejoice and flower.
> Like the crocus[4] it will flower;
> it will rejoice with rejoicing and singing.
> The glory of Lebanon will be given to it,
> the splendor of Carmel and Sharon. (vv 1-2)

That vv 1-2 are concerned with rain in Judah is indicated by the fact that when the description of the return of the diaspora to Jerusalem is presented in v 10, they are described as entering Zion with joy. That presumes Zion is at least as well supplied with water as the eastern desert through which the diaspora returns. In addition the description of the return of the diaspora does not begin till v 5 or even, more probably, v 6b.

Besides the rain in Judah, there will also be rain in the eastern desert so that the returning diaspora will have enough water as it returns on the Lord's highway:

> Yes, water will burst forth in the steppe;
> wadis (*nḥlym*), in the desert.

[2] For the opposition between *ʾdmh* on the one hand and *mdbr*, *ṣyh* and *ʿrbh* on the other, see A. Schwarzenbach, *Die geographische Terminologie im Hebraischen des Alten Testamentes* (Leiden: Brill, 1954) 133-36.

[3] Rd *yśśw* (ditto). For other explanations of the final *m* see F. M. Cross, *Canaanite Myth and Hebrew Epic* (Cambridge: Harvard, 1973) 170.

[4] The precise identification of *ḥbṣlt* is not possible. It is clearly some plant that blooms in connection with the first rains of winter. For G. Dalman's suggestions see *Arbeit und Sitte in Palästina* I (Gütersloh: Evangelischer Verlag, 1928) 96-97. Cf. M. Zohary, "Flora," *IDB* 2 (1962) 295.

The glaring desert will become a swamp;
the dry land, springs of water.
In the haunt where jackals dwell[5]
there will be a home[6] for the reed and papyrus.
A leveled highway will be there;
the Holy Road will it be called. (vv 6-8)

It would be possible here to think of all this as the result of water from ground-water sources, but in a context where Judah receives "the glory of Lebanon" and "the splendor of Carmel" (v 2), which is the product of rain, not ground water,[7] it is better to think of rain. Besides that is what a *nḥl* (v 6) is, a wadi that flows as a result of the winter rains and melting snow.[8] This interpretation will be confirmed by the total context of chaps. 34-35. The springs (*mbwʿy mym*) of v 7 are the result of the ground water being increased to excess by the rain. Note the west to east orientation of the rainstorm this analysis presumes. That also is true to nature. The same orientation will be met in the analysis of other rainstorms in what follows.

The chief interest here is with chap. 34 where we have sirocco theophany which is the foil for the rain of chap. 35. Everyone else gets blasted by the sirocco; only Judah and the returning diaspora receive the beneficent rain. Chap. 34 presents the picture of the Lord as a warrior destroying the nations (*kl hgwym*, v 2), the heavenly host (vv 4-5), and in a special way Edom (vv 5-17). That the Lord fights with a sword is clear (vv 2-3, 5-7). He also uses the engineer's line and plummet to select the key stones for removal in order to collapse the walls of Bozrah (vv 6, 11).[9] That this intervention of the Lord is accompanied by

[5] Rd *rābĕṣâ*. See GKC, § 145, k.

[6] Rd *ḥāṣēr*. See Isa 34:13.

[7] Ps 104:13.

[8] Schwarzenbach, *Geographische Terminologie*, 30-31.

[9] So Fohrer, *Jesaja* II, 144. The battle is over and the Lord sets to work as a wrecker. For a graphic illustration of this see the relief from Kujunjik (Y. Yadin, *The Art of Warfare in Biblical Lands* [2 vols.; New York: McGraw-Hill, 1963] 446) depicting Assyrian soldiers tearing apart the walls of a conquered Elamite city with crowbars while flames issue from the towers and gates which were partially made of wood. This interpretation is denied by W. Rudolph (*Joel, Amos, Obadja, Jona* [KAT 13/2; Gütersloh: Gerd Mohn, 1971] 234-35) who fails to see the utility of the engineer's line in wrecking as well as building walls. His discussion and gathering of the literature are useful.

the sirocco is clear from the effects. Chap. 35 speaks of the desert, the abode of desert beasts, being rained on and the desert beasts being removed (35:7, 9). But Edom ends up a desert (*tḥrb*, 34:10) where only desert animals (see especially *tnym* in 34:13 and 35:7) and demons live (34:11-17) and where no traveler passes because of the scarcity of water and fear of the animals and demons (34:10). The motif is common in sirocco contexts; it never occurs in rainstorm contexts (Part VII, Study 15). The text also speaks of the Lord's wrath (*ḥmh*, v 2) which is typical sirocco vocabulary and avoids rainstorms (Study 10).

V 9 points in the same direction:

> Her wadis will become pitch;
> her dust, bitumen;
> and her land, burning pitch.

The imagery here that presents the hot sirocco as turning dust to burning bitumen goes beyond the possibilities of any ordinary sirocco, but imagery of this type occurs with some frequency in sirocco contexts; never in a rainstorm (Study 18).

V 4 speaks of the effects of the sirocco on the firmament and the luminaries:

> The heavens will roll up (*gll*) like a scroll;
> all their army will wither and fall (*nbl*),[10]
> As the leaf withers and falls (*nbl*) from the vine,
> like foliage that withers and falls (*nblt*) from the fig tree.

The simile that mentions leaves withering and falling from the vine and fig tree belongs to the fall, to the months of October and November.[11] The falling of the leaves is a gradual process to which the summer dryness and the siroccos of the fall transition period contribute not a little. What precise understanding of "the heavens rolling up" and "their army (the luminaries) withering and falling" the comparison with falling leaves is supposed to suggest is not completely clear. Does the simile refer to both the heavens rolling up and the luminaries falling or to just the latter? It is impossible to be sure of this, but

[10] For the vegetal connections of *nbl* see Dalman, *Arbeit und Sitte* I, 100-1. It is used of leaves "withering and falling" and thus has points of contact with *ʾbl*, *ʾml* and *npl*.

[11] Ibid., 98-102.

I suspect the second is the correct interpretation.[12] The luminaries fall (*nbl*) like the falling (*nbl*) leaves of the vine and the falling foliage (*nblt*) of the fig tree.[13] Fohrer[14] has suggested that the "usage here is probably based on a mythical point of view that conceived of the stars as the fruit of a heavenly tree." Perhaps in view of the season of the year, the reference to the falling leaves of the vine and the usage of *nbl* it would be better to think of "leaves." That would fit the sirocco imagery which is otherwise clear.[15]

[12] This is the interpretation of Rev 6:13 where first the stars fall like figs shaken loose by a mighty wind and only then the heavens roll up. Viewed this way, *kspr*, the simile for the heavens rolling up, is balanced by *knbl* and *knblt*, the similies for the collapse of the luminaries. But it is clear that Rev 6:13 has varied the imagery somewhat.

[13] From the point of view of strict "logic" the collapse of the universe is hardly reconcilable with Judah's deliverance described in chap. 35. This is an indication that for the poet the imagery was precisely that. The impact of the imagery as a concrete expression of the Lord's power was an effect that meant more to the poet than strict "logic."

[14] Fohrer, *Jesaja* II, 142.

[15] It may be possible to suggest a partial model for the imagery here, the seven-branched lampstand, the menorah. C. L. Meyers (*The Tabernacle Menorah: A Synthetic Study of a Symbol from the Biblical Cult* [ASOR Dissertation Series 2; Missoula: Scholars Press, 1976]) on the basis of evidence gathered from all over the ancient Near East including the Aegean, has made even stronger the case for the architecture of this menorah being based on the stylized representation of the so-called sacred tree (see, e.g., E. A. S. Butterworth, *The Tree at the Navel of the Earth* [Berlin: de Gruyter, 1970]) with three pairs of branches issuing from a central axis. Note in this regard the vegetal terminology used to describe the menorah: *qnh*, *mšqdym*, *kptwr* (?), *prḥ* (p. 39). The evidence for the understanding of the "fruit" (not "leaves" as here) of this tree as the luminaries during this early period is not so clear, but a case can be made (p. 121). The evidence for this interpretation of the symbolism of the lamps of the menorah in the Greco-Roman period has been gathered by E. R. Goodenough (*Jewish Symbols in the Greco-Roman Period* IV [Bollingen Series 37; New York: Pantheon, 1954] 71-98). Reading this back into Isa 34:4 where the luminaries are leaves, is, of course, problematic; and the suggestion is offered with reserve. Perhaps echoes of the same motif can be heard in the language of Isa 14:12-19: morning star, son of the dawn, falls (*npl*) from heaven after having been cut down (*gdᶜ*) (12) and ends up like a detested branch (*knṣr ntᶜb*) (19). This symbol of the world tree is apparently the basis for the imagery of Dan 4:7-12 where it represents Nebuchadnezzar. It is described as a tree of great height at the center of the world. Its top reached the sky and it could be seen from the ends of the earth (7-8). The OT parallels for this have been gathered by L. F. Hartman and A. A. DiLella, *The Book of Daniel* (AB 23; Garden City: Doubleday, 1978) 176. However, the symbol was interpreted in detail in Mesopotamia, it would be easy for an Israelite poet to have developed his presentation here from a picture of the world tree like that on the

What about the image of "the heavens rolling up like a scroll"? Is that to be understood only psychologically: from fright? Perhaps, not. If the heavens are conceived of here as made of a hammered-out metal dome (*rqyᶜ*), that is precisely what such a vessel would do as the metal expands under the influence of heat. They would buckle and roll up at the ends—like a scroll.[16] In any case we do have a reference to the darkening of the heavens which is typical of sirocco contexts (Study 16), though explained here in an unusual way. Too much cannot be made of this guess at an interpretation of v 4, but it is clear from the rest of the imagery of the piece that a fall setting is presumed. That is especially true of the way in which the unit balances off *previously* dry land being rained on and producing flowers in chap. 35 against land being turned into a desert by the sirocco in chap. 34. The same opposition indicates the nature of the storm theophany in chap. 34.

V 8 also points in this direction:

> *ky ywm nqm lYhwh*
>   *šnt šlwmym lryb ṣywn*
> Yes, the Lord has a day of vengeance,
>   a year of requital for Zion's defense.

The verse is widely understood as an instance of the *ywm Yhwh* motif.[17] All the connections of this motif are with the sirocco; it never occurs in a rainstorm context (Study 20). In the context of the whole poem the *šnt šlwmym* has to be the eschatological, agricultural new year which brings prosperity to Zion and disaster to her enemies. That

Assyrian cylinder seal published by I. M. Casanowicz (*The Collection of Ancient Oriental Seals in the United States National Museum* [Proceedings of the United States National Museum 69/4; Washington: Government Printing Office, 1926] pl. 5, no. 2): 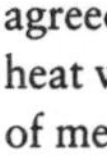 . For that there are numerous parallels. See the discussion of E. D. Van Buren, *Symbols of the Gods in Mesopotamian Art* (AnOr 23; Rome: Pontificium Institutum Biblicum, 1945) 94-104. It is a pity that the great picture book of ancient Near Eastern art has so little text to go with it.

[16] This suggestion is, of course, likewise tentative. I have discussed the imagery here with a metallurgical engineer, a sculptor whose specialty is metal and a welder. All agreed that under certain conditions a metal "dome" expanding under the influence of heat would behave this way. The interpretation presumes the poet had some knowledge of metal-working.

[17] E.g., G. von Rad, "The Origin of the Concept of the Day of Yahweh," *JSS* 4 (1959) 97.

is to say, the arrival of the new age of eternal joy (35:10) which can no longer be disturbed by any potential enemies (chap. 34) is presented with imagery derived from the contrasting storms of the fall interchange period which begins the agricultural cycle.[18] This again presumes a setting in the period after Sukkoth for the imagery of chaps. 34-35. Against this background the return of the diaspora as described in 35:10 could well be understood as a description of pilgrims coming up to Zion for Sukkoth, though it is clear they will arrive late:

> The ransomed of Yahweh will return;
>   they will enter Zion singing,
>   eternal joy upon their heads
> Happiness and joy will overtake them;
>   sorrow and groaning will flee.[19]

The whole of chapters 34-35 reflects the typically OT notion of bliss as evidenced in a text like 1 Kgs 5:5 (cf. Mic 4:4) when it describes, not without exaggeration, the success of Solomon's reign: "Thus Judah and Israel lived in security, every man under his vine or under his fig tree from Dan to Beer-sheba, as long as Solomon lived." Isaiah 34-35 expresses a hope for two things: freedom from outside oppression and rain to guarantee the success of the agriculture.[20] The text of 1 Kgs 5:5 gives us both these elements and in "everyman" probably adds a third, social justice. This last element is presumed by Isaiah 34-35.

The imagery of these chapters rather clearly reflects a time setting that looks forward to the/a coming fall interchange period when the arrival of the sirocco announces the coming of the rains. The Lord's coming in these storms it regards as the opening of the *šnt šlwmym*, which is in fact the opening of a new age. The best commentary I know

[18] See the remarks of J. C. de Moor (*New Year with Canaanites and Israelites* I [Kampen: Kok, 1972] 28) on "the eschatological New Year." With *šnt šlwm* || *ywm nqm lYhwh* of v 8 compare *šnt rṣwn lYhwh* || *ywm nqm lʾlhynw* of Isa 61:2. This text has in its immediate context the same motifs being noted here. The captives will be freed Israel will receive *šmn śśwn* (61:3); will be called oaks of justice, the Lord's garden (61:3). The destroyed cities will be rebuilt (61:4); the agriculture will flourish (61:5). If both texts are allowed to interpret one another, the *šnt rṣwn* of Isa 61:2 is likewise an agricultural new year.

[19] See the instructions regarding Sukkoth in Neh 8:8-12.

[20] For the combination see J. H. Eaton, "The Origin and Meaning of Habakkuk 3," *ZAW* 76 (1964) 161. This text will be studied below on pp. 82-97.

on the whole concatenation of ideas in these chapters is found in the words of Dalman. After describing the situation in Palestine at the end of the rainless summer, he writes: "In der Tat, wenn der Sommer zu Ende ging, erharrt man in Palästina den Regen wie eine Erlösung."[21]

2. Isa 30:27-33

27 Behold Yahweh['s name][a] comes from afar;
his nose burns and there is a heavy cloud.[b]
His lips are full of roaring (*zʿm*);
his tongue like consuming fire (*ʾš ʾklt*).
28 His breath (*rwḥ*) is like a rushing wadi
that reaches the neck.
He will shake the nations a terrible shaking,[c]
32d as he attacks them[d] with attacks that shake.

*

30 Yahweh will make his glorious voice heard;
he will display the lowering of his arm,
With angry wrath and flame of consuming fire,
a shattering rain and hailstones.
31 Yes, at the voice of Yahweh Assyria will be shattered;
with the rod he will be struck.[e]

*

32ab At every sweep of his chastising[f] shaft
which Yahweh will bring down upon him,
29abc You will sing
as on the night when the feast is celebrated.
Your heart will be joyful
like one marching with the flute,
32c with drums and harps,

[21] Dalman, *Arbeit und Sitte* I, 73. With the treatment of Isa 34-35 above, which presumes a clear and logical relation between the two chapters, contrast the treatment of H.-M. Lutz and the authorities he cites (*Jahwe Jerusalem und die Völker* [WMANT 27; Neukirchen-Vluyn: Neukirchener Verlag, 1968] 85-86). The real connection is missed because the meteorology is ignored. The texts brought into the discussion are, however, precisely the right ones because through them all runs the same meteorological imagery being analyzed here.

29d As you go about the mountain of Yahweh
toward the Rock of Israel.

*

33 Yes, his (Assyria's) fire pit[g] has long been ready;
indeed it[h] has been prepared for the king.
Deep and broad[i] is his hearth;[j]
the fire wood[k] has been heaped up.
The breath (*nšmt*) of Yahweh like a wadi of bitumen (*gpryt*)
will set it afire.

a) The imagery of the rest of the poem seems too anthropomorphic and concrete for *šm* to be original. b) The sense of *mśʾh* is uncertain. It is perhaps a dust cloud. See Judg 20:38, 40. c) Omit v 28b as a marginal gloss that disturbs the imagery pattern, though the plus does make some sense in the context. d) Rd Q. e) Rd *yukkeh*. f) Rd *mûsārōh*. g) Rd *toptōh*. h) Rd K. i) Rd *haʿmêq harḥēb*. j) Rd *mĕdūrātōh*. k) Perhaps understand *ʾš wʿṣym* as the equal of *ʿṣy ʾš*. Cf. the *dmmh wqwl* of Job 4:16 which apparently equals the *qwl dmmh* of 1 Kgs 19:12; and the *npṣ wzrm* of v 30 which may also be hendiadys.

The transpositions involved in the reordering of vv 29 and 32 are, of course, problematic. With slight alteration they are based on the *NAB*'s treatment which endeavored to give to the whole a logical sequence. In addition the present arrangement produces four sense units of 4, 3, 4 and 3 lines; and sets the six occurrences of the name, "Yahweh," in the first line of the first paragraph, the first and last line of each of the middle two paragraphs, and the last line of the final paragraph. That the piece might evidence the use of *mots crochets* in this way is indicated by the inclusion formed by *Yhwh . . . bʿr* in the opening line and *Yhwh . . . bʿrh* in the last line.[22]

The sense units are as follows. Strophe one presents the Lord coming in a sirocco to attack the nations. In strophe two the Lord attacks Assyria in a combined rain (*npš wzrm*) and hailstorm (*ʾbn brd*).[23] In the course of the storm lightning occurs. The phrase *lhb ʾš*

[22] I have no explanation for the presumed displacements in MT. The failure of other approaches to the text to make sense of it argues for the correctness of the *NAB* approach.

[23] For the combination hail and rain see Dalman, *Arbeit und Sitte* I, 202, 212, 235.

ʾwklh (v 30) can, in contrast to simple *ʾš ʾklt* of v 27, denote lightning (Study 12). The Lord's weapon here is a mace of some kind (*šbṭ*, v 31; see *mṭh*, v 32). Strophe three describes the joy experienced at the demise of the tyrant; and strophe four, how the pyre of Assyria is set on fire by the sirocco.

Whatever may be thought of these transpositions, the shifting meteorology of the piece is clear. Vv 30-31 present an unmistakable rainstorm. That is preceded by vv 27-28 and followed by v 33 where on the basis of the criteria worked out so far the theophany is presented as a sirocco theophany.

In v 28 the wind, which is clearly Yahweh's breath (see v 33), has the force of a rushing wadi. It comes out of his mouth and his tongue is like an *ʾš ʾklt* (v 27). This verbal combination has clear sirocco connections; it does not occur in rainstorms (Study 12). The noun *zʿm* (v 27) is likewise typical sirocco vocabulary (Study 8).[24] The same is true of the presentation of the Lord as blazing (*bʿr*, v 27; Study 21) and having a hot nose (v 27; Study 9).

V 33 also presents the picture of Yahweh blazing (*bʿr*) at someone. This is typical sirocco vocabulary (Study 21). The *gpryt* motif of the same verse likewise belongs to the sirocco, not the rainstorm (Study 18). Besides, to understand v 33 as a continuation of the rainstorm of vv 30-31 defies logic. A pyre soaked by a tremendous rainstorm will not burn; or if a fire is started by a lightning bolt, it will be quickly extinguished.

This combined sirocco-rainstorm theophany fits either the fall or the spring interchange period. On the basis of the text itself, it does not seem possible to determine which period is meant.[25] But if the immediately preceding vv 23-26 are taken into consideration and allowed to supply the context out of which vv 27-30 are interpreted, it becomes clear that the period envisioned in that context for the theophany of vv 27-30 is the fall. V 23 (see v 25) looks forward to the coming period of

[24] Note how here where the Lord's breath (*rwḥ*, v 28; see *nšmt* in v 33) is the wind, where his tongue is like *ʾš ʾklt* (v 27) and where his *lips* are full of *zʿm*, *zʿm* almost has to have a concrete sense, "the roar of the sirocco." See Study 8.

[25] Most identify the feast of v 29 as Sukkoth, which I think probable. That would help solve the problem, but the identification is controverted. See Wildberger, *Jesaja*, 1220. The argument for assigning these alternating storms to the fall to be outlined below makes the Sukkoth connection even more probable.

salvation as a time when the Lord will send the rain—a useful one distinguished from the rainstorm of vv 30-31. The day of the Lord's intervention to save Israel not only means the removal of her enemies (vv 27-33), but also the coming of rain to guarantee the success of the agriculture. Both elements are already present in vv 23-26. V 25b describes the day of salvation as "a day of great slaughter when towers fall." Vv 27-33 are apparently meant as the commentary on v 25b.

The total picture here is very similar to the picture just seen in chaps. 34-35. In both texts the period of salvation begins with the doming of the rains in the fall. Israel gets rain for the agriculture; her enemies are destroyed by the Lord who comes. The one difference is that in chap. 34 the Lord coming to destroy Israel's enemies is accompanied only by the sirocco. The storm in which he comes to destroy Israel's enemies in vv 27-33 is a combined sirocco and rainstorm. The same picture will be seen again in what follows.

3. Hab 3:2-19

2 Yahweh, I have heard of your renown;
    I fear,[a] Yahweh, your work.
As the years approach (one another)[b] revive it!
    As the years approach (one another)[b] make it known!
    But in the tumult remember mercy!

*

3 God comes from Teman;
    the Holy One, from the mountains of Paran.
His glory covers the heavens;
    the earth is filled with his praise.
4 Brightness like the sun's appears;
    rays shine forth from him;
    therein is the covert of his might.
5 Before him goes Pestilence;
    Plague marches behind him.
6 He takes his stand and shakes the earth;
    he surveys the scene and makes the nations quake.
The eternal mountains are shattered;
    the ancient hills collapse

along his ancient paths.[c]
7 I see the tents of Cushan—
the tent curtains of the land of Midian are aflutter.
8 Against the rivers does there burn (*ḥrh*), Yahweh;
against the rivers (does there burn) your anger (*ʾp*);
against the sea (does there burn) your wrath (*ʿbrh*)?
Look![d] you mount your horses
and your chariot, victory.
9 Truly your bow is bared;
you fill with arrows your bowstring.[e]
With rivers you divide the earth;
10 the mountains see you and writhe.
A torrent of water passes over;
the deep lets its roar resound.
The sun forgets to rise;[f]
11 the moon stays in its palace,[g]
At the light of your flying arrows,
at the brightness of your lance of lightning.

*

12 In anger you bestride the earth;
in wrath you crush nations.
13 You come forth to save your people,
to save your anointed.
You smash the head[h] of the wicked;
you lay open[i] its base down to the neck.
14 You pierce with an arrow his head;[j]
his warriors are blown away.[k]
. . . .
. . . .[l]
15 You travel with your horses the sea,[m]
the churning deep waters.

*

16 I hear and my stomach is in turmoil;
at the sound my lips quiver.
Weakness enters my bones;
below I tremble as I walk.[n]
I groan[o] at the day of distress,
as it comes up against the people who attack us.

17 Even if the fig tree produces no fruit,[p]
if there is no yield on the vines,
If the effort of the olive tree deceives,
if the fields produce no grain,
If the flock is cut off[q] from the fold,
and there are no cattle in the pens,
18 Still will I exult in Yahweh;
I will rejoice in my saving God.
19 Yahweh, my lord, is my strength;
he has made my feet like the hinds';
he enables me to run on the heights.[r]

a) The expanded LXX text reflects both *yrʾty* and *rʾyty*. Perhaps, *rʾyty* fits the parallelism better and runs more smoothly into the next line. b) Perhaps rd *biqrōb*. For G-stem *qrb* of time see Lam 4:18; cf. Isa 13:6 and Exod 14:20 (*qrb zh ʾl zh*). See the discussion below. c) *tḥt ʾwn* (= because of sin) is taken as a plus; perhaps rd archaia *toḥtāʾûn* (3 m. pl.). See *HALAT*, 349. d) See the discussion below. e) For *šbʿwt mṭwt ʾmr* rd *śibbaʿtā maṭṭôt mêtārĕkā*; (*NAB*). f) For *rwm ydyhw nśʾ* : *šmš* rd *mzrḥw nšʾ šmš*. g) Rd *zĕbūlōh*. h) Omit *mbyt*. i) Joüon, § 79, p. The picture, perhaps, presents the skull and the material within it being cracked open vertically from the crown to the neck. j) Rd *bmṭh rʾšw*. k) Rd *yĕsōʿărû*, denominated from *saʿar*. l) Too problematic for any attempt at translation. m) GKC, § 144, m. n) Rd *ʾăšōr*. o) Rd *ʾānôaḥ*. p) Perhaps rd *tprh* for *tprḥ* in view of the parallelism; LXX, *karpophorēsei*. See below. q) Rd *gāzūr* or Qal pass. r) Rd *bmwt*, ditto.

Habakkuk's psalm has been and remains a difficult text. The difficulties are textual and philological on the one hand and concern the general organization of the argument and the context out of which it is to be understood on the other. Neither set of problems can be solved independently of the other set. The prime concern here can only be with the meteorology of the text and the temporal setting it presumes. They are treated along the lines first clearly elaborated by J. H. Eaton,[26] and the meteorology and temporal setting suggest a total

[26] Eaton, "Habakkuk 3," 144-71. Most useful for its thorough review of the older and recent literature is W. Rudolph, *Micha-Nahum-Habakuk-Zephanja* (KAT 13/3; Gütersloh: Gerd Mohn, 1975); see also B. Margulis, "The Psalm of Habakkuk: A Reconstruction and Interpretation," *ZAW* 82 (1970) 408-42; and T. Hiebert, *God of My Victory: The Ancient Hymn in Habakkuk 3* (HSM 39; Atlanta: Scholars, 1986).

interpretation that provides a frame out of which the numerous problems connected with Hab 3 can be approached. The translation presented is uncertain in not a few places because of both the state of the text and difficulties of interpretation. The discussion that follows will make every attempt to avoid basing conclusions on these uncertainties.

Subject matter and shifts in address immediately divide Habakkuk's psalm into sense paragraphs of 2 (v 2), 7 (vv 3-7), 7 (vv 8-11), 6 (vv 12-15) and 8 (vv 16-19) lines. In v 2 the speaker, addressing the Lord directly, recalls the Lord's past work (*šmᶜ*, *pᶜl*) and asks him to renew it. The speaker clearly has some awesome work in mind since in the coming tumult the Lord is asked to remember to pity—his people, presumably (see v 13).[27]

In vv 3-7 the speaker, addressing an indefinite addressee and speaking of the Lord in the third person, describes a sirocco (see below) theophany already seen. Or, better, the sirocco is in the process of being seen in a vision of some kind and prefiguring one still to come (see below) in which the Lord comes from the south. Both nature and men are affected. The Lord's instruments of destruction seem to be only nature forces.

In vv 8-11[28] the speaker, once again as in v 2 addressing the Lord directly, describes a rainstorm theophany. The direction from which the Lord comes is not directly indicated; but since a rainstorm is involved, the presumption is the west.[29] Here only nature is affected by the Lord's coming and the weapons used seem to be exclusively nature weapons—the clouds are the Lord's chariot (v 8; see v 15); lightning bolts, his arrows and lance (vv 9, 11).[30] The background for the imagery

[27] Cf. Nah 1:7-8; Joel 3:5. The former text was discussed in Part II; the latter text will be discussed in Part VI.

[28] Vv 8-11 and 12-15 have the same address pattern and deal with a rainstorm theophany. They could be regarded as one sense paragraph. But there is, however, a development of the argument in the two units. For this reason and because a division produces after the introductory prayer (two) sense paragraphs of almost equal length throughout the piece, they are here regarded as two units.

[29] W. F. Albright ("The Psalm of Habakkuk," *Studies in Old Testament Prophecy Presented to Prof. Theodore H. Robinson* [ed. H. H. Rowley; Edinburgh: Clark, 1950] 9) called attention to the distinct storms involved in vv 3-7 and 8-15: "This part of the Psalm [8-15] reflects the theophany of Yahweh in the north-west thunderstorm, with its torrents of water, which stands in sharp contrast to the disease-laden sirocco of Part II [3-7]." See 1 Kgs 18:44; Luke 12:54.

[30] Note how lightning is treated here as an arrow or a lance that is shot or thrown. This point of view is represented elsewhere in the OT (Ps 18:15 = 2 Sam 22:15; Ps 77:18;

involved in these shifting storms is precisely the meteorology of the fall interchange period as described in Part I. The reasons for assigning the meteorology to the fall rather than the spring will be discussed below.

Vv 12-15 continue the same pattern of address as that in vv 8-11. The rainstorm apparently continues. Note how in v 14 the Lord's enemies are blown away (*sʿr*). But in v 12 the Lord is no longer fighting from a chariot. He has dismounted after having reached land and now advances on foot (*ṣʿd*). The verb, *ṣʿd*, apparently always means this. It is never used of a chariot advancing on dry land or in the imagery that presents the Lord's chariot flying through the sky.[31] In addition, by contrast with vv 8-11 in vv 12-15 nature is not affected, but human enemies are. And the weapons of the Lord here seem to be principally (contrast *ysʿrw*, v 14) those of the human warrior rather than nature weapons. V 13 presents him as smashing (*mḥṣ*) heads. This is presumably done with a club, ax or striking sword. The same verse presents him as piercing (*nqb*) heads. This is presumably done with a real arrow or lance rather than the lightning of vv 9-11.

The way in which the translation of the two lines of v 8 has been handled is unusual. The fundamental problem is whether the question of the first line refers back to the sirocco of vv 3-7 or forward to the rainstorm of vv 8b-11. Does the question refer to a possible battle with the sea and its rivers[32] where, as in Ps 29:10, the Lord ends up enthroned on subdued *Mabbûl* or to the Lord's victory over the sea in which the sea is dried up as in Nah 1:4?

It is supposed here that the question refers back to the sirocco. In the first place the only natural phenomena "seen" to this point are sirocco phenomena. In addition *ḥrwn ʾp* and *ʿbrh* have clear connections to the sirocco, none to a rainstorm (Studies 9 and 19); the precise combina-

---

Gen 9:13) and in the iconography of the rainstorm god (*ANEP*, 490, etc.). The picture is different from the picture of hot wind issuing from the mouth of Yahweh just seen, e.g., in Isa 30:33 (see further Study 9).

[31] The typical sense of verbal *ṣʿd* = "to walk" is illustrated by 2 Sam 6:13; Jer 10:5; Prov 7:8. Something of a contrast is presented by 2 Sam 5:24 (= 1 Chr 14:15) where the wind rustling the tree tops is presented as the *qwl ṣʿdh* of the Lord's footsteps. That could be the picture here, as in Judg 5:4 and Ps 68:8, if the Lord is not marching precisely on the ground. The parallel verb (*dwš*) would seem, however, to require "walking on the ground" for Hab 3:12.

[32] See Rudolph, *Habakuk*, 244; J. Jeremias, *Theophanie* (WMANT 10; Neukirchen-Vluyn: Neukirchener Verlag, 1965) 93.

tion here is *ḥrh* + *ʾp* not *ḥrwn ʾp*; and the connections of verbal *ḥrh* + *ʾp* to the sirocco are not so clear (Study 9). In addition, an answer to the question asked in v 8a is needed. The answer comes in v 8b, not in words but in the switch in the direction and nature of the storm. The whole answer is not in v 8b; it comes in the unfolding of the theophany as viewed in vv 8b-15. This answer is introduced by deictic emphasizing *ky*.[33] Finally, the problem of the reference of v 8a almost has to be resolved this way, if, as I think likely, the image used to present the Lord coming in a sirocco from the southeast is the sun disk glaring through the dust (v 4). The manner of the Lord's advance is described differently in vv 8b-15. Note that for the first time in v 8b (see 15) the speaker sees the Lord mounted/mounting[34] on his cloud chariot and it is with v 8b that the rainstorm from the west begins. See below.

Interpreted this way the whole of vv 3-15 presents the following picture. The speaker describes his vision of the coming of the Lord in a sirocco advancing from the southeast[35] toward the Mediterranean (vv 3-7). People and nature are affected by the storm; but about the Lord's ultimate intentions the speaker has doubts. He addresses the Lord and asks whether he comes this time as of old to dry out the sea (v 8a), which

[33] A parallel for the use of the particle *ky* here is Ruth 1:10. When Naomi tells her daughters-in-law to leave her, they answer: *ky ʾtk nšwb lʿmk*. The recent translation of E. F. Campbell (*Ruth* [AB 7; Garden City: Doubleday, 1975] 61; see the discussion on p. 66 and the literature cited there) renders this: "No! with you we will return to your people." The particle *ky* does not, of course, mean "No," or as translated above "Look" or "that" or "because" or, as in Hab 3:17, "if." It is a deictic or emphasizing particle for which there is no precise equivalent in English. The sense comes out of the context. In the present context the speaker sees the Lord coming in a sirocco and wonders about the Lord's intent; and his first suspicions are removed by the switch to a rainstorm theophany in which the Lord comes in his chariot to destroy Israel's enemies (12-14) and bring rain to Palestine (17), "Look" seems a fair rendering. "No" would be equally good here; and "Look now!" with overtones of insistence would work in Ruth 1:10. For the use of *ky* see J. Muilenburg, "The Linguistic and Rhetorical Usages of the Particle *ky* in the Old Testament," *HUCA* 32 (1961) 135-60. Cf. Gen 37:35.

[34] For the sense of *rkb ʿl* see G. Schmuttermayr, *Psalm 18 und 2 Samuel 22* (SANT 25; München: Kösel, 1971) 64-67 and the literature cited there.

[35] If the storm comes from the south and is expected to hit the Mediterranean, the direction meant has to be southeast. OT Hebrew does not have words for southeast, northwest, etc. See H. Klein, "Das Klima Palästinas auf Grund der alten hebräischen Quellen," *ZDPV* 37 (1914) 317-18. Neither Teman nor Paran can be localized with precision, but they are part of Edom. See Rudolph, *Habakuk*, 243.

here, at least, is the Mediterranean. The Lord does not answer. But the speaker sees the vision change, and in this change is his answer. The wind shifts; the sirocco is replaced by a tremendous rainstorm and the Lord comes in his cloud chariot, "victory,"[36] to destroy not the sea, but human enemies. He comes from the west, dismounts from his chariot and attacks his enemies with human weapons (vv 8b-14). The direct answer to the question in v 8a is, of course, not presented till vv 12-14.

This raises the question why v 15 again speaks of of the Lord traveling over the sea, the churning deep waters, with his chariot. Other explanations are possible,[37] but it can be wondered whether the whole picture in vv 8b-15 is not the progression of a westerly rainstorm coming off the Mediterranean, reaching land and then disappearing to the east. This presumes that the Lord remounts his chariot and departs toward the east finally to disappear. In this regard note how the storms come to an end with v 15. Note too how the poem to this point has presented a picture of *moving* storms. The sirocco comes from Teman and Paran (v 3). It sets the tent curtains of Cushan and Midian aflutter (v 7). It threatens the Mediterranean (v 8).[38] The rainstorm comes off the Mediterranean and the Lord reaches land (v 12).

This interpretation presumes that while *ym* in v 8 is the Mediterranean, *ym* in v 15 is the/an eastern sea.[39] See, e.g., Ps 72:8:

> May he rule from sea to sea,
> from the river to the ends of the earth.

[36] The ambiguity of *yšwʿh* ("victory" or "salvation") might well be intended here. Note *lyšʿ* in v 13. While the real meaning of the Lord's coming is not completely clear till vv 12-14, it is already hinted at in v 8b.

[37] E.g.: "(This is why) you travel." The picture presumed is low clouds scudding over the sea (Ps 77:19-20).

[38] The precise geographical relation of Teman-Paran to Cushan-Midian cannot be determined, but the mention of the Mediterranean at the end of the list clearly implies movement out of the south-east.

[39] I share the view of Rudolph (*Habakuk*, 248-51) that in the context of the whole of Habakkuk the nations (v 12) whom the Lord crushes in order to save his people (13) are in the first place the Chaldeans (see 1:6). In other words the context supplied by the whole book presumes the storm reaches at least as far as Babylon. That the speaker can "see" events at this distance is not a problem. He has already "seen" events in Teman, Paran, Cushan, and Midian. That would be another argument for regarding the sea of v 15 as an eastern sea. See the discussion below.

The second colon refers to the (then known) inhabited world from Mesopotamia (the Euphrates or the Tigris) to the inhabited islands/coastlands of the West. In the first colon one sea has to be the Mediterranean; the other is, perhaps, the Persian Gulf. In any case, the context demands that *mym ʿd ym* mean from one end of the world to the other.[40]

In vv 16-19 the speaker describes his reaction to the vision. Once again there is a shift in address. The speaker addresses an indefinite addressee and speaks of the Lord in the third person. In v 16 he describes his own personal fear. The coming of the Lord is so awesome that even those like himself who have reason to rejoice at it are frightened (see v 2). In v 17 the speaker reviews important aspects of the coming agricultural cycle. He treats first of the fruits in the order of their ripening (the early figs in June and the late figs in August; the grapes in August; the olives in September[41]). He treats last of the herds which prosper most through the rainy winter and early spring when the grass is fresh and abundant and which give a steadily decreasing supply of milk during the rainless summer.[42] In between he reckons with the possibility that there will be no *ʾōkel* in the *šdmwt*. In this lineup where the staples of the Palestinian diet are being reviewed, even though it is not clear what precise kind of agricultural land *šdmwt* refers to,[43] it seems clear that *ʾōkel* has to refer to cereals, as it frequently does elsewhere.[44] To be noted here is that the poet is rather clearly thinking in terms of the agricultural cycle which starts with the rains of October-November insofar as he presents the elements of the food supply in precisely the reverse order of their becoming available

[40] See H.-J. Kraus, *Psalmen* (BKAT 15/1-2; 2nd ed.; Neukirchen: Neukirchener Verlag, 1961) 498; H. W. Wolff, *Dodekapropheton 2, Joel und Amos* (BKAT 14/2; Neukirchen-Vluyn: Neukirchener Verlag, 1969) 380.

[41] Dalman, *Arbeit und Sitte* I, 561.

[42] Ibid., 519-20; VI (1939) 291.

[43] In Isa 37:27 *šdmh* is probably to be changed to *šdph* of the parallel text in 2 Kgs 19:26. In Isa 36:8 and Deut 32:32 *šdmwt* refers to land on which vines grow. Jer 31:40 (Q) and 2 Kgs 23:4 probably favor "slopes" or the like, but it is not necessary to read this into Isa 16:8 and Deut 32:32. Vineyards in Palestine are not necessarily set out on mountain sides. See ibid., IV (1935) 308-9.

[44] Gen 41:35; etc. BDB and F. Zorell, *Lexicon hebraicum et aramaicum Veteris Testamenti* (Roma: Pontificium Institutum Biblicum, 1963) s.v., specifically identify *ʾkl* in Hab 3:17 as "cereals," presumably for the reasons indicated.

or, in the case of milk, available in abundance: the fruits of summer, the cereals of the spring and the milk products of winter and early spring. The speaker affirms that even if all these staples fail to materialize, still he will trust in the Lord who is his strength.

Possibly the speaker has in mind here a whole series of possible causes for the failure of the various parts of the Palestinian agricultural economy (locusts, blight, lack of rain, etc.). But the context supplied by the whole text, namely the fact that rain is in sufficient supply and at the right time was the most important factor determining the success or failure of the agriculture.[45] The fact that a lack of rain is the one factor that would undermine most directly each of the aspects of the agriculture mentioned, would indicate that what the speaker has in mind is principally the insufficiency of the winter rains. The temporal sequence envisioned by the text here would then be very similar to that envisioned by Deut 11:11-17 which is a review of the Palestinian agricultural year that has for a starting point the arrival of the early rains:

> The land into which you are crossing over to take possession of is a land of hills and valleys that drinks in rain from the heavens. It is a land which the Lord, your God, looks after from the beginning of the year to the end. . . . I will give the seasonal rain to your land, the early rain (Oct.-Nov.) and the late rain (Mar.-Apr.) (as well as the rain in between), that you may have your grain (in the spring), wine (in the late summer), oil (at the end of the summer) to gather in. And I will bring forth grass in your fields (during the winter and early spring) for your animals. Thus you may eat your fill. But be careful . . . not to serve other gods. . . . For then the Lord will close up the heavens, so that no rain will fall, and the soil will not yield its crops, and you will soon perish from the good land he is giving you.[46]

That vv 3-7, which are distinguished from the rainstorm theophany of vv 8-15 by the shift in address, in fact describe a sirocco is, perhaps, not immediately evident. To some extent the identification is based on the other combination-sirocco-rainstorm theophanies already examined and still to be examined. In addition there is no mention of rain or thunder or lightning. The storm approaches from the south where the sirocco is supposed to come from.[47] There is a wind involved which

[45] Dalman, *Arbeit und Sitte* I, 115-54.

[46] See also Lev 26:4-5; Ps 104:13-15.

[47] The other Yahweh-comes-from-the-south passages are: Judg 5:4; Ps 68:9; Deut 33:2.

sets the tent curtains aflutter (v 7). The motif of the earth shaking and the mountains being knocked over (v 6) could go either with a rainstorm or a sirocco,[48] but again it indicates a wind is involved. Finally there is the motif which presents the Lord coming in the company of Plague and Pestilence (v 5). This motif belongs exclusively to the sirocco theophany (Study 2) and is the clear indication of the nature of the storm. See also the discussion of v 8a above.

One other indication that different natural phenomena are involved in vv 3-7 and vv 8-15 is found in vv 3c-4 which possibly can be meteorologically rationalized. Though vv 10-11 are in part textually corrupt, they indicate clearly enough that the sun and the moon are blotted out by the clouds of the rainstorm of vv 8-15. The meteorological facts are not presented that way, but that is what is meant. It is true that in some sirocco theophanies the sun and the moon are thought of as darkened by the blowing dust (Study 16); but the sky is apparently not thought of as darkened in vv 3c-4:

> His glory covers the heavens;
> the earth is filled with his praise.
> Brightness like the sun's appears;
> rays shine forth from him;
> therein is the covert of his might.

The glory (*hwd*) of the Lord that covers the heavens and the praise (*thlh*) of the Lord that fills the earth are, perhaps, the dusty haze and

In Judg 5:4 Yahweh comes from Seir/Edom (southeast) and it rains! If the text is correct, it bursts the bounds of experienced meteorology. Cross (*Canaanite Myth*, 100-1), however, for reasons that have nothing to do with meteorology regards *gm ʿbym nṭpw mym* as secondary and for the rest revocalizes mention of rain out of the text. Contrast M. D. Coogan's treatment ("A Structural and Literary Analysis of the Song of Deborah," *CBQ* 40 [1978] 146). In Ps 68:8-9, which has verbal connections with Judg 5:4 and in which the Lord marches from the Sinai desert at the head of his people, the text as vocalized by the masoretes presumes rain. Again Cross (p. 101) revocalizes mention of rain out of the text. True rain is present in v 10, but it is not clear whether different storms are described in vv 8-9 and 10. It should be noted, however, that here the direction from which the Lord comes is southwest and a southwest wind can bring rain. The text of Deut 33:2, where the Lord comes from Sinai, Seir and the hill country of Paran is too disturbed for certain interpretation, but it is clear that no rainstorm is involved. See n. 49 below for a possible connection to the sirocco.

[48] See v 10 where the mountains writhe (*ḥyl*) during the rainstorm theophany.

the noise of the wind that raises the dust (v 3). The imagery of v 4 is apparently based on the picture of the hot sun blazing through the haze in a sirocco as described in Part I. The Lord is thought of as appearing under the cover (cf. *ḥbywn*) of the blazing fireball of the sun that produces the heat characteristic of sirocco periods.[49]

[49] The picture in Deut 33:2 could be similar. There the Lord shines (*zrḥ*) and displays beams of light (*hwpyʿ*) as he comes from Sinai, Seir and the mountain country of Paran. The verb *zrḥ* is clear solar vocabulary; hiph. *ypʿ* has connections with light, none with lightning. In Ps 50:2-3 it may be used of the Lord appearing in a sirocco, again presented as the blazing sun:

From Zion perfect in beauty
God shines forth (*hwpyʿ*).
Our God comes;
he will not be silent.
Fire (*ʾš*) before him consumes (*tʾkl*);
round about him there is a great storm (*nśʿrh*).

The combination *ʾš* + *ʾkl* is attested in patent sirocco contexts; never in a rainstorm (Study 12). The point of view that has the sirocco originate on Zion is not, of course, experienced meteorology, but it has a clear parallel in Amos 1:2 where Yahweh roars (*yšʾg*) and gives forth his voice (*ytn qwlw*) from Zion. This produces the withering (*ʾblw*) of the pastures and the drying up (*ybš*) of Carmel (Study 7).

A good parallel for the picture in Hab 3:3-4 may, perhaps, be found in any locality where the sun is partially covered by haze or smog. The viewer squinting at it gets the impression of rays coming forth from its edges.

It is sometimes denied (e.g., A. Jirku, "Die Gesichtsmaske des Mose," *ZDPV* 67 [1945] 43-45; W. F. Albright, "The Psalm of Habakkuk," 14) that *qrnym* in v 4 can denote "rays (of light)." Though witness to this usage is limited to the present text, the parallelism calls for "rays" and this sense is presumed by the denominated verb *qrn* in Exod 34:29, 30, 35. Here as U. Cassuto pointed out (*A Commentary on the Book of Exodus* [Jerusalem: Magnes, 1967] 418-49), with *ʿwr pnyw* as subject *qrn* cannot mean "to have horns." It has to mean something like "to shine" (so LXX, Syr., *Tg. Onq.*). K. Jaroš ("Des Mose 'strahlende Haut'," *ZAW* 88 [1976] 275-80), who is determined to keep the cult mask here, suggests that *ʿwr* was originally the skin of the mask and that *qrn* originally meant "to have horns." Only P's handling of the text makes *qrn* mean "to shine." How P could make a word denote what it did not denote, he fails to explain. The interpretation of personal names on the basis of false etymologies is something quite different and not a parallel. The dual *qrnym* in Hab 3:4 does not necessarily indicate only two rays (Joüon, § 91, e). The picture intended may be influenced in part by an iconography related to the presentation of Mesopotamian Šamaš on cylinder seals with rays issuing from his shoulders or sides (*ANEP*, 683-86). See J. Jeremias, *Theophanie*, 87. For a somewhat different view of *qrnym* here see M. Dahood, *Psalms* I (AB 16; Garden City: Doubleday, 1966) 108; and W. H. Propp, "The Skin of Moses' Face—Transfigured or Disfigured?" *CBQ* 49 (1987) 375-86.

The combined rainstorm-sirocco theophany of the poem makes the time period assumed by the meteorology of the piece either the spring or the fall interchange period. Other indications point more directly to the fall. In the first place v 9 speaks of the Lord as dividing up the earth with rivers (*nhrwt*). This is probably a reference to rivers like the Jordan which had dwindled to streams during the dry summer beginning to flow with force after the first rains. The situation envisaged is the opposite of that presumed by Isa 11:15 where the Lord turns the Euphrates (*hnhr*) into seven wadi-like streams (*nḥlym*) which can be crossed on foot. Perhaps too, it is possible to understand the imagery here as hyperbole. The wadis (*nḥl*) which had completely dried up during the summer are turned into veritable rivers (*nhrwt*).[50] V 2 presents the speaker requesting the Lord to revive (*ḥyyhw*) and make known (*twdyᶜ*) his work (*pᶜl*) "as the (two) years meet (*biqrōb* [MT, *bĕqereb*] *šnym*)."[51] The work to be revived is rather clearly that done in the vision. The phrase *bqrb šnym* is unparalleled and the interpretation difficult. Eaton[52] has interpreted it as referring to the transition from the old year to the new, i.e., the period after Sukkoth when the new agricultural year begins with the coming of the first rains. That view is followed here. This immediately fits in with the list of the products of the agriculture listed in reverse order in v 17 and discussed above. In addition, note how the success of the agriculture is still completely in doubt (v 17). If the spring interchange period were involved, the progress of the agriculture during the rainy season would already have given a good indication of what the prospects were.

In the course of this discussion the suggestion has been made that what is being described in vv 3-15 is a theophany already seen or, better, in the process of being seen and foreshadowing a "real" one still to come. It is clear that something, at least, is still expected to happen. In v 2 the speaker calls on the Lord to *renew*, to *make known* his work. This work has something to do with the future occurrence of sufficient rain to guarantee the appearance of fruit on the fruit trees and the vine during the coming summer, to guarantee grain in the fields in the spring, and to supply the cattle with fresh grass during the winter and

[50] This can also happen in the spring. See the spring storms described by Dalman, *Arbeit und Sitte* I, 202.

[51] For the sense of *qrb* presumed here see text note *b* on p. 84 above.

[52] Eaton, "Habakkuk 3," 147.

spring and with water for the summer; and this issue is still in doubt (v 17). Furthermore, it does not seem reasonable to suppose that the poem presumes that the sirocco, which in the words of the Palestinian proverb brings the west wind,[53] comes as soon as the prayer of v 2 has been uttered.

On the other hand, the speaker who at first thought that the Lord's coming in the sirocco might be directed at the sea (v 8), already knows (vv 12-15) that the Lord's anger is directed at human enemies. There is a ready explanation for this, if the theophany in one way or another has already been witnessed.

In this way it might be possible to explain the difficult concatenation of tenses throughout the chapter. The vision (vv 3-15) in process is presented with action perfects or converted imperfects describing what has just been seen, stative perfects describing the present situation, and action imperfects describing the present vision as it unfolds. The shifting tenses, perhaps, are intended to convey a sense of excitement.[54] The prophet's reaction to the vision (v 16) is described with stative perfects and converted imperfects as well as imperfects, all reflecting present time. That leaves to be explained only the tenses in v 2 and vv 17-19 where the orientation is toward the future. In v 2 the tense usage is straightforward. The speaker has heard of (*šmʿty*) and now fears (*yrʾty*)[55] the Lord's work. He asks for its renewal. Vv 17-19 can also be explained with relative ease. Even if the fig trees do not produce fruit (*tprh*; MT, *tprḥ*) next summer, and if the effort of the olive tree will have deceived (*kḥš*, fut. pf.),[56] and the fields will not have produced grain (*ʿśh*, fut. pf.), and the flock will have been cut off (Qal pass., fut.

[53] Dalman, *Arbeit und Sitte* I, 103-4.

[54] Rudolph (*Habakuk*, 241; similarly Eaton, "Habakkuk 3," 163-65) understands the tense oppositions here as the mixing of a description of a vision already *completely* past with a description of the future events it foreshadows. But in v 8 the vision is not over. Habakkuk does not yet know what the Lord's intentions are. And if he does not know these intentions or understand the vision fully, he cannot be said to be describing the future. The prophet's whole concern here is to understand what he is seeing. The understanding of the future implications of the vision comes only with its full unfolding. This is not said directly, but is implicit in the argument of the piece. Of course, from the start Habakkuk knew something of the possibilities. He had heard the tales of what the Lord did when he came in similar theophanies in the past (v 2).

[55] Or "has seen," if *rʾyty* is read. See text note *a* on p. 84 above.

[56] To express the fut. pf. both *qṭl* and *yqṭl* are possible (Joüon, § 112, i; 113, b) and can be combined in the same context: Isa 4:4; 6:11; 2 Sam 15:33-34.

pf.; MT *gāzar*) from the fold, the speaker will still exult and rejoice (*ʾʿlwzh . . . ʾgylh*) in the Lord; for the Lord is his strength, has made (*wayyāśem*) his feet like the hinds' and has continually directed him (*ydrkny*) on the heights. No matter what fate the immediate uncertain future holds in store, the speaker's past experience of the Lord and the vision just seen are for him sufficient guarantee that ultimately he has good grounds to trust in providence (cf. Job 1:21).

Viewed in the light of Isaiah 34-35 and Isa 30:(23-26+) 27-33, the first two texts examined where the sirocco and the rainstorm appear in combination, Habakkuk 3 presents a peculiar picture. In Isaiah 34-35 the enemies of the Lord and of the Lord's people get blasted by the sirocco (v 34); the Lord's people get rain (v 35). In Isa 30:27-33 the Lord attacks Assyria in a combined sirocco and rainstorm while his people receive the needed fall rain (vv 23-26). Both texts reflect the twofold desire of the Israelite farmer as he looks forward to the coming fall interchange period: freedom from outside oppression and the success of the agriculture.

By contrast the speaker in Habakkuk 3 sees a vision in which the Lord comes in a combined fall sirocco and rainstorm to save his people by destroying its enemies (vv 12-14). But in describing his own reaction to the vision he expresses his doubts about the success of the agriculture (v 17); and at the same time professes his loyalty to the Lord (vv 18-19). How is this to be understood?[57] The question can be answered on two levels: 1) by regarding Habakkuk 3 as an independent unit; 2) by regarding Habakkuk 3 as the conclusion of Habakkuk 1-3—either as an original part[58] or as a secondary plus, perhaps with adaptations (the doubts about the success of the agriculture in v 17) occasioned by the new context.

Level 1: The speaker has seen a vision of the Lord coming in a sirocco and rainstorm. The vision of the Lord makes clear to the speaker that the Lord will indeed come to remove his and his people's

[57] Some eliminate v 17 and with it the problem. Rudolph (*Habakuk*, 240-41) says it stands completely isolated in chap. 3 and has no connection with anything that precedes. He translates *ky* as "Denn"; and claims that v 17 was added to chap. 3, once it had become a community psalm, in order to make it useful not only when there was danger of enemy attack, but also when the agriculture failed. It is difficult to conceive of an editor inserting v 17 in such an awkward place, if that were the intent behind the insertion.

[58] Ibid., 240.

enemies (unspecified) and by implication that the same rainstorm will bring the needed rain to prosper the agriculture. But while the vision has made clear to the speaker that the Lord will come, it has not made clear to him the time. Naturally he hopes the Lord will come this year. But if that does not happen (v 17), if in the coming agricultural year or years the rain does not come in sufficient supply and the agriculture fails, and if by implication the does not remove the enemies of his people, he still trusts the Lord. He knows both his desires will be fulfilled—someday.

Level 2: Here I follow closely Rudolph's analysis.[59] Habakkuk complains to the Lord about rampant injustice in Judah (1:2-4). The Lord answers he will send the Chaldeans to remedy the situation (1:5-11). That the cruel Chaldeans should be the instrument of the Lord's punishment causes the prophet further problems (1:12-17). The Lord explains to the prophet that he will punish the Chaldeans too (2:1-5), but the possibility of a delay is to be reckoned with (2:3). Through all this the just man will survive by his *ʾmwnh* (2:4). As 1QpHab expressed it commenting on the text here: "The Lord told Habakkuk what would happen to the last generation, but the precise time he did not announce to him" (VII, 1-2). The prophet is satisfied and after directing five woes against the Chaldeans (2:6b-20) closes chap. 2 with:

> The Lord is in his holy temple;
> silence before him, all the earth. (v 20)

The two elements here, certainty about the Lord's intervention to save his people from the Chaldeans and uncertainty about when precisely that intervention would take place, reflect perfectly the point of view of Habakkuk's psalm in chap. 3 as explained above. What chap. 3 adds to 1-2 is a specification of how, admittedly still rather mysterious, the Lord will deal with the Chaldeans. Nothing is said about this in chaps. 1-2.

This discussion of Habakkuk 3 has led off in directions which in part are not immediately germane to what is being attempted here, a clear isolation of the vocabulary and motifs that identify the sirocco. The text is difficult and there is no pretense that the interpretation suggested is definitive. The only point that must be emphasized to preserve the continuity of the overall argument from the texts that

[59] Ibid., 248-51.

preceded to the texts that follow is the distinction between the storms of vv 3-7 and 8-15. If everything else is wrong, that distinction seems clear. The next text is easier to deal with and the discussion can be straightforward.

4. Ps 18:8-10 (= 2 Sam 22:8-10)

Ps 18:8-17 is frequently read as a classic example of a rainstorm theophany. There is reason, however, to think that what is actually being described is a combined sirocco-rainstorm theophany. The opening vv 8-9 describe rather a sirocco than a rainstorm. In v 7 the Lord is said to have heard the speaker's complaint. The description of the theophany follows immediately:

8 The earth shook and quaked;
the foundations of the mountains trembled;
they quaked because he was angry (*ḥrh lw*).
9 Smoke rose from his nose (*ʾpw*);
fire (*ʾš*) from his mouth consumed (*tʾkl*);
embers (*gḥlym*) were set ablaze (*bʿrw*) by him.
10 He parted the heavens and descended;
a dark cloud (*ʿrpl*) was under his feet.

That vv 10-17 describe a rainstorm in which the Lord appears to draw the speaker out of the "deep waters" is sufficiently clear. But note how this part of the theophany seems to begin with v 10a: *wyṭ šmym wyrd*. Compare Ps 144:5 (the verbal connections with Psalm 18 are clear) where the psalmist's request for a theophany opens: *hṭ šmyk wtrd*. Unless this is a combined sirocco-rainstorm theophany like those already seen in Isa 30:27-33 and Habakkuk 3, it is difficult to explain why the effects of the Lord's coming from heaven should be described (8-9) before it is said that he comes. In other words, *wyṭ šmym wyrd* (10a) signals the same shift from an easterly sirocco to a westerly rainstorm as that signaled by *ky trkb ʿl swsyk mrkbtyk yšwʿh* in Hab 3:8b.

Individual elements of vv 8-9 also point in the direction of the sirocco. The presence of *ḥrh* in v 8 and *ʾp* in v 9 is, perhaps, an echo of *ḥrwn ʾp* which consistently appears in sirocco, but not in rainstorm contexts (Study 9). V 9 presents the Lord as fire-breathing. Smoke goes up through his nose; fire comes forth from his mouth. This motif belongs to the sirocco, not the rainstorm (Study 9). The combination *ʾš* + *ʾkl*, though it frequently describes the action of a sirocco, is not used of lightning (Study 12). This sirocco is a super-sirocco, which turns wood into burning embers (*gḥlym bʿrw mmnw*, v 9b).[60] Lightning can, of course, start fires, but in a downpouring rain they are quickly extinguished, and that does not seem to be what is meant here.

A serious objection can be raised to what has been suggested about the nature of the storm imagery involved in vv 8-9 that makes it different from the storm of vv 10-17. "Burning coals" are mentioned in both v 9 (*gḥlym*) and v 13 (*gḥly ʾš*);[61] and that would seem to forge a more intimate connection between vv 8-9 and 10-17 than the one envisioned here. It is necessary, however, to note the difference between *gḥlym* (9) and *gḥly ʾš* (v 13). In v 9 it is apparently a question of wood on earth being turned into "burning coals" by a super-hot sirocco. That never happened, of course, but the exaggeration clearly fits the nature of this hot storm. Thus, the *gḥlym* of v 9 are the result of the theophany, not a constitutive part of it.

In v 13 the *gḥly ʾš*, if the text is in order, almost have to be understood as lightning, i.e., as part of the theophany.[62] Every time that *ʾš* is paired

[60] For the probable sense of *gḥlym bʿrw mmnw* see the description of fire-breathing Behemoth in Job 41:13 and the discussion of P. Dhorme, *Le livre de Job* (Paris: Lecoffre, 1926) 581-82. In Ps 18:9 it would be possible to think of a prairie fire or forest fire driven by the sirocco. Such fires are characteristic of the dry season (from May - June on) and become increasingly more dangerous as the vegetation dries out through the summer (see Dalman, *Arbeit und Sitte* II [1932] 340-41; and Study 12). Some (e.g. Cross, *Canaanite Myth*, 158) translate: "Coals flamed forth from him." That is possible; but if one thinks in terms of the sirocco, less easy to rationalize. In any case the presentation of the Lord as "blazing (*bʿr*)" has connections with the sirocco, not with the rainstorm (Study 21).

[61] They are mentioned again in v 14, but the *brd wgḥly ʾš* of v 14 are missing in both the 2 Sam 22 version and the LXX of Ps 18; and the phrase in v 14 is probably a dittography. See F. M. Cross and D. N. Freedman, *Studies in Ancient Yahwistic Poetry* (SBLDS 21; Missoula: Scholars Press, 1975) 134; Cross, *Canaanite Myth*, 159; Schmuttermayr, *Psalm 18*, 77.

[62] There are, however, problems with the equation, *gḥly ʾš* = "lightning." The full phrase used here, *gḥly ʾš*, is never otherwise used of lightning in any clear text. In addition it is hard to understand how "burning embers" could ever be used as a figure for a lightning bolt. It would be possible to reconstruct v 13:

ngdw ʿbyw ʿbrw
brd wʾš mtlqḥt (Exod 9:24)
(or: *brd wʾš lhbwt,* Ps 105:32)

off with *brd* in this way it is clear it denotes lightning.[63] This would indicate that the meteorological phenomena described in vv 8-9 and 10-17 are in fact distinct.

To be noted about Psalm 18 is that in this royal psalm of thanksgiving the king thanks the Lord for his assistance in a *past* difficulty. Once again it is clear that the imagery of the theophany of vv 8-20 is simply that. This is so even if, as S. Mowinckel has argued, the theophany being described is in fact liturgical drama (see below). It does not seem possible on the basis of the purely geographical phenomena being studied here to tie the alternating storm imagery to any time period. For that reason no attempt will be made to do so.

It does seem pertinent to note, however, the immediate context into which the psalm has been inserted in the appendices to 2 Sam. The concluding chapters of 2 Samuel break down into the following divisions:

a) 21:1-14: The land has been ravaged by draught for three years due to bloodguilt. The bloodguilt is removed by the death of Saul's descendants in the spring interchange period (v 9); then the rains of the fall interchange period come (v 10).
b) 21:15-22: The victories of David and his warriors over the Philistines and four Rephaim.
c) 22:1-51: The psalm introduced (v 1) as sung by David after the Lord delivered him from all his enemies and Saul.
d) 23:1-7: The last words of David dealing with his relationship to the Lord and the consequent security of his house.
e) 23:8-39: David's warriors and their victories over the Philistines.
f) 24:1-25: David's census; he is given the opportunity to choose as his punishment three years of famine, fleeing from his enemies

---

Before him his clouds passed;
 there was hail and zigzagging lightning.
 (or: hail and bolts of lightning.)

The elimination of *mngh* as dittographic is a frequent correction (e.g., Cross and Freedman, *Studies*, 131; Cross, *Canaanite Myth*, 159; Schmuttermayr, *Psalm 18*, 73-76). The text produced is clear and straightforward. And it could be argued that a badly corrupt v 13 was corrected on the basis of v 9. The process is observable in the 2 Sam version of v 13. But both the Ps version and 2 Sam 22 as well as the versions reflect *gḥly* (the Ps version doubly so), and it is almost impossible to eliminate it from the text here with any degree of confidence.

[63] Exod 9:24; Isa 30:30; Ps 105:32; Ps 148:8.

for three months, or three days of pestilence. He chooses the third and it comes in the spring interchange period (vv 15, 20).

That these appendices have been structured is clear from the way section *a* parallels *f* (God's punishment of Israel and its removal); and *b* parallels *e* (the victories of David over the Philistines). It is also clear that throughout the complex run elements that have recurred in the materials being dealt with here. The spring and fall interchange periods are very much in the picture (21:9, 10; 24:15, 20). So too are the first rains of the fall interchange period (21:10) or at least adequate or abundant rain (21:1, 14; 24:13). So too is pestilence, characteristic of periods of sirocco (Study 2); here located in the spring sirocco period (24:13, 15, 20). So too is success against external political foes (21:15-22; 23:8-39; contrast 24:13). The psalm, of course, is principally concerned in its present context with victories over enemies, a prime concern of the combined sirocco-rainstorm pieces already looked at and still to be examined. But there is also the suggestion from the materials the editor associates with the psalm that he saw implied in it undercurrents that the modern eye less familiar with the material fails to see. In particular the way in which he connects the psalm to the spring and fall interchange periods and with a spring plague (Study 2) is suggestive of the combined sirocco-rainstorm character of the storm imagery involved in the psalm as analyzed here.[64]

5. Isa 29:1-8

There is no intention here to enter in detail into the numerous problems of interpretation connected with this difficult text.[65] The only real concern is the storm theophany of vv 5c-6 and how it fits into the probable time sequence presumed by vv 1-8 in the received text. This time sequence supplies a framework which helps tie the whole together, either as an original unit or one that is the product of editing.[66]

[64] I would suggest tentatively that what the editor had in mind in bringing together these materials was to say his "yes" (*b* and *e*) and "no" (*a* and *f*) to the presentation of the Lord's unconditional support of the monarchy reflected in *c* and *d*. The complex thus serves as the transition to the sorry story of 1-2 Kings. To pursue the question would broaden the scope of this investigation unduly.

[65] See Kaiser, *Isaiah 13-39*, 263-68; Lutz, *Jerusalem und die Völker*, 100-10; Wildberger, *Jesaja*, 1097-111.

[66] The text is probably an editorial unit in which vv 1-5b (as far as: *wkmṣ ʿbr hmwn*

The text of vv 5c-6 reads:

5c *whyh lptʿ ptʾm*
mʿm Yhwh ṣbʾwt tpqd
6 *brʿm wbrʿš wqwl gdwl*
swph wsʿrh wlhb ʾš ʾwklh
Then suddenly in an instant
she will be visited by Yahweh of hosts,
In thunder and shaking and loud noise –
in tempest and storm and flame of consuming fire.

The mention of thunder in the first colon of the second line indicates that what is being described is a rainstorm. In the second colon *swph* and *sʿrh* make it clear that something quite different is being dealt with;[67] and combined with *lhb ʾš ʾwklh* they indicate that the second colon describes a sirocco. Both *swph* and *sʿrh* frequently are the sirocco; they do not occur in rainstorm contexts (Studies 3 and 4). While *lhb ʾš ʾwklh* can denote lightning, the phrase is also used of the sirocco (Study 12). The meteorology behind the description of this theophany is the interchange of the rainstorm and the sirocco in either the spring or the fall of the year.

It is perhaps possible to fit this theophany more precisely into the time sequence which seems to be presumed by the present form of the poem. In v 1 Jerusalem is told:

Add[68] year to year;
let the feasts go their round.

ʿryṣym) are expanded and reinterpreted by vv 5c-8. The best argument for this view is the shift in address. In vv 1-5b Jerusalem is addressed. The only exceptions are *spw* (1) for which 1QIsaᵃ has *spy* and the second *whyth* of v 2 which after the first *whyth* would be a simple enough copyist's error for *whyyt*. Even if this *whyth* is left, it is clear enough that vv 1-5b are addressed to Jerusalem. The addressee of vv 5c-8 is not specified. Here Jerusalem is referred to in the third person.

In addition: 1) Vv 4-5b read very much like a description of the fall of the city, though the description is vague enough to allow for the reinterpretation of vv 5c-8 which presume only a severe siege. 2) Vv 1-5b clearly presume that it is Yahweh who leads the attack on Jerusalem; vv 5c-8 presume that Yahweh comes (again?) to break the siege. 3) Vv 7 and 8 make the siege an attack of the *hmwn kl hgwym*. There is no indication in 1-5b that the army was so extensive.

[67] In the list of the prepositional objects which run through the line and where polysyndeton is the norm, note the lack of *w* before *swph*. The lack of the *w* could be understood as marking the division indicated.

[68] Rd *spy* with lQIsaᵃ. See n. 66.

The "adding of year to year" has been understood as the equivalent of "celebrate your New Year."[69] That could be right and might point to Sukkoth as the temporal setting for the words of the poem. Such a setting is readily harmonized with the time sequence presumed for what follows. In vv 2-3 the Lord is presented as a military commander laying siege to Jerusalem—according to vv 7 and 8 with a human army. The mention of (manned) *mĕṣūrōt* ("siege walls" or the like[70]) indicates the presence of an army already in v 3. The further fact that logistic and meteorological considerations generally dictated that campaigns start in the spring gives an indication of how the "let the feasts go their round" of v 1 is to be understood and how v 1 is related to vv 2-3 from a temporal point of view. This can be conceived of in two ways:

1) Celebrate this Sukkoth and the coming Passover and Pentecost (implied: that will do you no good; your feasts in my honor do not please me[71]) (v 1). I will be at your gates with an army next spring (vv 2-3).
2) Keep celebrating your Sukkoths, Passovers and Pentecosts. I will be at your gates with an army some spring.

This time sequence makes an immediate connection with v 4. The verse describes the effects of the difficult siege on Jerusalem. The fact that Jerusalem's speech during the siege is described as a low whisper (*tšḥ ʾmrtk*) or murmuring (*ʾmrtk tṣpṣp*) from the dust (*ʿpr*) calls for a setting anywhere during the dry summer. The noun *ʿpr* generally denotes "loose, dry earth"[72] and is a phenomenon of the summer.[73] The faint voice of exhausted Jerusalem during the siege is probably meant to contrast with the noisy jubilation of Jerusalem at the present Sukkoth feast.

V 5ab,

> The throng of your arrogant[74] will be like fine dust,
> like flying chaff (your) haughty ones,

[69] E.g., de Moor, *New Year* I, 20-21; Kaiser, *Isaiah 13-39*, 267. See Wildberger, *Jesaja*, 1106.

[70] LXX, Vg, Syr. and *Tg. Jon.* all have "siege wall" or the like here (as they do for the preceding *mṣb*). This is demanded by the context, though the precise sense of the military technical terms is uncertain.

[71] See 29:13-14 and especially v 13.

[72] Schwarzenbach, *Geographische Terminologie*, 123-27 and the summary on p. 138.

[73] Dalman, *Arbeit und Sitte* I, 521-23.

[74] Rd *zdyk* with 1QIsa^a. Yahweh does not begin to fight for Jerusalem till v 5c (*whyh lptʿ ptʾm*) which introduces the surprising shift in the action.

deals with the fate during the siege of Jerusalem's *zdym* and *ʿryṣym* who are the occasion of the Lord's anger. The imagery here is not easy to explain with certainty. It clearly belongs to the dry season. Both *ʾbq* (always "loose, dry earth"[75]) and *mṣ* are phenomena of the summer. Perhaps the comparison is only meant to indicate that Jerusalem's *zdym* and *ʿryṣym* will be as helpless to do anything about the siege as the "flying chaff" and "(presumably flying) dust" are before the wind of the dry season. It would also be possible to see here too a reference to a combined onslaught where the Lord not only brings an army to attack Jerusalem, but also fights himself in a spring sirocco. The picture would be similar to that in Isaiah 13 (see Part III). This second explanation would seem better. Understood this way v 5ab in addition to explaining why the Lord is angry (there are *zdym* and *ʿryṣym* in Jerusalem) also explains how the Lord removes them and why the Lord lifts the siege in vv 5c-8. The siege, though it fails to take the city, is sufficient to purge the city of her *zdym* and *ʿryṣym*. Presumably the purge is effected through disease, hunger, thirst and the fighting connected with the defense of the walls.[76] The imagery that involves dust and chaff flying before the wind is characteristic of sirocco theophanies; it does not occur in descriptions of rainstorms (Studies 6 and 11).

If what has been suggested here holds up, it would seem that the theophany of vv 5c-6 is to be located in the fall. The whole of Isa 29:1-8 presumes the following sequence. At one Sukkoth it is announced that Jerusalem will be put under siege the following spring or during some future spring. The siege will continue through the whole of the summer and will be lifted at the time of the next Sukkoth.

[75] Schwarzenbach, *Geographische Terminologie*, 129-30.

[76] If the whole of vv 1-5b presumes the Lord comes in a spring sirocco to destroy Jerusalem and if v5ab is a direct reference to that sirocco, there is a ready explanation for the choice of *ʾryʾl* = "hearth of the altar of holocausts" as the title by which Jerusalem is addressed (v 1). Jerusalem is *ʾryʾl* (synecdoche) because there holocausts were offered to the Lord especially on feasts (v 1). But these sacrifices do not please the Lord because there are *zdym* and *ʿryṣym* in the city. Consequently Jerusalem will become like an *ʾryʾl* in a different sense (v 2). Her inhabitants will be killed within her and consumed by the sirocco. See Isa 30:33 where the sirocco consumes the pyre of Assyria. Once these *zdym* and *ʿryṣym* are removed, Jerusalem will become worthy to bear the name *ʾryʾl* (v 7), the Lord will lift the siege, and the city will live in peace (vv 5c-8). Similarly H. Wildberger, *Jesaja*, 1107.

As indicated in n. 66 I think it probable that v 5ab closed out the poem of vv 1-5b and originally described the fall of the city.

Read this way Isa 29:1-8 is another agricultural new-year text like the first three studied in this section: Isaiah 34-35; Isa 30:27-33; Habakkuk 3. In Isaiah 34 the nations (v 2) and especially Edom get blasted by the sirocco as Yahweh attacks; this is in a context (chap. 35) where previously dry Judah and the eastern desert receive rain. The events take place on Yahweh's *ywm nqm* in his *šnt šlwmym* (v 8). In Isa 30:27-33 the nations (v 28) and especially Assyria are destroyed in a combined rainstorm and sirocco in an editorial complex where Israel receives the useful fall rain (vv 23-26). Hab 3 presents a vision of the Lord coming in a sirocco and rainstorm to crush the nations (v 12) in a context where the prophet looks forward to the coming of rain to guarantee the success of the agriculture. This is expected to take place *bqrb šnym* (v 2) which has been understood to refer to the period of the closing out of the old agricultural year and the beginning of the new one. Isa 29:1-8 speaks only of the Lord's defeat of the nation attacking Jerusalem. The parallel motif of the renewal of the agriculture is missing, though probably implied.

6. Psalms 96-97

In the discussion to this point we have consistently worked with five examples of the specific categories of sirocco dealt with. A sixth example of the rainstorm and sirocco in combination is added here because of the critical position Psalms 96 and 97 have taken in the discussion of the Israelite New Year since Mowinckel[77] and because here the rainstorm and the sirocco are combined in a different way, i.e., in consecutive psalms.

Both Psalms 96 and 97 are *Yhwh mālāk* psalms (96:10; 97:1); and the assumption being made here is that meteorologically they interpret one another. This meteorology would indicate a setting for their imagery in the fall interchange period.[78]

[77] S. Mowinckel, *Psalmenstudien II. Das Thronbesteigungsfest Jahwäs und der Ursprung der Eschatologie* (reprint of 1922 ed.; Amsterdam: Schippers, 1961).

[78] There is no possibility of entering here into the complicated question of the Israelite New Year or the many problems connected with it. For a critical, though not unsympathetic, presentation of Mowinckel's views and the ensuing discussion see H. Cazelles, "Le Nouvel An en Israël," *DBSup* 6 (1960) 620-45. The only concern is the meteorology of Psalms 96-97 and the temporal setting it presumes. The meteorology favors Mowinckel's connecting them to the fall interchange period. Mowinckel paid

In Psalm 96 the heavens and the earth rejoice (*yśmḥw, wtgl*); the sea and everything in it roar (*yrʿm*, v 11); the fields and everything in them rejoice (*yʿlz*); and all the trees of the forest shout for joy (*yrnnw*, v 12) before Yahweh, because he comes (v 13). The roaring sea indicates a storm theophany; the rejoicing fields and trees indicate that the storm is a rainstorm. The joy of the fields and forest is to be explained by the fact that what is being described is the first rain after the long dry summer.[79]

little attention to this meteorology because he was convinced it had little inner logic or relation to experienced natural phenomena. For him and more generally for the participants in the discussion of the Israelite New Year the details of theophanies are all *Beiwerk* and *Ornamentik* (*Psalmenstudien II*, 244-47). In addition he understood these storm theophanies as directly describing liturgical drama. That may be true; but behind the drama itself lies the meteorology of the fall interchange period and the nature mythology connected with it. This hypothesis can stand whether one accepts or denies the liturgical-drama hypothesis.

It does stand if the complicated meteorology of the fall interchange period begins to make sense of a whole series of complicated tests like those being discussed in this Part V and in Part VI. It does stand if the characteristic vocabulary and motifs of the sirocco are kept out of descriptions of rainstorms. Something is controlling that and nature suggests itself as the logical candidate. The isolation of these motifs and this vocabulary has been the prime concern throughout this study. That would hardly be possible if these theophany descriptions were all *Beiwerk* and *Ornamentik*. In addition Mowinckel's position is *a priori* improbable. A twentieth-century academic who works in a library can display this lack of concern for nature. The Israelite farmer will not have been much different from the Palestinian farmers cited by G. Dalman throughout the volumes of *Arbeit und Sitte*. They are interested in and know their meteorology.

So far as Mowinckel's New Year feast is concerned, my impression is that he would have been better served and spared himself considerable controversy had he spoken of "Sukkoth/the autumn festival standing before the opening of the new agricultural cycle/year" or the like. Much of the meteorological material dealt with to this point and still to be treated I too would regard as inspired by the liturgy of Sukkoth reflecting directly or in mythological terms the contrasting storms of the fall interchange period. This material shows not so much a concern with a New Year and the modern overtones the phrase brings to mind, but a concern with a new agricultural cycle. That is a valid point of view even in a period when Tishri is the seventh month.

[79] Isa 35:1-2, where the *mdbr* and *ṣyh* exult (rd *yśśw*), the *ʿrbh* rejoices (*tgl*), flowers (*tprḥ*) and shouts for joy (*wrnn*) at the coming of the first fall rain, was studied above. There as here the beneficent rainstorm was played off against a fall sirocco (Isaiah 34). Isa 42:10-17, which Mowinckel has interpreted as a prophetic imitation of his *Thronbesteigungspsalmen* (*Psalmenstudien II*, 49, 196), presumes the same temporal setting. There the sea and everything in it roar (rd *yrʿm*, v 10), the desert and its cities cheer (*yśʾw*, v 11), and the inhabitants of Sela shout for joy (*yrnw*, v 11) at the coming of the rain in a context where Yahweh threatens to wither vegetation and dry up bodies of

Ps 96 describes the good effects of the Lord's coming in the first fall rain. Ps 97 describes the Lord coming in a fall sirocco, this time to destroy his enemies. The theophany is described in vv 2-5:

> 2 Cloud (*ʿnn*) and darkness are round about him;
> justice and judgment are the foundation of his throne.
> 3 Fire (*ʾš*) goes before him;
> it consumes (*lhṭ*) his enemies round about.
> 4 His lightnings (*brq*) illumine the world;
> the earth sees and writhes.
> 5 The mountains melt like wax
> before Yahweh,
> before the Lord of all the earth.

The *ʿnn* (2) that surrounds the Lord cannot be a rain cloud, but frequently is the dust of a sirocco (Study 5). The fire (*ʾš*, 3) that goes before the Lord could be lightning, but v 5, which presents a picture of mountains melting (*mss*) like wax, presumes great heat, which is characteristic of the sirocco, not the rainstorm.[80] That makes the fire (*ʾš*) of v 3 the

water (v 15). Psalm 98 has the same relation to Psalm 97 as Psalm 96. There the sea roars (*yrʿm*, v 7), the rivers clap hands and the mountains shout for joy (*yrnnw*, v 8) before Yahweh as he comes to keep the earth in good order (*lšpṭ hʾrṣ*, v 9). The general west to east orientation of the rejoicing at the Lord's coming with *ym* at the head of the list in Ps 96:11-12, Ps 98:7-8 and Isa 42:10-11 (Ps 96:10 [*šmym*, *ʾrṣ*] *ym*) cannot be missed. That reflects nature too.

The same west to east orientation is also met in the description of the rainstorm theophany in Psalm 29. First affected is the Mediterranean (*hmym*, *mym rbym*, v 3). Then the storm reaches land and the thunder (and lightning) shatter the evergreen cedars of the Lebanon range (v 5). Next the storm makes the Anti-Lebanon (Sirion) dance (v 6) and finally reaches the desert (*mdbr*, *mdbr qdš*, v 8). Where precisely Kadesh is to be located is not certain, but it is clearly east of the Anti-Lebanon where the desert begins. Like Psalms 96-98, Psalm 29 speaks of the Lord as king (*melek*, v 10). As in Psalm 96 the description of the rainstorm presumes a fall setting. Note the reference to the deciduous trees losing their leaves in v 9. The west to east orientation of the rainstorm in Isaiah 35 (Judah, vv 1-2; the eastern desert, vv 6-8) was noted in the discussion above (Part V, 1).

This note has broached the question of the relation of 2 Isaiah to the so-called psalms of enthronement. The point cannot be pursued, but the tenor of the argument so far makes clear that a discussion in terms of dependency in either direction I tend to regard as a mistake. Both reflect materials that are as old as the hills.

[80] The sense assumed for *mss* here is that in Exod 16:21 where the manna melted (*mss*) whenever the sun grew hot (*wḥm hšmš*). The imagery is possibly based on a combination of the poet's knowledge of smelting ores and the hot sirocco. See n. 82.

sirocco as it frequently is elsewhere (Study 12). In addition *lhṭ* is typically used to describe the action of the sirocco; it is never used in a rainstorm context or of the effect of lightning (Study 22).[81]

The mention of *brqym* in v 4 is problematic. The explanation is probably given by Dalman's description of the sirocco he witnessed on Oct. 9, 1913 and described in Part I. There lightning flashed to the east in a sirocco that developed about 4:00 AM. Only at 6:00 AM did the wind shift and there followed a ten minute rainstorm accompanied by thunder and lightning. By 8:30 AM the wind was again coming out of the east while the temperature rose and the humidity fell.[82]

With the contrasting storms of Psalms 96 and 97 could be compared the more sober promise and threat of Deut 28:12 and 23-24. Since the texts deal with the question of whether the rains will or will not come, both have the fall interchange period as their point of departure. If Israel is obedient,

> The Lord will open for you his rich treasure house of the heavens, to give your land rain in due season, blessing all your undertakings (v 12).

If Israel is disobedient,

> The Lord will cause pestilence (*dbr*) to cling to you till he finishes you off from the agricultural land (*ʾdmh*) which you are setting out to occupy (v 21). The Lord will strike you with wasting (*šḥpt*), fever (*qdḥt*) and burning (*dlqt*); heat (*ḥrḥr*) and dryness (rd *ḥōreb*); blasting (*šdpwn*) and paleness (*yrqwn*). They will pursue you till you perish (v 22). The heavens above your head will be bronze; and the earth under your feet iron (v 23). The Lord will give instead of rain dust (*ʾbq*); and powder (*ʿpr*) will come down from the heavens till you are destroyed (v 24).

Vv 23-24 are meant to contrast with v 12; and v 24, which presents the picture of dust flying before the wind in a context where rain is awaited from the rain-bringing west wind, seems a reference to an easterly storm, the sirocco (Study 6).

[81] The language of Joel 2:3,

lpnyw ʾklh ʾš
wʾḥryw tlhṭ lhbh,

which describes the Lord coming in a sirocco is particularly close to Ps 97:3. This text will be studied in Part VI. See also Ps 50:2-3 discussed in p. 92, n. 49.

[82] Dalman, *Arbeit und Sitte* I, 107. See further the discussion in Part I. P. Reymond,

It is possible that the afflictions threatened in vv 21-22 should also be connected with the sirocco. As was seen in Part I, high incidence of disease is characteristic of sirocco periods; and *dbr* (v 21) has been mentioned in the sirocco texts studied to this point (Study 2). In v 22 the seven afflictions are grouped by homophony[83] into three sub-groups. The first (*šḥpt*, *qdḥt*, *dlqt*) deals with human disease,[84] probably spec-

---

(*L'eau, sa vie, et sa signification dans l'Ancien Testament* [VTSup 6; Leiden: Brill, 1958] 83) has also tried to give a meteorological analysis of the imagery of this text. He claims that Ps 97:3-5 is a description of erosion. Whether he regards the whole of the description of the theophany of vv 2-5 as modeled on a rainstorm he does not say, but that for the reasons indicated is impossible. If Reymond is right, it would be possible to analyze vv 2-3 as crafted on the model of the sirocco and vv 4-5 as crafted on the model of the rainstorm. That would immediately explain the reference to lightning in v 4, and would turn the imagery of Ps 97:2-5 into the combined-sirocco-rainstorm imagery which is the immediate concern of the present discussion.

The problem is *mss* has no clear connections with erosion or the rainstorm. The common derived use of the heart "melting" is not relevant in the present context. The same is true of Ps 112:10 where *mss* is used of the wicked "pining away" or the like with grief. In Judg 15:14 the *ʿbtym* and *ʾswrym* of Samson "disintegrate (?)" like flax burnt (*bʿr*) by fire. Note here how the comparison implies heat. In Ps 68:3 the wicked perish (*ʾbd*) before Yahweh like wax melting (*mss*) before a fire. The comparison again brings heat into the picture and if storm imagery is involved, the storm ought to be the sirocco.

The other two texts where *mss* is used of mountains are Isa 34:3 and Mic 1:4. Isa 34 was the first text studied in this section, and the storm there is clearly the sirocco. But v 3 does not present the results of the sirocco. Rather it is a question of the mountains dissolving in the vast amount of gore that begins to putrefy:

> The mountains will grow mushy (*mss*) with their blood;
> and all the hills (rd *hgbʿwt*) will putrefy (*mqq*).

Mic 1:3-4 is the closest parallel for the present text:

> Look! Yahweh comes forth from his place;
> he descends and treads upon the heights of the earth.
> The mountains melt (*mss*) under him;
> and the valleys are divided (*bqʿ*),
> Like wax before the fire
> as with waters poured down (*ngr*) a slope.

Again note there is heat in the picture. If there is a storm involved, it is rather the sirocco. In any case there is no suggestion of rain.

If the sirocco is involved, the imagery might be rationalized as follows: The Lord comes in a super-hot sirocco, hot enough to melt ore (see n. 80) like wax. The molten lava runs down the side of the mountains like water down a slope and divides the valleys with rivers. Cf. the related use of *bqʿ* in Hab 3:9.

[83] Like *taʾăniyyâ waʾăniyyâ*, etc.

[84] See Lev 26:16. The denotation is typical for the nominal pattern, *qaṭṭalt*, which is related to *qaṭṭil* > *qiṭṭēl* (Joüon, § 88, H, a).

ifying *dbr*. Dalman[85] connects the epidemic here to the month of October when most cases of malaria occur. He explains this as due to bodily fatigue occasioned by periods of sirocco.

The third group (*šdpwn*, *yrqwn*) deals with harm to vegetation;[86] and *šdpwn* at least, can be caused by the east wind.[87] In the case of the second group (*ḥrḥr*, *ḥōreb*), etymological considerations and an attempt to find a middle ground between groups one and three might suggest "heat" and "dryness"/"low humidity," two of the chief characteristics of sirocco periods.[88]

The texts discussed in this Part V are so reminiscent of the legend of Elijah's contest with the prophets of Baal in 1 Kings 18 that this section cannot conclude without a brief reference to it. In v 38 the *ʾš Yhwh* "falls" (*npl*) after Elijah's prayer and consumes (*ʾkl*) the holocaust (*ʿlh*), wood, stones and dust, while it licks up (*lḥk*) the water. This is followed by the coming of the first rains off the Mediterranean (*miyyām*) in vv 44-45. The time setting of the legend can only be the fall interchange period. Behind the *ʾš Yhwh* there could ultimately lie the sirocco, though clearly this is no hyperbolic presentation of a relatively normal sirocco to contrast with the rainstorm that follows. If the sirocco is in the background, a parallel would be the *nšmt Yhwh* that sets ablaze the pyre (rd *toptōh*) of Assyria in Isa 30:33, a text just examined. But the narrative presents here material of legend so far removed from normal meteorology that it is impossible to be sure whether behind this *ʾš Yhwh* lies the sirocco or lightning or even supranatural fire. For present purposes the text is best left out of consideration. Job 1:16, the only other text where *ʾš* is the subject of *npl*, presents the same problem. The text also has a fall setting (1:14).

[85] Dalman, *Arbeit und Sitte* I, 106-7.

[86] 1 Kgs 8:37 (= 2 Chr 6:28); Amos 4:9; Hag 2:17.

[87] Gen 41:6. See Dalman, *Arbeit und Sitte* I, 158.

[88] The noun *ḥōreb* generally occurs in contexts where weather is being discussed. In Gen 31:40 and Jer 36:30 "*parching* heat" (*ḥōreb*) is opposed to *qeraḥ*. In Isa 4:6 "*parching* heat" is opposed to *zrm* and *mṭr*. In Judg 6:37, 39, 40 the presence of dew on Gideon's fleece is contrasted with *ḥōreb* on the ground and vice versa. See Study 1 for *ḥōreb* in Jer 50:38.

The mention of *šdpwn* apparently presumes a period when the grain has begun to grow, i.e., after the first rain (Dalman, *Arbeit und Sitte* I, 158-59; and Gen 41:6). Thus the whole of Deut 28:22-24 (clearly for v 12) cannot be set in the fall interchange period. Dalman thinks of an east-wind period without rain like those of Jan. 22 to Feb. 21, 1902 and Nov. 1 to Dec. 14, 1923. Both periods of drought had serious consequences for the grain crop.

PART VI

Joel 1–4

The book of Joel presents contrasting siroccos and rainstorms very much like those met in Part V. Joel, however, is given a separate treatment because: a) the whole book is organized around the shifting meteorological conditions of the seasons of the year; b) it takes us through two fall interchange periods in which these contrasting storms play a role; and c) it makes the connection between a normal fall interchange period introducing a normal agricultural year and an eschatological fall interchange period introducing a new age. Thus Joel is a clear illustration of the development of the imagery based on the contrasting storms of the fall interchange period into eschatological imagery.[1] The discussion must be summary and concern primarily geography, but the essential points can be made.

The treatment here presumes that the received text as it stands is for all practical purposes the prophet's book.[2] The only significant exception to that is 4:4-8 which is quite clearly a plus.[3] The seasonal

[1] The eschatological character of Joel 3-4 is universally recognized. See, e.g., J. A. Bewer, *Obadiah and Joel* (ICC; New York: Scribner, 1911) 64-65; J. Bourke, "Le Jour de Yahvé dans Joël," *RB* 66 (1959) 5; H. W. Wolff, *Dodekapropheton 2, Joel und Amos* (BKAT 14/2; Neukirchen-Vluyn: Neukirchener Verlag, 1969) 15; W. Rudolph, *Joel-Amos-Obadja-Jona* (KAT 13/2; Gütersloh: Gerd Mohn, 1971) 23.

[2] So, e.g., Rudolph, ibid., 24.

[3] Ibid.

sequence to be discussed here makes the case for the unity of Joel stronger. But even if the present Joel is the product of serious editing, that makes no difference. The seasonal sequence to be described at least guided the hand of the editor. Since the issues to be discussed here can be handled independently of the difficult question of the date of the book, the problem is ignored. The date only becomes significant in discussing the sources of Joel's language. But for present purposes it makes no difference whether Joel is quoting or being quoted or drawing on the same traditional language used by others. The only essential point of interest is the similarity of the language and the context in which it is used.

In Joel 1 the prophet calls for an assembly in Jerusalem to pray for relief from the failure of the agriculture which the community had just experienced (v 14). The causes of the disaster were two: locusts (vv 4-7) and insufficient rain (vv 10-12). Though we are not in a position to define with absolute certitude in each case the precise sense of *gzm*, *ʾrbh*, *ylk*, and *ḥsyl* in v 4, with some degree of probability we can think of the various stages of the locust.[4] It is also possible that the four terms are simply synonymous, general terms for locusts. The argument here does not depend on a solution to this problem. Such plagues are a phenomenon of the spring.[5] Generally the appearance of the locust is sporadic and localized,[6] but in this instance we are probably to infer a tremendous, widespread invasion like that in 1915 about which we are well informed.[7]

The time sequence in 1915 can be presumed to be similar to that in Joel. Reports of the first fliers began to arrive in Jerusalem at the end of February. By the middle of March they were seen in Jerusalem. The first wave did little damage, but laid vast numbers of eggs, though not

[4] See *HALAT*, s.v., and the literature cited there. The problem is complicated by the different order in 2:25.

[5] Dalman, *Arbeit und Sitte in Palästina* I (Gütersloh: Evangelischer Verlag, 1928) 393.

[6] Dalman could report having seen them in significant numbers only once, and that in Moab (ibid.).

[7] J. D. Whiting, "Jerusalem's Locust Plague," *The National Geographic Magazine* 28 (1915) 511-50; L. Bauer, "Die Heuschreckenplage in Palästina," *ZDPV* 49 (1926) 168-71; Dalman, ibid., 393-94. The first two are eyewitness accounts. The beautiful pictures that accompany the first account make it possible to grasp the seriousness of the situation described by Joel.

in the Jerusalem area. About forty days later the larvae hatched and thereafter in a series of molts passed through the pupa stage with developing wings and finally reached the flying stage. During each of these stages they ate voraciously. By May 28 the larvae, already passing into the pupa stage, had reached Jerusalem. The grain crop was being harvested and suffered little damage. But starting with the grape vines and figs they ravaged almost everything else in sight. The first young fliers appeared in early June and it was this group that attacked the olive trees. In late June and early July they departed with the wind leaving the countryside almost completely barren. Fortunately the preceding winter of 1914-15 had brought abundant rain and the trees and the grape vines with their deep roots were able to find sufficient water to put forth leaves again.

Because of the insufficient rain of the previous winter (see the discussion of Joel 1:20 below), possibly combined with spring siroccos or meteorologically related heatwaves (vv 10-12), this was apparently not the case in Joel's time. Note the vocabulary used to describe the state of the agriculture in vv 10-12; *ʾdmh ʾblh* (v 10), *ybš* (vv 10, 12, 12), *ʾml* (vv 10, 12), as well as *šdd* (vv 10, 10) and *ʾbd* (v 11).[8] The first three are typical sirocco vocabulary (Study 7) and clearly refer to the effect of dry heat and/or lack of rain upon vegetation. The last two, though more general terms, can have such connections.[9] Vv 19-20 are also significant in this regard. The vocabulary *ʾš* + *ʾkl* (Study 12) and *lhbh* + *lhṭ* (Study 22) and the effects referred to are typical of the sirocco. In addition the two very close parallels supplied by Ps 50:3 and 97:3 are probably descriptions of a sirocco;[10] and we have the same language in Joel 2:3 where a fall sirocco is described (see below).[11]

[8] Contrast the vocabulary used to describe the work of the locusts in 1:4-7 and 2:25.

[9] For *šdd* see p. 55, n. 25 and note *šd* with reference to the *ywm Yhwh*, which is the day of the sirocco, in 1:15. For *ʾbd* see Jonah 4:10 where *ʾbd* equals *ybš* in 4:7.

[10] See above p. 92, n. 49, p. 107, n. 81.

[11] G. A. Smith, *The Historical Geography of the Holy Land* (reprint 1931 ed.; London: Collins, 1966) 64, connects Joel 1:18-19 to a prairie or forest fire. That fits the season, but neither dries up water sources (v 20). It is interesting to note the differences in the use of this language in the four passages brought together here. In Joel 1:19-20 the language is used to describe a sirocco, a heatwave or at least the hot summer sun. In Joel 2:3 it is applied to the Lord's army that comes in a sirocco; in Ps 50:3 and 97:3 it is the Lord himself who comes in a sirocco.

It would be possible to vary the scenario somewhat. Vv 4-7 would still refer to a spring invasion of locusts and vv 10-12 would still describe the results of the insufficient rains of the previous winter and possibly periods of severe spring sirocco or *samūm*. But vv 18-20 could be understood in the light of Chaplin's[12] description of the situation in Jerusalem in the fall of 1868 which was cited in Part I. In that year the first rains came on Nov. 2 after sirocco had prevailed for thirty days. Vv 18-20 could then refer to such a second severe fall sirocco period following upon the one of the previous spring (vv 10-12). Unfortunately Joel's audience knew the facts of the situation. He had no need to describe it in the detail we would wish. It is clear, then, that Joel speaking at the end of the summer (see below) in addition to the locust problem attributes the present lack of water and the failure of the agriculture during the summer to a lack of rain during the previous winter. Whether part of the whole picture is a period of severe spring sirocco (vv 10-12, 19-20) or whether we are to regard vv 19-20 as a reference to a second period of sirocco in the fall are both uncertain, but they are distinct possibilities.[13]

In any case vv 18-20 do make it clear that the rain during the preceding winter was insufficient. Food and water for the flocks are always in short supply in Palestine during the rainless summer and the situation grows worse as summer draws to an end. But about the normal situation no one can complain. In this particular year due in part to the locusts and in part to the drought the supply was even more meager than usual. Not only the large cattle which need better food but also the sheep and goats which can eat almost anything cannot be fed (note *gm* before *ʿdry hṣʾn*) and even the wild animals,[14] normally considered able to fend for themselves, cannot find anything to eat or drink,

> Because the *ʾpyqy mym* have dried up (*ybš*),
> and fire has devoured (*ʾš ʾklh*) the pastures of
> the steppe. (v 20)

The whole context presumes that the *ʾpyqy mym* are water sources normally available to wild animals through the rainless summer, now

[12] T. Chaplin, "Observations on the Climate of Jerusalem," *PEFQS* (1883) 17.

[13] *Tg. Jon.* paraphrases *ʾš* in 1:20 with *qdwm tqyp kʾšʾ*, which is the sirocco. See p. 58, n. 27.

[14] The climactic character of the argument demands "wild animals." See 1 Sam 17:44.

dried up because the ground water had not been built up sufficiently during the preceding winter.

This description of the state of the agriculture, the vegetation and the water supply implies a temporal setting for Joel 1 in the late summer or early fall prior to the early rains. The setting is similar to the late summer and early fall of 1925 after the deficient winter rains of 1924-25 as described by Dalman.[15] In a context where he is speaking of the importance of the cisterns for men and animals in the late summer he reports how in that year toward the end of summer no water from any source was available in many households. Whole villages moved to the Jordan with their flocks and water had to be brought to Jerusalem by rail to be sold in small amounts.[16] The situation in 1925 and Joel 1 is the same as that presumed in Jer 14:1-10 which speaks of empty cisterns (v 3) and the distress of the wild animals (v 5).[17]

The disasters spoken of in Joel 1 are clearly past disasters. The tense usage is without problems. All the finite tenses referring to the disasters that have occurred are either action perfects with a past reference or stative perfects presenting the resulting situation.[18] The one exception to that is 1:15:

> Alas, the day!
> Indeed near (*qrwb*) is the *ywm Yhwh*.
> It is coming/will come (*ybwʾ*) as destruction
> from the Destroyer.[19]

The orientation here is toward the immediate future.

This motif of the day of the Lord is picked up by the description of the day of the Lord in 2:1-11 which is bound by the inclusion formed by *ywm Yhwh* in vv 1 and 11. Once again the orientation is toward the immediate future. The tense usage is completely different from that in

[15] Dalman, *Arbeit und Sitte* I, 70-73, 176, 194-99.

[16] Ibid., 70-73.

[17] Ibid., 296-97. With the sequence of events in Joel 1 could also be compared the sequence of the visions in Amos 7:1-9 + 8:1-3. The first vision concerns a locust plague. The second, where fire consumes (*ʾš* + *ʾkl*) the *thwm*, can only be modeled on the sirocco. The third concerns an invasion after the spring interchange period; the fourth, a basket of summer fruit. See p. 59, n. 30, and p. 173.

[18] In 1:7 for MT *wĕhiślîk* rd *wĕhaślēk*.

[19] The word play suggests Joel intended this interpretation of *šdy* here, whatever its etymology may be. See Wolff, *Joel*, 22.

chap. 1. The day is coming (*bāʾ*, ptc.), is near (*qrwb*, 1). For the rest there are a few perfects among recurring imperfects. V 3, for example, reads:

> Before it fire (*ʾš*) has consumed (*ʾākĕlâ*);
> behind it flame (*lhbh*) burns (*tlhṭ*).

And v 10 reads:

> Before it the earth quaked (*rāgĕzâ*);
> the heavens shook (*rʿšw*).

This I interpret as the language of vision.[20] The prophet, after relating the agricultural disasters that have already occurred, the locusts and the drought (perhaps, siroccos or heatwaves), announces signs of still worse things to come, the *ywm Yhwh*.[21] He sees that day in one way or another as already dawned for some, now dawning for others (2:6), on its way toward Judah and Jerusalem and soon to arrive there.

The problem of what precisely is being described in 2:1-11 has been much debated.[22] The view to be defended here is that Joel is speaking in the late summer and is describing the coming of a tremendous sirocco in the fall interchange period which is about to open. After the disasters of the preceding year the one hope for relief lay in the coming of the rains in Oct.-Nov., the more abundant the better, and in a normal or abundant fall of rain through the whole of the rainy season. Whether the *ywm Yhwh*, the day of the sirocco, here is to be thought to have particular eschatological connections or not is not completely clear and unimportant for present purposes. But to be noted in this regard is the fact that when the prophet is finally able to announce that the rains will come, that there will not be any spring locusts and that the agriculture will prosper (2:19-27), he does this in quite normal, non-extravagant terms. At the same time, in one sense at least, 2:1-11 is eschatological. After the disasters of the previous year, a prolonged fall eastwind period delaying the rains and introducing another year of drought could easily be presumed to be the end, or almost that, of Judah. Also to be noted in this regard is the peculiar fact that in contrast to other presentations already seen of the Lord coming in a

[20] A similar explanation for the shifting tenses of Hab 3:3-16 was suggested on pp. 94-95.

[21] So, for example, Wolff, *Joel*, 39.

[22] Contrast, for example, Wolff, ibid., 47-50 and Rudolph, *Joel*, 53-54.

sirocco at the head of an army, in 2:1-11 neither the Lord nor his army do any fighting with weapons in the strict sense of the word. All that is needed to finish Judah is for the east wind to blow and the rains not to come.

It is frequently argued that what is being described in 2:1-11 is a plague of locusts, to be interpreted either figuratively or literally. It is readily admitted that the presentation of the sirocco is in part modeled on the locust plague of chap. 1. Thus in 2:4 the Lord's army has the appearance of horses (horse-drawn chariots are meant) and locusts look like horses.[23] Locusts seem to advance in ranks[24] and so does the Lord's army (2:7-8). In 1:6 the locusts are a *gwy . . . ʿṣwm*; in 2:2 the army is an *ʿm rb wʿṣwm*. This is no accident. The army of locusts and the drought of chap. 1 were the signs that foreshadowed and revealed to Joel the imminent *ywm Yhwh*, the day of the Lord's *army* coming in the *dry* sirocco, and so have influenced its description.

The reasons why 2:1-11 cannot be a description of locusts and must be a description of the sirocco are basically four:[25]

1. The timing is wrong for locusts or locust imagery. The advancing summer is not the time to warn against them. The next critical period is the fall-interchange period and the question of burning concern is whether the west wind will come with the early rains or whether the east wind will blow and prevent them from coming. Joel would have been regarded as crazy or totally irrelevant had

[23] Rudolph, ibid., 56. Cf. German "Heupferd" and Italian "cavalletta."

[24] Prov 30:27.

[25] Wolff's treatment (*Joel*, 47-49) underlies a good deal of what is said here. But note his completely different approach: "Dann aber ist in dem angesagten Feind ein apokalyptisches Heer zu sehen. . . . Was von seinen Wirkungen zu sagen ist, ist wesentlich nicht aus Naturbeobachtungen geschöpft, sondern bietet Traditionselemente der überlieferten Theophanieschilderungen, der Androhungen eines Feindes von Norden und der Feinddarstellungen in den Prophetien vom Tag Jahwes" (p. 49). But the way in which descriptions of rainstorms, surely "aus Naturbeobachtungen geschöpft," are balanced off against descriptions of siroccos here (see below) and in Part V, and the way in which these contrasting storms fit into typically Palestinian meteorology suggest that Joel 2:1-11 is also "aus Naturbeobachtungen geschöpft." This is not generally recognized because the nature observed is not European or American. That the description of the sirocco is traditional is clear. Descriptions of storms tend to become that in any language.

he spoken of locusts to Jerusalem's practical farming community at this point.

2. The *ywm Yhwh* is not elsewhere a day of locusts. It is typically the day of the sirocco (Study 20).
3. The characterization of the Lord as coming at the head of an army of locusts is foreign to the OT.[26] The characterization of the Lord as coming in a sirocco at the head of an army is typical biblical imagery.
4. The imagery of 2:3, 10 simply cannot be made to fit locusts. Locusts do not scorch vegetation. Locusts do not shake mountains. But the language here and through the whole of 2:1-11 fits descriptions of the sirocco and evokes parallels that have ties to such storms. And it is impossible to compromise here and combine locusts with the sirocco. Joel well knew what the wind does to locusts (2:20).

The genuinely important arguments are the second and the fourth and they must be gone into in sufficient detail to make clear the pedigree of the language involved. We will start here with 1:15.

Joel 1:15

The language has connections to: a) Isa 13:6: the sirocco character of the language was discussed in Part III;[27] b) Ezek 30:2-3: the *ywm lYhwh* is a *ywm ʿnn*. That *ʿnn* (never a rain cloud) is the dust of the sirocco (Study 5) is indicated by v 12 where the Niles are turned to *ḥrbh* (Study 1); c) Zeph 1:7: the motif of the killing of the fish (v 3) probably implies the drying out of the waters and so the sirocco (Study 13). In v 18 the earth is consumed (*ʾkl*) by the fire (*ʾš*) of the Lord's jealousy on the day of his wrath (*ʿbrh*). This is typical sirocco language (Studies 12 and 19). See further Zeph 1:14-15 discussed immediately below.

[26] Joel 2:25 where the Lord speaks of the locusts of 1:4-7 as "my army" will not help here. The Lord says he sent (*šlḥty*) that army, not that he led it.

[27] The numerous parallels between Isaiah 13 and Joel 2:1-11 have been systematically presented by Wolff (*Joel*, 55-56) who thinks Joel is borrowing freely from Isaiah 13. Wolff may have the relationship between the two correct, but this is not brought into the discussion because it would needlessly complicate the argument and because the date of Joel is too problematic.

Joel 2:1-2

The language has connections to Zeph 1:14-15. Note that the *ywm Yhwh* is again the *ywm ʿnn* (never a rain cloud).

There is an effective use of oxymoron involved in comparing the dust of the sirocco rising over the mountains to the east to the "dawn (*šḥr*) spread over the mountains." This day of the Lord is a day of darkness (vv 2, 10) like Amos' (Amos 5:18). Both the dawn and the sirocco come from the east.

Joel 2:3

The language has connections to Joel 1:19-20; Ps 50:3; Ps 97:3. The sirocco character of this language was discussed above. Note again the oxymoron involved in comparing Judah in its present lamentable situation to a *gn ʿdn*. It is a veritable garden of Eden compared with what it will be. Note how the language here reverses the language of Isa 51:3 which presumes rain. See what Joel 4:10 does to the language of Isa 2:4 and Mic 4:3. It is possible to bring in from other languages examples of the effects of locusts being compared to the effects of fire upon the vegetation,[28] but that is not an OT speech pattern.

Joel 2:4-5

Horse-drawn chariots are brought into the picture because the imagery that presents the Lord coming in the dust clouds of the sirocco has been transferred to the Lord's army (Study 14). Note how the language describing the Lord's coming in Ps 50:3 and 97:3 is transferred to his army in Joel 2:3. The combination *lhb ʾš* + *ʾkl* is sirocco language (Study 12); so too is *ʾkl* + *qš* (Study 11).

Joel 2:6

The verse has connections to Isa 13:8 and Ezek 30:16. See the relation of Isa 13:6 and Ezek 30:2-3 to Joel 1:15 noted above.

[28] Bewer, *Joel*, 96.

Joel 2:7-9

Here Joel begins to describe the physical advance of the Lord's soldiers and their attack on Jerusalem. Since the wind does not have a body it is impossible to continue the description in sirocco language. But note v 9: They enter through the windows like a thief. That might well be inspired by the tendency of wind-blown dust to find the smallest openings in even shuttered (Gen 8:6; 2 Kgs 13:17) windows.[29]

Joel 2:10

The language has connections to Isa 13:10, 13 discussed in Part III; to Ps 18:8 discussed in Part V; and to Joel 4:16 which is likewise a description of the sirocco (see below). Sirocco texts that speak of the darkening of the heavens are gathered in Study 16. It is also to be noted that locusts generally do not move in the cool of the night. That can only occur when the temperature is unusually warm. This makes the locusts a less likely explanation for the darkened moon and stars.[30]

Joel 2:11

While *ntn qwl* is also used of thunder in a rainstorm (Ps 77:18, etc.), the phrase refers to the roar of the sirocco in Amos 1:2; Jer 25:30; and Joel 4:16 (see below). These texts were treated in the course of the discussion of Jer 25:30-38 in Part III.

In the light of this analysis of the language and motifs of Joel 2:1-11 it does not seem that the text can be anything else but a description of a tremendous sirocco in the imminent fall interchange period. This immediately forges the connection to the argument as it continues to unfold. The text does not indicate who precisely constitute the Lord's army. The only plausible identification would seem to be angels.

After the description of the impending day of the Lord, Joel renews his call for an assembly to pray for relief from what has happened and

[29] Dalman, *Arbeit und Sitte* I, 133. The *tymrwt ʿšn* of 3:3, if they are "dust devils," might furnish another approach to the picture here. See the discussion below and Thomson's remarks in n. 45.

[30] Whiting, "Jerusalem's Locust Plague," 533. See Nah 3:17 and the comments of Dalman, ibid., 95.

may still happen (2:12-17).[31] There is no description of the assembly, but it was surely held.[32] For in 2:18 it is recounted how the Lord took pity on his people and in 2:19-27 the prophet can announce that the rains will come, the locust plague will not be repeated, and there will be abundance. Joel starts by announcing that the Lord will send grain (in the spring), wine (in the late summer) and oil (at the very end of the summer). Granted the temporal setting he means the early rains in the first place, and by this metonymy of effect for cause in a shorthand way he guarantees that the rains when they come will be effective (2:19). Note how the order (grain, wine, oil) shows he is thinking in terms of the agricultural cycle.

In 2:20 he turns to the second problem of the year that lay behind, the locusts. If/when they show up, they will be blown away. Note how in 2:20 *hym hqdmny* and *hym hʾḥrwn* presume the Lord controls the west and east winds, a conception which is otherwise in the context here. Whatever else he may mean by characterizing the locusts as *hṣpwny*, the locusts of 1915 came from the northeast first[33] and according to Whiting[34] that is the normal situation in the Jerusalem area. In 2:21-24 he returns to the description of the effects of the winter rains. Again everything is in the order of the agricultural cycle. The grass of winter will grow; the trees will produce fruit in summer—first the fig and then the vine (v 22). The Lord will send the early rains and the late rains (v 23); and there will be an abundance of grain, wine and oil, again in the order of the harvest (v 24).

With 2:25 Joel returns to the locust problem of the preceding spring. The damage done by the locusts in this year of drought will take several years to undo. Thus the Lord's promise to make good the years (*šnym*) eaten by the locust implies that more than one year of successful agriculture is promised (see *ʿwlm* in v 26).[35]

[31] I agree with Rudolph (*Joel*, 53) that in 2:17 *lmšl bm gwym* can only mean "with the nations mocking them." That is demanded by the immediate and more general context.

[32] There is a certain economy in Joel's style whereby he leaves to the imagination what is readily implied. See below.

[33] Bauer, "Die Heuschreckenplage in Palästina," 168.

[34] Whiting, "Jerusalem's Locust Plague," 513.

[35] There is nothing in 1:4-20 to suggest the events described were spread out over a period of years.

Just as Joel was able to see in the locusts and drought of chap. 1 signs of the coming of the tremendous fall sirocco described in 2:1-11, he is able to see in the promise of the coming of the rains in 2:19-27 signs of another happy fall interchange period to come, this time an eschatological one, which he describes in chaps. 3-4. The connection between the two parts of the book is highlighted by the way 2:27 is picked up by 4:17 and in other ways to be detailed in part below.

The major divisions of chaps. 3-4 (3:1-5; 4:1-3 + 9-14a; 4:14b-21), which are distinguished by subject matter, are marked by the time indicators: *whyh ʾḥry kn* (3:1) which is picked up by *bymym hhmh* (3:2); *bymym hhmh wbʿt hhyʾ* (4:1); and *qrwb ywm Yhwh* (4:14) which is picked up by *whyh bywm hhwʾ* (4:18). The time indicators in 3:2 and 4:18 serve to split the first and last units into sub-units. These major divisions will be discussed in reverse order.

Joel 4:14b-21

14b Yes, near is the day of Yahweh
    in the valley of decision!
15 Sun and moon are darkened;
    the stars withhold their brightness.
16 Yahweh roars from Zion;
    from Jerusalem his voice resounds;
    the heavens and the earth quake.

*

But Yahweh is a refuge for his people;
    a stronghold for the sons of Israel.
17 And you will know that I am Yahweh, your God,
    the one who dwells on Zion, my holy mountain.
Jerusalem will be holy;
    and strangers will never pass through her again.

* *

18 And it will come to pass on that day,
    the mountains will drip with wine,
    and the hills will flow with milk.
All the wadis of Judah
    will flow with water.

A fountain will issue from the house of Yahweh,
and water the Valley of Shittim.

*

19 Egypt will be a desert;
and Edom will be a desert waste,
Because of the violence done to the sons of Judah;
because they shed innocent blood in their land.
20 But Judah will abide forever;
and Jerusalem for all generations,[36]
21 with Yahweh dwelling[37] on Zion.

Vv 14b-21 immediately break down into four sense paragraphs of three lines each. The first speaks of a sirocco in the fall interchange period (see below). The second speaks of the Lord protecting his own, presumably from the sirocco. What happens to the others is not specified. The third speaks of the start of the rains in the fall interchange period (see below) and a river to water Judah. The fourth specifies the disastrous results of the sirocco for the nations; this time Egypt and Edom are named and their crime is mentioned. It also speaks of the results of Yahweh's protection and the rains for Judah and Jerusalem/Zion.

Insofar as paragraphs 1 and 3 speak of contrasting storms in the fall interchange period, they complement one another. Insofar as 2 and 4 speak of the results of these storms they complement one another. This

[36] I omit *wnqyty dmm lʾ nqyty* as a corrupt and misplaced doublet of *dm nqyʾ* in v 19. This kind of radical surgery is only a tentative solution, but MT cannot be made to yield a satisfactory sense. And if this is supposed to be about the punishment of the nations, it is too late in the course of the argument for that. Note too the very harsh shift in address involved in a line like:

wnqyty dmm lʾ nqyty
wYhwh škn bṣywn.

The shift in address between v 16 and v 17 is different. The omission is primarily motivated by the structures it reveals in the piece (see below) — especially the way in which it allows each of the parallel halves of the unit to end with Yahweh dwelling on Zion and Jerusalem safe (v 17); with Jerusalem and Judah safe and Yahweh dwelling on Zion (vv 20-21). The "paragraphs" indicated tend to begin or end in tricola. The omission is of little importance for the main concern here.

[37] The shift to the ptc. here emphasizes the durative character of the Lord's dwelling and its simultaneity with Jerusalem's abiding. See Joüon, § 121, h; 159, d.

relation between 1-2 and 3-4 is marked, by *mots crochets* which bind 1-2 and 3-4 together as sub-units.

Beginning	*End*
14) *ywm Yhwh*	17) *Yhwh . . . škn bṣywn*
18) *bywm hhwʾ*	21) *Yhwh škn bṣywn*

Note too how the second two paragraphs widen the geographical perspective of the first two. The first two are concerned with what is happening in the valley of decision in the Jerusalem area (4:14b); the last two with what is happening in the rest of Judah (4:18, 19, 20) and Egypt and Edom (4:19) as well.

In addition each of the paragraphs is marked off by the use of *mots crochets*. *Yhwh* occurs in the first and last line of paragraph 1; in the first line of paragraph 2; in the last line of paragraph 3; in the last line of paragraph 4.[38] Jerusalem/Zion and *byt Yhwh*[39] are mentioned at the end of paragraph 1 (Zion, Jerusalem), 2 (Zion, Jerusalem), 3 (*byt Yhwh*) and 4 (Jerusalem, Zion).[40]

That the time setting for the piece is the fall interchange period is indicated by 4:18 which presumes that the mountains and valleys just begin to flow with rain waters. That the storm described in paragraph 1 is a sirocco is made clear by its results. Egypt is turned into a *šmmh*; Edom, into a *mdbr šmmh* (4:19). Joel here picks up the vocabulary that describes the effects of the sirocco in 2:1-11. See *mdbr šmmh* in 2:3. The language and the motif are typical of the sirocco (Study 15). Egypt's becoming a desert presumes the Nile was dried up. That introduces the sirocco motif of bodies of water being dried up (Study 1). What made Egypt fertile was known to Joel. See Deut 11:10-11 and below.[41] These effects immediately connect to the darkening of the sun, moon and stars (4:15) which are blotted out by the dust of the sirocco (Study 16). That storm likewise shakes (*rʿš*) heaven and earth (4:16).

The sirocco character of the storm described in paragraph 1 is likewise indicated by the connection of the *ywm Yhwh* (4:14) to that storm (Study 20). The way *qrwb ywm Yhwh* of 4:14 echoes 1:15 (see 2:1-2, 11)

[38] Apart from this it occurs once more in v 17.

[39] This is a legitimate substitution for Jerusalem/Zion because Zion here is the Lord's holy mountain (v 17).

[40] Apart from this the terms are not mentioned at all.

[41] See p. 37, n. 34.

elucidated in 2:1-11 indicates Joel had something similar in mind. In addition note the echoes of 2:10 in 4:15-16; and the echo of 2:11 in 4:16 (*ytn qwlw*). The connection between 2:11; 4:16 and Amos 1:2; Jer 25:30, both descriptions of the sirocco, was discussed above. It seems clear that Joel intends both 2:1-11 and 4:14b-16a as parallel descriptions of a sirocco in the fall interchange period.

The first two major divisions of chaps. 3-4, 3:1-5 and 4:1-3 + 9-14a, presume that all the nations apart from the Judeans will be destroyed on this day of Yahweh (3:5; 4:2, 9, 11, 12). Why then the specific mention of only Egypt and Edom in 4:19? Whatever other considerations brought them into the picture here, geography played a role. The problem of the drought in chap. 1 was occasioned in part by Judah's almost complete dependence for water on the winter rains which had been deficient. The Lord's promise to remedy such situations in 4:18 resolves this problem in two ways. Judah will receive the winter rains and it will also have a river. The implication is it will flow summer and winter since the progression of the argument demands that it is something in some way better than the *ʾpyqy yhwdh* already mentioned. Note that Joel 4:18 does not betray the negative evaluation of a land that depended on a river for water met in Deut 11:10-11. This is followed by 4:19. Egypt where the agriculture depends not on rain, but on the Nile, is turned into a desert by the sirocco. Edom where the agriculture depends on winter rain as in Palestine will suffer the same fate. Thus Egypt and Edom are, in part at least, chosen to represent the nations of the world because they represent the two possible bases for life and civilization in the world Joel knew. These water sources are denied the rest of the world and given to Judah.

A further word needs to be said about 4:14b:

> Yes, near is the day of Yahweh
> in the valley of decision!

For formal reasons the line was joined to what follows. It in fact marks the transition from 4:1-3 + 9-14a to what follows. The second section (4:1-3 + 9-14a) presents the Lord deciding to judge ("to battle" is meant) the nations (4:1-3); issuing orders to declare war, to summon the nations and to prepare for battle (4:9-13). The recipients of these orders are presumably the angels (see 4:11b). V 14a presents us with the results of all this activity:

Crowd upon crowd
in the valley of decision.

At this point the day of Yahweh is imminent (v 14b). It opens with the sirocco described in vv 15-16. This sirocco starts from Jerusalem (v 16) and the valley of decision (v 14b) and passes on to the rest of the world (v 19).

There was occasion to note previously a tendency toward economy in Joel's style. He leaves to the imagination what can be implied. Thus, the call for an assembly of 2:12-17 is not followed by an account of the assembly that surely took place, but by an account of the Lord's reaction and his answer (2:18-27). Similarly in 4:9-11 the Lord sends his messengers to declare war and to summon the nations to the valley of decision. There is no account of the events that followed; but in 4:14a they are simply in place ready for the battle. Similarly in 4:13 the Lord commands his own warriors to get ready for battle. But when the battle comes (4:15-16, 19), there is no mention of the role of the angels. What they do in the course of the battle Joel simply leaves to the imagination. The important point here is that viewed in this way the total picture of the Lord and his angels coming in a sirocco is very much present in 4:15-16, 19 and the presentation is even closer to 2:1-11. The one difference is that the second sirocco theophany involves bloodshed.

There is nothing of meteorological import in this second major division of chaps. 3-4, but note that the imagery in which the Lord tells his troops to prepare for battle is grape-harvest imagery (4:13), which fits the period just before the fall interchange. I suspect that the imagery is completely that of the grape harvest. This has the advantage of consistency.[42]

The first major division of chaps. 3-4, 3:1-5 serves as its introduction and presents themes to be developed in what follows: a) blessings for

[42] The sense of *mgl* is uncertain. In its other occurrence (Jer 50:16) it is the sickle, but its cognates in Aram./Syr. and Arab. can denote "pruning knife." The LXX with *drepana* (see *trugētos*) interpreted it that way here. While *qṣyr* overwhelmingly denotes "grain harvest," it is the "grape harvest" in Isa 18:5; 16:9. The Peshitta with *qṭpʾ* interpreted it that way here. The key word, however, is *bšl*. In its other occurrence with the denotation "to be ripe" it is used of grapes (Gen 40:10). This harmonizes with the usage in later Hebrew and with the cognates in Aram./Syr. and Akk. where it is used of fruits which have to "cook" in the summer sun to ripen. So far as I can determine in none of these languages is *bšl* used with reference to grain.

the Judeans (vv 1-2); b) the terrible wonders of the day of Yahweh (vv 3-4); c) protection for the Lord's own on that day (v 5).

Only the middle section is of concern here.[43]

> I will work wonders in heaven and on earth:
> blood, fire and pillars of smoke.
> The sun will be turned to darkness;
> and the moon to blood,
> At the coming of the day of Yahweh,
> the great and terrible day.

The wonders in the heavens are the darkening of the sun and moon. Here as throughout Joel (2:2, 10; 4:15) this is caused by the dust of the sirocco. The moon, partially obscured, turns dirty brown, the color of dried blood.[44] The wonders on earth are: blood, fire and pillars of smoke. The first seems to be a reference to the work of the Lord's soldiers. Whether the second and third are to be thought of as the work of the Lord's army starting fires, or the work of a super-hot sirocco, or both, is not clear. Thomson, at least, has interpreted the *tymrwt ʿšn* as "dust devils."[45]

Jer 10:10 + 12-13 is a lovely commentary in a different type of text on the whole of the meteorology of Joel. Jer 10:1-16 contrasts the powerlessness, really the non-existence, of the pagan gods with the might of

[43] In the light of 4:18 it may be wondered whether the outpouring of the Lord's spirit in 3:1-2 implied more than is directly said. See Isa 44:3-4:

> I will pour out water on the thirsty ground;
> and streams on dry land:
> I will pour out my spirit on your offspring
> and my blessings upon your descendants,
> They shall spring up amid (rd *mbyn*) the grasses
> like poplars by streams of water.

Here the coming of the rain is likewise combined with the pouring out of the Lord's spirit and influences the presentation of its consequences. For other plausible solutions to the *bbyn* problem see A. Schoors, *I am God your Saviour* (VTSup 24; Leiden: Brill, 1973) 79. See Isa 32:15-16.

[44] So W. M. Thomson, *The Land and the Book* I (New York: Harper, 1880) 142.

[45] "The pillars of smoke are probably those columns of sand and dust raised high in the air by local whirlwinds, which often accompany the sirocco. On the desert of northern Syria, and also in Hauran, I have seen a score of them marching with great rapidity over the plain, and they closely resemble 'pillars' of smoke." Ibid.

Yahweh. It is not necessary to fear them. They cannot do harm or good (v 5). But Yahweh can do harm. He can send the sirocco (v 10):

> Yahweh is the true God;
> he is the living God, the eternal king.[46]
> At his anger (*qṣp*) the earth quakes;
> the nations cannot endure his wrath (*zʿm*).

The shaking of the earth indicates a storm is involved. Its sirocco character is indicated by *zʿm* (Study 8). He can also do good. He it is who sends the rains (vv 12-13):

> He it is who made the earth by his power,
> established the world by his wisdom,
> by his knowledge stretched out the heavens.
> He thunders and the waters roar in heaven;
> he brings up clouds from the end of the earth.
> He made lightning and rain;
> he leads out the wind from his storerooms.[47]

The same contrast is found in Ps 107:33-35:

> He makes rivers a desert;
> fountains of water thirsty ground;
> Fruitful land a salty desert,[48]
> because of the wickedness of its inhabitants.
> He makes the desert a pool of water;
> desiccated ground into springs of water.

[46] The text combines the kingship of Yahweh, his superiority over all other gods, the destruction of his enemies, the sirocco and the rainstorm in the same way as Psalms 96 and 97 studied in Part V.

[47] Whoever inserted the Aramaic plus in v 11 recognized how what is described in v 10 is distinct from what is described in vv 12-13. The same is true for the hand responsible for secondarily inserting Jer 10:12-16 into Jeremiah 51 (vv 15-19). He also knew where to split the text. The whole of Jeremiah 50-51 is filled with sirocco imagery, which was partially treated in the analysis of Jer 51: 34-37 + 42-45 in Part II. The only rain in these two chaps. is in the insert from Jeremiah 10. It can be explained as an attempt to emphasize the omnipotence of Yahweh as the Lord of the west as well as the east wind. Jer 10:10 + 12-13 as interpreted here are very close to Amos 9:4-6 discussed on p. 167, n. 14.

[48] A. Schwarzenbach, *Die geographische Terminologie im Hebräischen des Alten Testamentes* (Leiden: Brill, 1954) 104; Dalman, *Arbeit und Sitte* II, 20.

Ezek 17:24 presents the contrast with beautiful succinctness:

> I wither (*ybš*) the green tree;
> I make the withered (*ybš*) tree bloom.

And the Lord's claim to omnipotence in Job 38:23-24 will be much the same:

> Where is the path along which the wind[49] is dispersed;
> along which the east wind (*qdym*) scatters[50] over the earth?
> Who cleft a channel for the downpour;
> a way for the thunderstorm?

[49] Rd *rwḥ*.

[50] Rd *yāpûṣ* with LXX and Syr.

PART VII

Vocabulary and Motif Studies

Study 1
ybš/ḥrb Used of Bodies of Water

The texts gathered here present bodies of water being dried up in a certain or probable storm context. The storm involved can only be the sirocco.

The following texts were specifically singled out for study: Hos 13:15 (Part II, 1); Nah 1:4 (Part II, 2); Isa 19:5-6 (Part II, 3); Isa 50:2 (Part II, 4); Jer 51:36 (Part II, 5); Joel 1:20 (Part VI).

In the course of the discussion the texts where the same vocabulary and motif are met received cursory treatment: Exod 14:21 (in Part IV);[1] Isa 51:10 (in Part IV); Ps 106:9 (in Part IV); Isa 42:15 (in Part V, pp. 105-6, n. 79); Ezek 30:12 (in Part VI).

Without the specific vocabulary the motif is implicit in numerous other texts already discussed. For example: Lam 2:13 (Part III, 5); Isa 15:6 (in Part III, p. 55, n. 25); Joel 4:19 where Egypt becomes a desert (Part VI); Isa 13:9 where Babylon becomes a desert (Part III, 1).

Other instances with the typical vocabulary are:

Study 1

[1] The different notations, "Part VI" and "in Part VI," are intended to distinguish between texts singled out for discussion and texts treated in passing either in the introductions to the Studies of Part VII or in the analysis of another text. The difference will be marked throughout the Studies of Part VII.

1. Isa 11:15

The Lord dries up (*ḥrm* = *ḥrb*)[2] the tongue of the sea of Egypt.[3] This is in a context where a shoot comes forth (*yṣ*ʾ) from Jesse's stump and a bud blossoms[4] from his root (v 1), the grass grows (v 6) and Israel draws water from the fountain of salvation (12:3). The imagery presumes rain will fall on previously dry ground and indicates a temporal setting in the autumn interchange period. This makes the drying up the work of a fall sirocco. Note too that the whole of 11:1-12:6 presumes that justice and peace will be established in Judah and Ephraim. The text has all the hallmarks of the agricultural-new-year texts already seen.[5]

2. Jer 50:38[6]

In 50:35-37a the population of Babylon is threatened with the sword (*ḥrb*, 4 times).[7] In v 37b Babylon's treasure houses are likewise threat-

[2] In Isa 11:15 *whḥryb* is usually read for *whḥrym*. That may not be necessary. Cf. *ʾml* = *ʾbl* = to wither; *mrʾ* = *brʾ* = to be fat. And note *dymwn* twice for *dybwn* in Isa 15:9 which is occasioned by the *m* alliteration of the first colon: *ky my dymwn mlʾw dm*. The same explanation could apply here: *whḥrym Yhwh ʾt lšwn ym mṣrym*; *r*, *m*, *y*, *y*, *m*, *m*, *r*, *m*.

[3] Unfortunately *bʿym rwḥ* in the next colon is still unexplained. If it does mean "by the force of his wind" or the like (so LXX, Vg, Syr.), the reference to the sirocco is clear. See the discussion of H. Wildberger, *Jesaja* (BKAT 10/1-3; Neukirchen-Vluyn: Neukirchener Verlag, 1965) 464.

[4] Rd *yprḥ* for *yprh*.

[5] The editorial character of Isa 11:1-12:6 does not undermine what has been said. The meteorology of the piece as interpreted here may only reflect the view of the editor(s), but that is sufficient. The closing out of Isaiah 1-12 with the imagery of the agricultural new year is similar to the close of Habakkuk, Joel, and Isaiah 34-35, the finale of Isaiah 1-35, examined in Parts V and VI. See the remarks of S. Mowinckel, *Psalmenstudien II. Das Thronbesteigungsfest Jahwäs und der Ursprung der Eschatologie* (reprint of 1922 ed.; Amsterdam: Schippers, 1961) 36, n. 2.

Note too the very natural connection between the sirocco imagery here and the similar imagery in Isaiah 13 studied in Part III, 1. There is a good deal of sirocco imagery running through the whole of the prophecies against the nations (chaps. 13-23)—for example, Isa 19:1-7 studied in Part II, 3; Isa 15:1-6 discussed on p. 55, n. 25. Though the point cannot be pursued, I think it clear that the editor viewed the prophecies against the nations as part of the agricultural-new-year pattern of chaps. 11-12.

[6] Jeremiah 50 and 51 both contain oracles against Babylon. The sirocco character of the imagery in Jer 51:34-37, 42-45 was examined in Part II, 5. See p. 127, n. 47.

[7] In view of the masculine suffix, *ʾl swsyw wʾl rkbw* is probably a plus based on 51:21.

ened with the *ḥereb* and it is said that they will be plundered. Here the *ḥereb* is arguably a "crowbar" or the like.[8] The list closes out in v 38a: *ḥōreb ʾl mymyh wybšw*, "Dryness upon her waters that they may dry out." Sometimes MT *ḥōreb* here is revocalized *ḥereb* for the sake of symmetry; and the colon is understood as a reference the inability of the decimated population to keep in order the canals.[9] That is possible. But the masoretes, who apparently understood *ḥōreb* as the *dry* sirocco, may still be right. Note how the next two verses bring in the motifs of Babylon being destroyed like Sodom and Gomorrah and being inhabited not by humans, but only desert beasts (vv 39-40). Both motifs are typical of sirocco contexts (Studies 18 and 15) and the correct commentary on the text could well be Jer 51:36 studied in Part II, 5. Vv 39-40 do seem to presume Babylon has became a genuine desert and that would not be so unless the Euphrates itself were dried up.[10] See *šmh* in v 3; *mdbr, ṣyh, ʿrbh* in v 12; *šmmh* in v 13; *šmh* in v 23 (Study 15).

3. Ezek 29:10

Ezek 29:10 may well be the same as 30:12 (see above). In v 8 the Lord is presented as bringing a sword against Egypt. Egypt will become a desolate desert (*šmmh wḥrbh*, v 9). The motif is common in sirocco contexts (Study 15). V 10 presents the Lord attacking the "Niles." He turns Egypt into *ḥrbwt ḥrb šmmh*.[11] That can only be due to the drying up of the Nile. If a storm is involved, it is the sirocco. For other texts with *ḥrbh*, "desert," see Study 15.

* * *

Study 2
Disease (*dbr, qṭb, ršp*) and the Sirocco

The specific texts studied where the connection is blatant are: Hos 13:14 (Part II, 1); Deut 32:24 (Part III, 4); Hab 3:5 (Part V, 3). Deut 28:21 was

[8] See Ezek 26:9. The other possibility is that the *ḥereb* is used on the guards of the treasure houses.

[9] W. Rudolph, *Jeremia* (HAT 12; 3rd ed.; Tübingen: Mohr, 1968) 304-5.

[10] See the discussion of *ḥōreb* on p. 109, n. 88.

[11] The LXX reflects *lḥrbh* (*wḥrb*, ditto) *wšmmh* and that is probably original. See v 9.

also treated in the discussion of Part V, 6. That is not a large number of texts, but the correctness of the connection is confirmed by modern observation (Part I). There is no text that brings disease into a rainstorm context.

In addition there are some disease texts where the modern reader generally fails to see a storm, but where on the basis of the vocabulary and motifs connected with the sirocco and isolated in this study, it is probably present. Only two examples will be cited, Jer 21:4-7 and Ezek 7. Both texts foretell the destruction of Judah at the hands of the Babylonians; and they do it in a way similar to Lamentations 2's presentation of the events, then already past (Part III, 5). It is the Lord who attacks his people; he hands them over to the Babylonians.

1. Jer 21:4-7

The Lord turns back Israelite weapons (v 4); he fights against Jerusalem with *yd nṭwyh* and *zrwᶜ ḥzqh* in *ḥmh* (v 5). He will strike man and beast with *dbr* (v 6) and after that will hand the city over to Nabuchadnezzar (v 7). The combination—Yahweh as warrior, *dbr* and *ḥmh* (Study 10; here "anger")—probably indicates that the imagery is derived from the picture of Yahweh, the warrior, who comes in the sirocco. The noun *ḥmh*, whether understood concretely or abstractly has clear connections to the sirocco.

2. Ezek 7

The only protagonist in the first part of the text is the Lord. In v 21 he hands his people over to the Babylonians and then they go to work. The text is a *ywm Yhwh* text (v 19; see vv 7, 10). That is typically the day of the sirocco (Study 20). As in Isa 13:9 and Zeph 1:15, 18 the day is the day of Yahweh's *ᶜrbh* (v 19), again typical sirocco vocabulary (Study 19).[1] The same is true of *ḥrwn* in vv 12 and 14 (Study 9). V 8 speaks of pouring out (*špk*) wrath (*ḥmh*); both the noun and the combination are typical sirocco vocabulary (Study 10). Into this picture fits *dbr* mentioned in v 15.

Study 2

[1] The closest relation is to Zeph 1:18. I doubt this is a case of dependency. The language is the traditional language of the myth that both texts reflect.

This sirocco imagery immediately makes the connection to the strange verbs used of "lawlessness (rd *hammuṭṭeh*)" and "insolence" in v 10: "Lawlessness has blossomed (*ṣyṣ*); insolence has blossomed (*prḥ*)." The figure turns them into plants in full bloom to be withered by the sirocco. See further: Jer 21:6 (Study 10); Ezek 5:12 (Study 10); Ezek 38:22 (Study 13); and possibly Isa 28:2 (Study 4).

***

Study 3
swph

Scott[1] defined *swph* as "(1) a *destructive storm-wind* . . . (2) specifically the *Scirocco* or *Khamsin wind-storm*, a violent wind." It is possible to be more precise. It is frequently the sirocco; perhaps, sometimes another strong wind without rain. There is no evidence at all to indicate it can ever be a rainstorm.

The following texts where the *swph* is the sirocco were studied in detail: Nah 1:3 (Part II, 2); Jer 4:13 (Part III, 2); Isa 29:6 (Part V, 5).

To these texts can be added:

1. Isa 17:13

Here *mṣ* and *glgl* are driven before the *swph*. The motif never occurs in a rainstorm; it is typical of the sirocco (Study 11).

2. Amos 1:14

The opening section of Amos, the judgment of the nations, runs from 1:2 through 2:16. The book opens with the Lord roaring from Zion and the vegetation withering (v 2; *ʾbl, ybš*). The motif is typical of the sirocco (Study 7). In 1:14 the Lord says he will kindle a fire (*ʾš*) upon the wall of Rabbah and it will consume (*ʾkl*) its towers which were par-

Study 3

[1] R. B. Y. Scott, "Meteorological Phenomena and Terminology in the Old Testament," *ZAW* 64 (1952) 24. H. Lugt, "Wirbelstürme im Alten Testament," *BZ* 19 (1975) 195-204, also studies *swph* and *sʿr* (discussed in Study 4). The treatment is too limited in conception to be helpful.

tially made of wood. This combination (*ʾš* + *ʾkl*) is typical sirocco vocabulary (Study 12). The attack takes place *bywm mlḥmh* in a *sʿr* on a *ywm swph* (v 14). Like *swph* the noun *sʿr* is typical sirocco vocabulary (Study 4). In this context the *ʾš* of 1:4, 7, 10, 12; 2:2, 5 is likewise the sirocco. There is a good deal of sirocco language running through the rest of Amos, though that cannot be pursued here. Note how the epilogue describes the restoration in terms of the magnificent success of the agriculture, which presumes abundant rain (9:13-15).

3. Ps 83:16

The nations of the world threaten the Lord's people (vv 2-9). The Lord is asked to make them like *glgl* and *qš* before the wind (v 14). The motif is typical of sirocco descriptions (Study 11). The Lord is compared to an *ʾš* which burns (*bʿr*) up the forest; and to a *lhbh* which consumes (*lhṭ*) the mountains (v 15). The vocabulary here consistently appears in sirocco contexts. For *ʾš* and *lhbh* see Study 12; *bʿr*, Study 21; *lhṭ*, Study 22. In v 16a the Lord is requested to pursue them in his *sʿr*, which is typically the sirocco (Study 4). The whole context serves to identify the *swph* of v 16b.

4. Isa 21:1

The *swpwt* here come from the Negeb which is the right direction for the sirocco.

5. Isa 66:15

The language and imagery of this final chapter are in part inspired by the meteorology of the fall interchange period. The Lord will cover Jerusalem with *šlwm* like a *nhr*; with the wealth of the nations like a *nḥl šwṭp* (v 12). The bones of her sons will "blossom" (*prḥ*) like *dšʾ* (v 14). At the same time the Lord will "judge" all mankind with the sirocco:

> Behold Yahweh will come in *ʾš*—
> his chariots like the *swph*.
> He will exercise in *ḥmh* his wrath;
> his anger in *lhby ʾš*.

Yes, with *ʾš* and sword Yahweh
will judge all flesh;
and many will be slain by Yahweh. (vv 15-16)

The vocabulary *ʾš*, *lhby ʾš* and *ḥmh* are typically used of the sirocco (Studies 12 and 10). The same is true of the *zaʿmô* (MT *zāʿam*) which v 14 says will be made known to the Lord's enemies (Study 8). Whether *mrkbtyw* should be viewed a plural of majesty (Hab 3:8) with reference only to the Lord's chariot or as a real plural with reference to his and the angelic army's chariots is not clear. In either case this imagery does occur in sirocco contexts (Study 14). What is being described is a sirocco (*swph*) theophany in which Yahweh, the warrior, comes to destroy his enemies.

6. Isa 5:28

Here swiftly moving chariot wheels raising dust are compared to the *swph*. The motif of dust being blown before the wind is typical of the sirocco (Study 6).

7. Job 21:18

The motif of *tbn* and *mṣ* being driven by the wind identifies the storm as the sirocco (Study 11).

8. Job 27:20

The *swph* is defined by the parallel *qdym* in v 21. See Study 4, p. 139, n. 10.

9. Job 37:9

mn hḥdr tbwʾ swph
mmzrym qrh
From the chamber comes the *swph*;
from the scatterers, the cold.

The translation presented is as literal as possible. Some, e.g. Dhorme,[2] understand the "scatterers" as northerly winds which typically drive

[2] P. Dhorme, *Le livre de Job* (Paris: Lecoffre, 1926) 514.

clouds from the Palestinian sky and bring the cold.[3] Dhorme also understands *ḥdr* as "south" in the light of *ḥdry tmn*, "Chambers of the South," a southern constellation or a group of southern constellations (9:9).[4] The *swph* interpreted as the sirocco, the contrast for the cold north wind, would fit that analysis. There is a clear reference to the wind clearing clouds from the sky in v 21, and to the sirocco from the south in v 17.

Against this background the *swph* could be the sirocco in Hos 8:7; Prov 1:27 (see Study 13, p. 177, n. 8); 10:25 (see Study 19), though there is little in the immediate contexts to help identify the storms.

***

Study 4
sʿr (śʿr) / sʿrh (śʿrh)

That these synonyms can denote the sirocco is clear from the way they appear in parallel or context with *swph* in sirocco texts already examined: Nah 1:3 (Part II, 2); Isa 29:6 (Part V, 5); Ps 83:16 (Study 3); Amos 1:14 (Study 3). The sirocco was also identified in Jer 25:32 (in Part III, 3). This denotation is called for in other texts.

1. Jer 30:23 and 23:19

Jer 30:23-24 reads:

> Behold the *sʿrh* of Yahweh!
> *ḥmh* has come forth.
> A whirling[1] *sʿr*
> bursts over the heads of the wicked.
> The *ḥrwn*[2] *ʾp Yhwh* will not turn back,
> until he has accomplished and fulfilled the plans
> of his heart.

[3] G. Dalman, *Arbeit und Sitte in Palästina* I (Gütersloh: Evangelischer Verlag, 1928) 240-41.

[4] Dhorme, *Job*, 514.

Study 4

[1] Perhaps rd *mitḥôlēl* with 23:19.

[2] Jer 23:20 omits *ḥrwn*. Even if *ḥrwn* is secondary here, it fits the context.

In a context with *ḥmh* and *ḥrwn ʾp Yhwh*, both with clear sirocco connections (Studies 10 and 9), *sʿrh* and *sʿr* are that storm. Possibly *ḥmh* and *ḥrwn ʾp Yhwh* are to be interpreted concretely.

The whole of Jeremiah 30 reads very much like some of the agricultural-new-year texts already seen. Everyone is scared stiff (v 6) because of the great day (*gdwl hywm*[3]), the likes of which has never been seen (v 7). But Jacob will be safe (vv 7, 10)[4] when the Lord, presumably coming in a fall sirocco (vv 23-24), makes an end of the nations (v 11). The Lord's land and people will be rebuilt (vv 18-21). The motif of the agriculture flourishing because of the rain is missing in chap. 30, but it is present in chap. 31 (vv 5, 9, 12).

Jer 23:19-20 is an almost exact parallel for Jer 30:23-24 and it refers to the same kind of storm. It may likewise be an agricultural-new-year text, though it promises Judah not prosperity but disaster. V 10 speaks of a withered (*ʾbl*) land and desiccated (*ybš*) pastures. That could well be a description of Judah at the end of the summer following upon a winter of deficient rain.[5] In v 12 the Lord promises to bring on the *šnt pqdtm*. V 14 compares the prophets and people of Jerusalem to the inhabitants of Sodom and Gomorrah. The motif is typical in sirocco contexts (Study 18). V 13 (see v 27) speaks of Samaria's prophets prophesying by Baal, the god from whom rain might be expected. The *šlwm* promised (v 17) certainly included rain. Instead of the fall rains there will come a fall super-sirocco (vv 19-20).

2. *Isa 40:24*

The Lord blows (*nšp*) on recently planted plants. They wither (*ybš*) and the *sʿrh* carries them off like *qš*. The withering vegetation and the picture of *qš* flying before the wind are typical sirocco motifs (Studies 7 and 11).

3. *Zech 9:14*

Zech 9:9-17 speaks of the Lord destroying the enemies of his people and bringing them prosperity. V 14 reads:

[3] Whether this is a *ywm Yhwh* text or not is unimportant. But it is clear that the combination of materials here is similar to those brought together in Joel and the other texts of that category. See Study 20.

[4] See Nah 1:7 (Part II, 2); Hab 3:2 (Part V, 3); Joel 3:5 (Part VI).

[5] The setting would be the same as that presumed for Joel 1:19-20 (Part VI).

Yahweh will appear over them;
his arrows will shoot forth like *brq*.
The Lord Yahweh will sound the trumpet;
he will come in *sʿrwt tymn*.

The storm comes from the right direction for the sirocco. The simile *kbrq* may be occasioned by the connection between lightning and the sirocco noted in the discussion of Part I.

Note the motifs of the universal kingship of Yahweh (vv 9-10), the destruction of his enemies in a sirocco (v 14) and rain for the agriculture (v 17). These were the same motifs noted in Psalms 96-97 (Part V, 6) where the imagery is also based on the meteorology of the fall interchange period.

4. *Ezek 13:11, 13*

The repair of house walls which had dried out and cracked during the dry season is an activity of the late summer.[6] That probably makes the *gšm šwṭp*, the *ʾbny ʾlgbyš*, and the *rwḥ sʿrwt* distinct storms of the fall interchange period: the rainstorm, the hailstorm and the sirocco.

In a similar way the lists of Ps 148:8 (*ʾš wbrd*, *šlg wqyṭwr*, and *rwḥ sʿrh*) and Isa 28:2 (*zrm brd*, *śʿr qṭb* and *zrm mym*) seem to present distinct meteorological phenomena. The *śʿr qṭb* could easily be the sirocco. The blowing dust "stings" the face; or possibly better, the storm brings disease (Study 2).[7]

5. *Isa 41:16*

The imagery here presents vegetation on the mountains and hills being; threshed till it ends up like *mṣ*. This is winnowed and then scattered by the *sʿrh*. The storm contrasts with the rainstorm presumed in v 18. The meteorology is probably that of the fall interchange period; and the *sʿrh* is probably the sirocco. The motif of flying *mṣ* is typical of sirocco contexts (Study 11).

[6] G. Dalman, *Arbeit und Sitte in Palästina* I (Gütersloh: Evangelischer Verlag, 1928) 188.

[7] Literally "storm of a sting" (KB, *qṭb* = Syr. *qwrṭbʾ*, Arab. *quṭb*; cf. Dalman, ibid., 166, 322); or "storm of disease." See the discussion of J. Blau "Über homonyme und angeblich homonyme Wurzeln II," *VT* 7 (1957) 98. Both interpretations fit the sirocco.

In Jonah 1:4, 12 and Ps 107:25, 29 the *sʿr/sʿrh* occurs during the summer seafaring period. That probably eliminates both the rainstorm and the sirocco. It is a summer gale.[8]

The other texts where the vocabulary occurs are: 2 Kgs 2:1, 11; Ezek 1:4; Ps 55:9; Job 9:17; 38:1; 40:6. The context is in each case insufficient to identify the storm. Note that in Ezek 1:4 *sʿrh* occurs in conjunction with *ʿnn*, which is not a rain cloud (Study 5).[9]

In sum the evidence indicates that *sʿr/sʿrh* is a strong wind, frequently the sirocco. It is very doubtful that it can be a rainstorm.[10]

* * *

Study 5
ʿnn

The discussion here can be abbreviated because the necessary conclusions have been drawn by Scott[1] and confirmed by Reymond.[2] Of *ʿnn* Scott writes:

[8] It is possible to think of a gale out of the north/northwest like those described by W. Bascom, *Deep Water, Ancient Ships* (Garden City: Doubleday, 1976) 32. For the east wind (*rwḥ qdym*) sinking ships in Ezek 27:26 and Ps 48:8 see Dalman, *Arbeit und Sitte* I, 109, 316. Neither text supplies sufficient *meteorological* data for identifying the temporal setting presumed.

[9] I doubt that Ezekiel 1 has anything but the remotest of connections to experienced meteorology.

[10] What has been said about the nominal forms of *sʿr/śʿr* squares well with the verbal forms. The reference is generally to a strong wind without any indication of rain. The wind has been identified as the sirocco in Ps 50:3 (p. 92, n. 49) and in Job 27:20-21 where a *qdym* (|| *swph*) sweeps a man away (*śʿr*) (Study 3). The sirocco is probably also involved in Zech 7:14. The Lord blew away (rd *wāʾăsāʿărēm*) his people among the nations. Their land is a desert (*nšmh, šmh*) which no one travels through (Study 15). But now the Lord is filled with *ḥmh gdwlh* (8:2; Study 10) for his people. He will return to Jerusalem (v 3). This is the time of peaceful sowing (*zrʿ hšlwm*), i.e. the fall. The vine will produce grapes; the land, its yield. And the heavens will give dew (v 12). The text has the characteristics of the agricultural-new-year in a rainstorm context is Hab 3:14 (Part V, 3). For another vocabulary oddity in that text see p. 142, n. 3.

Study 5

[1] R. B. Y. Scott, "Meteorological Phenomena and Terminology in the Old Testament" ZAW 64 (1952) 24-25.

[2] P. Reymond, *L'eau, sa vie, et sa signification dans l'Ancien Testament* (VTSup 6; Leiden: Brill, 1958) 14-15.

> *ʿnn*, *cloud* or *mist* in general, *cloud-stuff as* extended rather than defined (*not* »a cloud «), (only once plural, Jer 4:13, intens.) a *cloud-mass* or *overcast*, *mist* or *fog* as opaque and obscuring; seldom if ever cloud bringing rain. . . . the *overcast* and *dust-filled* air of the Scirocco, Jer. 4:13; Ezek. 30:18; Nah. 1:3. . . . [3]

This he contrasts with *ʿb*, "*a distinct* cloud, in most cases *a rain-cloud* or *thunder-cloud*. . . ."[4]

It is true that to some extent *ʿb* and *ʿnn* can overlap. Thus, for example, the *ʿnn bqr* of Hos 6:4 is a morning mist like the *ʿb ṭl* of Isa 18:4.[5] In Job 26:8 the Lord binds up water in his clouds (*ʿb*); and the cloud-stuff (*ʿnn*) is not rent under its weight. But the important point is that there is never mention of an *ʿnn* in a context where rain falls.[6] The closest one can come to that is Gen 9:13, 14 combined in v 14 with denominated, verbal *ʿnn*; but here the reference is to rained-out clouds in which a rainbow shines.

[3] Scott, "Meteorological Phenomena," 24. The learned study of *ʿnn* by G. E. Mendenhall (*The Tenth Generation* [Baltimore: Johns Hopkins, 1973] 32-66) gets off on the wrong foot by starting with texts like Exod 14:24 in an attempt to analyze OT usage. That text is impossible to rationalize at least, at present. What the models for the presentation here were is not known. The word is an obvious piece of meteorological vocabulary and ought to be analyzed on that basis first. The comparison of Yahweh's *ʿnn* with the *melammu* or *puluḫtu* of Mesopotamian divinities is helpful for some texts, though there is obvious difference. The *melammu* is something that shines; the *ʿnn* darkens, obscures. Failure to note the difference between *ʿnn* and *ʿb* turns Jer 4:13 (see Part III, 2), Joel 2:2 (see Part VI) and Zeph 1:15 (discussed in Part VI) into rainstorms. The same is true of the mysterious Sinai theophany (see p. 33, n. 20).

[4] Scott, "Meteorological Phenomena," 25.

[5] G. Dalman, *Arbeit und Sitte in Palästina* I (Gütersloh: Evangelischer Verlag, 1928) 311.

[6] That an agriculturally based society should have words to denote different types of clouds with distinctions like the one made here is not surprising. See the different Palestinian Arabic words for clouds listed by Dalman, ibid., 111-12. While Heb. *ʿnn* is not a rain cloud, it can have this denotation in Aram./Syr. The Targum renders *hʿbym* in Qoh 11:3: *ʿnnyʾ*; the Peshitta: *ʿnny mṭrʾ*. In KTU 1.10:II:33 Baal is, perhaps, referred to as *h?d dʿnn*. The other Ugaritic occurrences of *ʿnn* denote "servant" or the like (J. C. de Moor, *The Seasonal Pattern in the Ugaritic Myth of Baʿlu* [AOAT 16; Neukirchen-Vluyn; Neukirchener Verlag, 1971] 129-30); though the attempt has been made to relate this ultimately to Heb. *ʿnn* (T. W. Mann, "The Pillar of Cloud in the Reed Sea Narrative," *JBL* 90 [1971] 19-22), this effort has been persuasively discredited (R. M. Good, "Cloud Messengers?" *UF* 10 [1978] 436-37). Dalman (ibid.) notes similar shifts in the denotations of Palestinian Arabic words for clouds.

The texts where *ʿnn* has been identified as the dust cloud of the sirocco are: Nah 1:3 (Part II, 2); Jer 4:13 (Part III, 2); Ps 97:2 (Part V, 6); Joel 2:2 (Part VI); Ezek 30:3 (in Part VI); Zeph 1:15 (in Part VI).

See further: Ezek 30:3, 18 (Study 10); Ezek 38:9, 16 (Study 13); Ezek 32:7 (Study 17).

***

Study 6
Flying Dust

The motif cannot and does not appear in any rainstorm context. It is typical of the sirocco and along with other indications of the nature of the storm served to identify the sirocco in: Nah 1:3 (*ʾbq*; Part II, 2); Isa 19:7 (Part II, 3); Isa 29:5 (*ʾbq*; Part V, 5); Joel 3:3 (Part VI); Deut 28:24 (*ʾbq*, *ʿpr*; in Part V, 6); Isa 5:28 (Study 3). The motif is implicit in all those texts gathered in Study 16 where it is a question of the heavens being darkened by the sirocco; and in Study 11 where it is a question of chaff flying before the wind. The usual term is *ʾbq*: "Very fine dust which because of its lightness can rise and build clouds."[1]

See further Jer 18:17 (in Study 11); Isa 41:2 (Study 11).

***

Study 7
Withering Vegetation

The vocabulary involved here is: *ʾml*, *qml*, *ʾbl*, *nbl*, *ḥrb* and *ybš*. The texts studied where this motif was encountered are: Nah 1:4 (*ʾml*; Part II, 2); Isa 19:6-7 (*qml*, *ybš*; Part II, 3); Jer 4:28 (*ʾbl*; Part III, 2); Isa 34:4 (*nbl*; Part V, 1). In the course of the discussion the following texts were given summary treatment: Amos 1:2 (*ʾbl*, *ybš*; in Part III, 2); Isa 15:6 (*ybš*; in Part III, p. 55, n. 25); Isa 42:15 (*ḥrb*, *ybš*; in Part V, pp. 105-6, n. 79); Ezek 17:24 (*ybš*; in Part VI); Isa 40:24 (*ybš*; in Study 4).

The motif is implicit in any sirocco context but most directly in those that speak of drying out bodies of water (Study 1) or present the

Study 6

[1] A. Schwarzenbach, *Die geographische Terminologie im Hebräischen des Alten Testamentes* (Leiden: Brill, 1954) 129.

sirocco as "fire" consuming (*ʾkl*, *lhṭ*) vegetation (Studies 12 and 22). Since the motif infallibly identifies a storm, a lengthy discussion of other examples is not required. I cite only Isa 40:78; Ezek 17:10; 19:12 which require no discussion since specific mention is made of the *rwḥ Yhwh* or the *rwḥ hqdym*.

See further: Ps 102:5, 12 (Study 8); Job 18:16 (in Study 9); Job 13:25 (Study 11); Hos 4:3 (Study 13).

***

Study 8
zʿm

This noun occurs some 23 times in the OT and is widely understood as an abstract denoting "anger" or the like. BDB (s.v.), for example, interprets it as "indignation."[1] There are two things peculiar about the word: 1) Save for Hos 7:16[2] it always is a question of Yahweh's *zʿm*. 2) It very frequently occurs in clear sirocco contexts—only once in a rainstorm context (Hab 3:12).[3] It has been suggested already (Part II, 2) that *zʿm* sometimes, at least, ought to be interpreted concretely, i.e. "the roar (of the wind)" and specifically the sirocco. But even if that is not acceptable it is still clear that for whatever reason *zʿm* (either the abstract "anger" or the concrete "roar") tends to occur in sirocco texts and can be used to identify them. Why it should avoid rainstorm contexts is not particularly clear. I can only suggest that the noisemaker there was thunder.

The evidence upon which this conclusion is based is the following:[4]

1) Verbal *zʿm* not only means "to be angry" but also "to curse" (Num 23:7-8; || *qbb* and *ʾrr*) which involves noise. In this it is like

Study 8

[1] *HALAT*'s (s.v.) "Verwünschung," which is based on J. Pedersen (*Der Eid bei den Semiten in seinem Verhältnis zu verwandten Erscheinungen sowie die Stellung des Eides im Islam* [Strassburg: Trübner, 1914] 81-82), is too narrow.

[2] The text here is partly in disorder and *mzʿm* could be an error (see, e.g., *BHK*), though it need not be.

[3] On p. 139, n. 10 the unique use in a rainstorm context of the root *sʿr*, albeit a verbal form, in Hab 3:14 was noted.

[4] The evidence here is in part derived from G. R. Driver ("Linguistic and Textual Problems: Ezekiel," *Bib* 19 [1938] 69) who interpreted *zʿm* in Ezek 22:24 as "angry weather."

Syr. *zʿm* which means "to denounce" and the like. Cf. Arab. *zǵm* in the fifth form used of the roaring of a camel or angry speech.

2) Heb. *zʿp*, a cognate of *zʿm* (like *plṭ* = *mlṭ*), produces *zaʿap* the "raging/roaring" of the sea in Jonah 1:15. Cf. *rwḥ zlʿpwt* (Ps 11:6) which is probably the sirocco (note *gpryt*; and Study 18) and *zlʿpwt ṣpwn* (Sir 43:17), the north wind.
3) Aram. *zʿp* can mean "to storm." The Targum to Ps 50:3 renders Heb. *nśʿrh*[5] with *tzʿwp*; and the *rwḥ gdwlh . . . mʿbr hmdbr* in Job 1:19 with *zʿpʾ*.
4) The prime argument is OT usage and that will be detailed below.

The evidence indicates that: a) *zaʿam* sometimes, at least, ought probably to be interpreted concretely as the sirocco, though it is very difficult here to defend against the poet saying "anger" and by metonymy of cause for effect meaning "sirocco"; b) sometimes the concrete "roaring sirocco" or the abstract "anger" will do; c) sometimes "anger" is the denotation required. The kind of semantic development presumed here will be paralleled in Studies 9 and 10 where *ḥrwn ʾp* and *ḥmh* are treated. If this semantic development took place in a myth-related context where the sirocco is thought of as issuing from some god's mouth and nose, there would be a ready explanation why *zʿm* should be almost exclusively Yahweh's *zʿm* and consistently appear in sirocco contexts.

The sirocco texts involving *zʿm* examined to this point are the following: In Isa 30:27 (Part V, 2) the Lord's lips are full (*mlʾ*) of *zʿm*; his tongue is like an *ʾš ʾklt*. Here *zʿm* almost demands the interpretation "roaring." Nah 1:6 (Part II, 2) denies that anyone can stand firm (*ʿmd*) before the Lord's *zʿm* or face (*qwm*) his *ḥrwn ʾp*. His *ḥmh* is poured out (*ntk*)[6] and cliffs are shattered by him. Here *zʿm*, *ḥrwn ʾp* (Study 9) and *ḥmh* (Study 10) could easily be the "roaring sirocco," the "scorching sirocco" and the "hot sirocco." Similarly in Jer 10:10 the Lord's *zʿm* which the nations cannot endure (*kwl*) could be the Lord's "roaring" (treated in the discussion of Part VI);[7] the *kly zʿm* of Isa 13:5 (Part III, 1) and Jer 50:25 (treated in the discussion of Part III, 1), the Lord's "roaring weapons"; and the *zʿm ʾp* of Lam 2:6 (Part III, 5), "the roar of the

[5] The storm involved here is a sirocco. See p. 92, n. 49.

[6] For *ntk* used in connection with the wind see p. 32, n. 19.

[7] For the verb *kwl* used in this context see Joel 2:11 where no one can endure (*kwl*) the day of Yahweh, which is the day of the sirocco (Part VI). See Study 20.

Lord's nose." The phrase *zʿm ʾp* finds its parallel in *ḥrwn ʾp*, "the heat of the Lord's nose," discussed in Study 9. Isa 66:14 (rd *zaʿmô*; nose Study 3) says the Lord's *zʿm* will be revealed to his enemies in a context where the Lord comes in *ʾš* and his chariots are like a *swph* (v 15). At the same time it is clear that in almost all of these texts "anger" will work too.

To these texts where *zʿm* appears in a sirocco context can be added the following:

1. Ps 102:11

Throughout the first part of the psalm runs sirocco imagery. The speaker is described as withering like grass (v 12; *kʿśb ʾybš*); has been struck like grass (*hwkh kʿśb*) and has withered (v 5; *wybš*). The speaker's days come to an end in smoke (*ʿšn*); the bones are scorched (*nḥrw*) as if by fire (v 4; *kmwqd*). The motif of withering grass has clear sirocco connections (Study 7). The speaker mourning is compared to a desert owl (*qʾt mdbr*), an owl inhabiting ruins (v 7, *kws ḥrbwt*). This has connections to the motif of the sirocco turning cities into deserts inhabited only by desert birds and beasts (Study 15). V 11 reads:

> *mpny zʿmk wqṣpk,*
> you picked me up and cast me aside.

Whether *zʿm* here is to be interpreted abstractly or concretely is not clear.

The next psalm, Ps 103:15-16 supplies a lovely commentary on the text:

> The days of a man are like those of the grass;
> he blooms like a flower of the field.
> The wind sweeps over him and he is gone;
> his place knows him no more.

The *rwḥ* here can only be the sirocco.

2. Ps 78:49

In Ps 78:44-51 there is found a review of the plagues of Egypt. Though not all the plagues are represented, the plagues are the traditional plagues of Exodus ordered differently and with some variations in detail. The first ordering principle is the progression from the least to the most severe; the second involves the groupings: one line devoted to bodies of water being turned into blood (v 44; plague 1); two lines devoted to insects and small animals (vv 45-46; plagues 4, 2, 8); four lines devoted to storms, two to a hailstorm (vv 47-48) and two to the sirocco (vv 49-50a; plagues 7 and 9, the darkness; see below); two lines devoted to the death of animals and the first born (vv 50b-51; plagues 5 and 10).

44 He turned their rivers to blood;
their streams too, so that they could not drink.

*

45 He sent against them flies that devoured them;
and frogs that destroyed them.
46 He gave their crops to the locust;
their toil to the grasshopper.

*

47 He killed their vines with hail;
their sycamores with hailstones.[8]
48 He subjected to the hail their beasts;
their flocks to lightning.

*

49 He sent against them *ḥrwn ʾpw*,
ʿbrh wzʿm wṣrh,
An embassy of messengers of woe
50 to level a path for his anger.

*

He did not save them from death;
their animals he subjected to the pest.
51 He struck every first born in Egypt,
the first fruits of manhood in the tents of Ham.

It is to be noted that the language throughout describes the Lord's activity in very concrete terms. The Lord changed rivers to blood (v 44); sent flies and frogs (v 45); handed over to locusts (v 46); killed with

[8] Though *ḥnml* is uncertain, the parallelism suggests "hailstones."

hail and lightning (vv 47-48); subjected to the pest and slew (vv 50b-51). The context argues for a concrete interpretation of vv 49-50a. In addition *ḥrwn ʾp* (Study 9), *ʿbrh* (Study 19), and *zʿm* are vocabulary typical of sirocco descriptions and avoid rainstorm or hailstorm contexts. It would be very easy here to interpret vv 49-50a:

> He sent against them the heat of his nose,
> outburst, roar, trouble,
> An embassy of messengers of woe,
> to level a path for his anger.

Note how the presence of the sirocco in the first line here immediately explains how the path is leveled in the second. This is the path upon which the Lord comes to kill the Egyptian first born in v 51.

I have connected the sirocco here to plague 9, the darkness (Exod 10:21-29). Whether the darkness there is really to be attributed to the sirocco is problematic, but plague 9 could easily have been interpreted that way by the psalmist (Study 16), especially in the light of Exod 14:21 and Exodus 15 (Part IV).

3. Zeph 3:8

In 3:6 the Lord speaks of his past accomplishments as proof of what he still can do:

> I destroyed nations;
> their battlements became desolate (*nāšammû*).
> Their streets I made a desert (*heḥĕrabtî*)
> with no one passing through.
> Their cities became a desert (*niṣdû*)
> without a man,
> without an inhabitant.

The motif of the Lord turning inhabited land into an uninhabited desert (*šammâ*, *ḥorbâ*[9]) is typical of sirocco contexts (Study 15). Though *ṣdh* is attested only here, it means the same thing. Cf. Arab. *ṣadiya* = "to be thirsty"; Aram./Syr. *ṣdʾ* = "to be desolate"; Syr. *ṣdyʾ* = "desert."

[9] A. Schwarzenbach, *Die geographische Terminologie im Hebräischen des Alten Testamentes* (Leiden: Brill, 1954) 107-10.

In v 8 the Lord describes what he intends to do:

> Yes, wait for me, says the Lord,
> for the day when I rise up as plaintiff.[10]
> Indeed it is my decision to gather the nations,
> to assemble the kingdoms.
> I will pour out[11] on them my *zʿm*,
> all my *ḥrwn ʾp*.
> Yes, through the fire (*ʾš*) of my jealousy
> all the earth will be consumed (*ʾkl*).

The *ʾš* + *ʾkl* combination is sirocco vocabulary (Study 12). Even though the fourth line here is probably the result of a reworking of the text,[12] it is consistent with the imagery of the verse and immediately makes the connection to *zʿm* and *ḥrwn ʾp* (Study 9). The concrete effects of *ʾš* could well argue for a concrete interpretation of *zʿm* and *ḥrwn ʾp*. If the day when the Lord 13 rises up is to be interpreted as the *ywm Yhwh*,[13] that would be another argument for seeing the sirocco here (Study 20). See Zeph 1:7-8, 14-18. Note by way of contrast how the description of the restoration that follows 3:1-8 speaks of the pasturing of flocks (v 13), which presumes rain.

4. Ezek 22:24, 31

Ezek 22:23-31 is closely related to the text just studied, Zeph 3:1-8.[14] The imagery pattern will be much the same. This is the text where Driver identified *zʿm* (v 24) as "angry weather."[15] In the light of the present discussion it can probably be defined more narrowly. Much like Lamentations 2 (Part III, 5) the text describes the events of 587 now past

[10] Rd *lĕʿēd*.

[11] The verb *špk* can be used of the wind. See *špk* + *rwḥ* in Ezek 39:29; Joel 3:1-2.

[12] W. Rudolph, *Micha-Nahum-Habakuk-Zephanja* (KAT 13/3; Gütersloh: Gerd Mohn, 1975) 290.

[13] So H.-M. Lutz, *Jahwe, Jerusalem und die Völker* (WMANT 27; Neukirchen-Vluyn: Neukirchener Verlag, 1968) 99.

[14] D. H. Müller, "Der Prophet Ezechiel entlehnt eine Stelle des Propheten Zephanja und glossiert sie," *WZKM* 19 (1905) 263-70; W. Zimmerli, *Ezechiel* (BKAT 13/1-2; Neukirchen-Vluyn: Neukirchener Verlag, 1955-69) 521-22.

[15] See p. 142, n. 4.

as the work of Yahweh, the warrior, coming in a sirocco. The Lord had sought someone to build a wall and to stand in the breach so that he would not destroy[16] the land, but he found no one (v 30). So Judah ended up a land "not rained on"[17] *bywm zʿm* (v 24). The Lord poured forth (*špk*) his *zʿm*; he finished them off with his *ʾš ʿbrh* (v 31). Note how the text disassociates rain and *zʿm*. The *ywm zʿm* and the *zʿm* that is poured out could easily be interpreted concretely: "the day of the roaring sirocco," "the roaring sirocco." The noun *ʾš* is typical sirocco vocabulary (Study 12); the same is true of *ʿbrh* (Study 19). The combination *ʾš ʿbrh* could be interpreted concretely, "fiery blast."

A lovely commentary on this text from the opposite direction is supplied by Ezek 34:25-27:

> I will make a covenant of peace with them. I will banish evil beasts from the land. They will dwell securely in the pasture land (*mdbr*) and sleep in the forests. . . . I will send them the rain in season and the rain will be a blessing. The trees of the field will bear fruit and the land its crops.

5. Ezek 21:36

The only other occurrence of *zʿm* in Ezek is very similar. The Lord will pour forth (*špk*) his *zʿm* and will *blow* (*pwḥ*) with *ʾš ʿbrh* against the Ammonites (Studies 12 and 19).

6. Isa 26:20

The Lord's people are told to hide until *zʿm* passes (*ʿbr*).[18] This is in a context where the wish is expressed that the Lord's enemies be consumed by fire (v 11; *ʾš* + *ʾkl*; Study 12) and where it is said that the Lord is coming forth from his place to punish the iniquity of the inhabitants of the earth (v 21).

[16] Pi. *šḥṭ* can take a vegetal object (Jer 12:10) and can be used of the effects of the sirocco (Lam 2:6; Part III, 5).

[17] Rd with the LXX *mĕmuṭṭārâ*.

[18] The verb *ʿbr* can be used of the wind and specifically the sirocco. See Ps 103:16 and the discussion of *ʿebrâ* in Study 19.

7. Ps 69:25

The psalmist prays that the Lord pour out (*špk*) his *zʿm* upon them and that the Lord's *ḥrwn ʾp* catch up with the psalmist's enemies. Like *zʿm*, *ḥrwn ʾp* is typical sirocco vocabulary (Study 9).

The texts where *zaʿam* is more likely to mean or clearly means "anger" are: Isa 10:5; 10:25; Jer 15:17; Ps 38:4; Dan 8:19; 11:36. It is possible or even probable that the net has been cast too widely in identifying texts where the noun denotes or probably/possibly denotes "the *roaring* sirocco." But two things I think are certain. The word avoids rain contexts (the only exception is Hab 3:12); it consistently occurs in contexts with vocabulary and motifs characteristic of the sirocco. For present purposes that is enough. The next two Studies will treat *ḥrwn ʾp* and *ḥmh*. Both can have the denotation "anger"; and both avoid rainstorm contexts even more rigidly than *zʿm*. They likewise can denote "the *hot* sirocco." That is further support for what has been said about *zʿm*.

A few final remarks must be made about verbal *zʿm* which can have a human subject. With Yahweh as subject it generally means "to be angry" or "to curse": but the connections of *zaʿam* to the sirocco may be the solution for the difficult verse, Prov 25:23:

> *rwḥ ṣpwn tḥwll gšm*
> *wpnym nzʿmym lšwn str.*

The north wind that brings rain has to be a northwest wind.[19] In view of what has been said about the connections of *zaʿam* to the east or southeast sirocco, it would be possible to see in *nzʿmym* a verbal form denominated from *zaʿam*.[20] The way in which *rwḥ ṣpwn* and *lšwn str* echo one another (*r*, *ṣ*, *ōn* echoes *š*, *ōn*, *s*, *r*) would indicate that *rwḥ ṣpwn* and *lšwn str* are the things being contrasted in a very compact fashion. I would suggest that what the proverb means is: The northwest wind (= kindly speech) gives birth to the (smile-bringing) rain; the back-biting tongue (= the east/southeast wind) gives birth to a

[19] F.-M. Abel, *Géographie de la Palestine* I (Paris: Gabalda, 1933) 119; but contrast G. Dalman, *Arbeit und Sitte in Palästina* I (Gütersloh: Evangelischer Verlag, 1928) 246: "Nordwind setzt in Angst Regenguss," which is what the north wind, which clears away rain clouds, does.

[20] Cf. Ps 50:3 where *nśʿrh*, denominated from *śaʿar*, means "the sirocco raged." See p. 92, n. 49.

sirocco-blasted (= unsmiling) face. If the interpretation were not so uncertain, it would be clear proof that *zaʿam* can denote concretely "the *roaring* sirocco."[21]

***

Study 9
ḥrwn (*ʾp*)

The vocabulary, *ḥrwn ʾp* (33x), *ḥrwn* alone (5x), *ḥrwnym* (1x), is met some 39 times in the OT.[1] There are 14 occurrences in prose, always *ḥrwn ʾp* save for *ḥrwn* in Neh 13:18. The other 26 are in poetry.[2] If only the prose occurrences had been preserved, there would not be any reason to go beyond the denotation "anger" or the like. 1 Sam 28:18 is typical. There Saul is rebuked for not having executed the Lord's *ḥrwn ʾp* against Amalek. The strangeness of the phrase "heat of the nose" might raise a query as to its origin, and one might suspect this is a phrase with a story behind it. But there are phrases like that in any language: dressed to the nines (elegantly), to hit the needle (right on target), before you can say Jack Robinson (in a moment); and there would hardly be reason to attempt to get behind the stage of usage presented by the prose texts with any hope of success or degree of certainty.

But when the more abundant instances from the poetry are brought into consideration, other factors become evident and the picture changes. In all the occurrences of the vocabulary in prose and poetry

[21] Dalman's (see n. 19 above) interpretation of the first colon could also be reconciled somewhat less felicitously with the suggested interpretation of the second: a backbiting tongue is/produces a sirocco-blasted face. There may be an etymological word-play (false or correct makes no difference) between *ṣpwn* and *str*. The northwest wind gives birth *secretly* to the rain insofar as no one has seen the birth but just its results. This contrasts with the tongue that speaks ill of a man secretly. See J. van der Ploeg, "Prov. XXV 23," *VT* 3 (1953) 189-91. Biblical Hebrew has no words for northeast, southeast, etc. For a review of the literature on this difficult proverb see W. McKane, *Proverbs* (Philadelphia: Westminster, 1970) 582-83.

Study 9

[1] The count presumes *ḥrb hywnh* for *ḥrwn hywnh* in Jer 25:38. See Part III, 3. Ps 58:10 is omitted as too corrupt to deal with.

[2] The poetry count includes the elevated prose of Ezek 7:12, 14 (*ḥrwn*).

the reference is exclusively to the Lord's anger. Many of the instances of this vocabulary in poetry appear in texts that, at least on the level of imagery, can be tied to the Palestinian sirocco with certainty or some degree of probability. Not a single one can be tied to a rainstorm.

In some texts a concrete interpretation of *ḥrwn* (*ʾp*) is clearly possible. For example, in Exod 15:7 (Part IV) the Lord sends forth his *ḥrn*; it consumes (*ʾkl*) his enemies like *qš* (Study 11) in a context where the waters are piled up by his *rwḥ ʾpym* (8) and the Lord blows (*nšp*) with his wind (v 10).[3] Jer 25:30-38 (Part III, 3) presents a picture of Yahweh, the warrior, coming forth with a sword (v 31) to attack his adversaries. That he comes in a sirocco is clear. He roars (*šʾg*) over the *nwh* from on high (v 30); a great storm (*sʿr*, Study 4) is unleashed from the ends of the earth (v 32). The *mrʿyt* and the *nʾwt hšlwm* are laid waste (*šdd*) and become desolate (*dmm*, Study 15) because of the *ḥrwn ʾp Yhwh* (vv 36-38). That the *ḥrwn ʾp Yhwh* here could also be the sirocco which issues from the Lord's nose is clear; that it could be a figure representing the storm is the manifestation of the Lord's anger is also clear. The problem is, of course, rooted in the fact that for Jeremiah the Lord is no nature force and myth has become imagery. In a similar way for the Christian, Jesus referred to as the *Sol Invictus* is no Sun. Nor is the Blessed Virgin the Moon in the anonymous:

> In gremio Matris residet Sapientia Patris.
> Luna fovet Solem cui Sol dedit ipse nitorem.[4]

In dealing with texts like these the modern interpreter can never know precisely what was suggested or heard in their original setting(s). He can only categorize roughly: Exod 15:7 comes pretty close to saying the sirocco issues from the Lord's mouth and nose; 1 Sam 28:18 has completely demythologized the language and there is no indication whether the writer knew or did not know where it came from; Jer 25:38 stands in the middle as regards *ḥrwn ʾp*. Whether it means "the heat of the nose" or "anger" is ambiguous, though it is clear in any case that vv 30-38 use materials from nature myth, specifically one concerned with the sirocco.

[3] With other language Ps 18:9 (= 2 Sam 22:9; Part V, 4) says the same thing even more explicitly: *ʿlh ʿšn bʾpw wʾš mpyw tʾkl.* Cf. *ḥrh lw* in v 8.

[4] Cited from H. Rahner, *Greek Myths and Christian Mystery* (New York: Harper and Row, 1963) 167.

The sole purpose of this attempt to tie *ḥrwn* (*ʾp*) interpreted as "the heat of the nose" ultimately to the language of myth is to try to explain the facts that the phrase is a peculiar one, that *ḥrwn* (*ʾp*) is used only of divine anger and that when it is used in texts where storms are involved and there is sufficient description to be certain or almost so about the nature of the storm, it is invariably the sirocco. There is no indication that it can ever be used in a rainstorm context. The origin of the language in a myth about a sirocco-breathing deity coming in that storm would explain these facts. That is speculative, of course. What is not speculative is the connection of this language to the sirocco and nature myth(s) concerned with it. That is clear and for present purposes sufficient.

The best examples of *ḥrwn ʾp* (Nah 1:6 [Part II, 2]; Jer 51:45 [Part II, 5]; Isa 13:9, 13 [Part III, 1]; Jer 4:8, 26 [Part III, 2]; Jer 25:37, 38 [Part III, 3]; Jer 30:24 [Study 4]; Ps 78:49 [Study 8]; Zeph 3:8 [Study 8]; Ps 69:25 [Study 8]) and *ḥrwn* (Exod 15:7 [Part IV]; Ezek 7:12,14 [Study 2]) in a clear sirocco context have already been treated. There follows a complete list of the other poetic passages where the vocabulary appears. The sirocco is not so blatantly in evidence here, at least to the modern interpreter, but the list serves useful purposes.

The phrase *ḥrwn* (*ʾp*) continues throughout to pick up the vocabulary and motifs being treated in these Studies and renders graphically clear the tight package of materials being dealt with. In addition, the list highlights the ultimately unresolvable problem of delimiting the precise denotations and connotations of this kind of language in many cases. It has been argued here: 1) in, some cases *ḥrwn* (*ʾp*), the "heat of the nose," denotes the sirocco issuing from the Lord's nose; 2) in some cases it denotes "anger," but is still tied to contexts where sirocco imagery is evident; 3) generally in prose texts as in 1 Sam 28:18 it simply denotes "anger" and connection to the sirocco is probably/possibly lost. Unfortunately the amount and kind of documentation needed to take certain decisions is not available. The problem can again be illustrated by the Christian use of materials from Greek and Latin solar cults. Most Christians in the pew at an Easter vigil fail completely to connect their presence there at that time, the *Lumen Christi* ceremony, etc. to these cults. But the documentation is available in abundance for those who wish to make use of it. The interpreter of the materials being dealt with here lacks that wind of documentation. In part it can be made up for by bringing into the discussion vocabulary and motifs not directly connected to meteorology, but that cannot be attempted now. The problem exists for the other materials dealt with in this study. It is spelled out specifically here.

1. Hos 11:9

Israel sacrificed to the Baals (v 2) and so was punished. But now the Lord pities Israel. He will not treat him like Admah and Zeboiim (v 8; Study 18). He will not exercise his *ḥrwn ʾp* (v 9). He will not blaze against him (*bʿr*, 9; Study 21).[5] The sirocco imagery in Hos 13:14-15 was discussed in Part II, 1. Note how in the promise of assistance that closes out the book when the Lord's *ʾp* turns away (14:5), the Lord becomes Israel's dew (*ṭl*) and he blossoms like the *šwšnh* (v 6), etc. All this presumes rain.[6]

2. Zeph 2:2

The opening chapter is filled with motifs and vocabulary being treated in these Studies. It closes with a reference to *kl hʾrṣ* being consumed by fire (*ʾš* + *ʾkl*, Study 12) on the Lord's *ywm ʿbrh* (1:18; Study 19) which is the *ywm Yhwh* (1:14; Study 20). V 2:2 speaks of the coming of the *ḥrwn ʾp Yhwh* as the coming of the *ywm ʾp Yhwh* (Study 20; see also v 3). On that day Ashkelon will be a *šmmh* (v 4; Study 15).[7] See the discussion of *ḥrwn ʾp* (3:8) in Study 8 and 2:14-15 in Study 15.

3. Jer 12:13

"Shepherds" destroyed the Lord's vineyard, Judah. They left it a *mdbr šmmh* (v 10). This is presented as the work of the Lord's sword (v 12). But there is more involved. V 13 reads:

> They sowed wheat; *qṣym* they reaped;
>   they toiled for naught.
> Dismayed are they at their crop[8]
>   on account of the Lord's *ḥrwn ʾp*.

[5] MT is in disorder. Rd *ʾābôʾ ʾăbāʿēr* or *ʾôbeh baʿer*.

[6] See pp. 26-27, n. 7.

[7] V 2:2a is corrupt. The picture of flying chaff fits the sirocco context (Study 11). See, e.g., *BHK*'s and *BHS*' emendation: *bṭrm lʾ tiddāḥēqû kmṣ ʿōbēr*. The LXX renders: *pro tou genesthai humas hōs anthos paraporeuomenon*.

[8] Rd *mtbwʾtyhm*.

Analyzing the imagery Dalman comments simply: the east wind destroyed the wheat; only thorns were left in the field.[9] The *qṣym* are thorns that need less water to survive than wheat.[10] The image presents the devastation of the "shepherds" as the work of the Lord's sirocco, just as Lamentations 2 (Part III, 5) presents the Babylonian destruction of Jerusalem as the work of Yahweh, the warrior, coming in a sirocco. Dalman compares Isa 32:12-13 where the overconfident ladies are told to lament[11] because the grain and wine harvests will fail and only *qwṣ* and *šmyr* will grow. This situation will last till *rwḥ* is poured forth from on high. Then:

> The *mdbr* will become *krml*,
> and the *krml* will be reckoned a *yʿr*. (v 15)

That presumes rain in abundance.

4. Jer 49:37

In this prophecy against Elam the Lord is presented as bringing the four winds and scattering her people to the corners of the earth (v 36). Elam's enemies are involved (v 37), but one gets the impression the destruction is wrought by both Yahweh and these enemies. The second line of v 37 reads:

> I will bring (*whbʾty*) on them *rʿh*,
> the *ḥrwn ʾpy*.

The verb *hbʾty* is the same verb used for the sending of the four winds in v 36. And in Jer 25:32 (Part III, 3) *rʿh* is used as a synonym for *sʿr* (Study 4) in a clear sirocco context.

5. Ps 85:4

Ps 85:4 reads:

> *ʾspt kl ʿbrtk*
> *hšybwt mḥrwn ʾpk.*

[9] G. Dalman, *Arbeit und Sitte in Palästina* I (Gütersloh: Evangelischer Verlag, 1928) 407.

[10] Ibid., 51. See Judg 8:7, 16: *qwṣy hmdbr*.

[11] Rd *sĕpōdâ*.

The tense usage is discussed. I am inclined to read both verbs as optative perfects with Dahood[12] and to regard the whole as a prayer for rain. In the second colon there are grammatical problems which can be resolved in various ways, but the sense is clear. For present purposes note *ʿbrh* (Study 19). In the oracular section of the psalm the cult prophet announces:

> The Lord will give *hṭwb*
> and our land will produce its *ybwl*. (v 13)

In that context *ṭwb* connotes in part at least "rain."[13] The *kbwd* of v 10 is the "glory" of the Lord coming in the rainstorm as it is in Isa 35:2 (Part V, 1). See Ps 29:9.

6. Job 20:23

> He will send upon him his *ḥrwn ʾp*;
> *wĕyamṭēr ʿālêmô bilĕḥûmô.*

The second colon is very uncertain; but if one thinks in terms of *ḥrwn ʾp* as the sirocco the text adjustment in *BHS* elaborated in the note to Job 18:15 gains further support.[14] In 20:23 it reads *wymṭr ʿlyw mbl ḥmw*, "He will rain down upon him the fire of his wrath," or the like. It may not be necessary to go outside the Hebrew lexicon to resolve the *mbl* problem. The root *nbl* (Study 7) has clear sirocco connections and *mbl* < *mnbl* could be related to it. For a vocalization it would be possible to think of an Aramaic-style verbal noun, *miqtal* (Joüon, § 49, 1), like *miqqaḥ šōḥad* "the taking of a bribe" (2 Chr 19:7). In the light of Jer 17:8, *ḥm* could arguably be vocalized *ḥummô*. The colon *wĕyamṭīr ʿālāw mibbal ḥummô* could be rendered, "He will rain down upon him the withering of his heat," with metonymy of effect for cause. In the other text where *BHS* suggests the identification of *mbl* as "fire" (Job

[12] M. Dahood, *Psalms* II (AB 17; Garden City: Doubleday, 1968) 286. Contrast H.-J. Kraus, *Psalmen* (BKAT 15/1-2; 2nd ed.; Neukirchen: Neukirchener Verlag, 1961) 589; S. Mowinckel, *Zum israelitischen Neujahr und zur Deutung der Thronbesteigungspsalmen* (Oslo: Dybwad, 1952) 85. See Joüon, § 112, k.

[13] Dahood, ibid., 290. See Jer 5:24-25.

[14] The note to 18:15 reads: 1 frt * *mabbēl* cf akk *nablu*, ug *nblt* = *ignis*. Both notes are based on M. Dahood, "Some Northwest-Semitic Words in Job," *Bib* 38 (1957) 312-15.

18:15) there is met the *gpryt* motif (Study 18) and in the following verse roots dry up and branches wither (*ybš*, *mll* = *ʾml*; Study 7).

7. *Lam 1:12*

Lamentations 2 (Part III, 5) presents the destruction of Jerusalem in 587 as almost completely the work of Yahweh, the warrior, coming in the sirocco. Lamentations 1 is different. It clearly presents the events of 598[15] as the work of Jerusalem's enemies. But in part it also presents them from the Yahweh-did-it point of view of Lamentations 2. V 12c speaks of Jerusalem whom the Lord afflicted on the *ywm ḥrwn ʾpw*. V 13a continues:

> From on high he dispatched *ʾš*;
> he brought it down[16] into my bones.

That *ḥrwn ʾp* and *ʾš* (Study 12) can be the sirocco is clear. This could be understood to make contact with the pasture imagery of v 6b and the hunger of v 11. In v 21 Jerusalem prays that her enemies may suffer her own fate and the Lord is requested to bring on[17] the day he has proclaimed (*ywm qrʾt*). That could be the *ywm Yhwh* which is typically the day of the sirocco (Study 20). The same is true of *ywm ḥrwn ʾpw* in v 12c.

Finally there is the image (v 15c) of the Lord treading in the wine press virgin daughter Judah. This immediately recalls the wine-press imagery of Joel 4:13 (Part VI) where the imagery is that of the fall interchange period. Similar imagery was met in Jer 25:30 which has clear sirocco connections (Part III, 3). It is present in Jer 51:14 too. The whole chapter is filled with the kind of language being studied here. Jer 51:34-37, 42-45 was studied in Part II, 5. The only mention of rain in the chapter in the plus of 51:15-19 was explained in Part VI, p. 127, n. 47.

Isaiah 63 presents the Lord returning from Edom with reddened garments like those of the treader of the wine press (v 2). His own arm did the fighting (v 5). He trampled there *bḥmh* (v 3); his *ḥmh* supported him (v 5); he crushed [18] in *ḥmh* (v 6). The noun *ḥmh* frequently occurs

[15] W. Rudolph, *Das Buch Ruth. Das Hohe Lied. Die Klagelieder* (KAT 17/1-3; Gütersloh: Gerd Mohn, 1962) 193-99, 209-11.

[16] Rd *wayyōrīdennâ*.

[17] Either regard *hbʾt* as optative perfect or rd *hābēʾ ʾet*.

[18] Frequently MT *wʾškrm* is corrected to *wʾšbrm* with the manuscripts. Whether

in sirocco contexts; not in rainstorms (Study 10). All this happened on the *ywm nqm*, in the year of his people's redemption (*šnt g'wly*, v 4). There is enough material here to suggest that there is sirocco imagery in Lamentations 1 too and that it has points of contact with a mythology connected with the fall interchange period and Sukkoth. Against that background the designation of the Babylonian army as a *mw'd* (v 15b) in the immediate context of the Lord treading the wine press (v 15c) and the more remote context of the absence of Israelite pilgrims (*b'y mwʿd*, v 4a) is even grimmer irony. See the discussion of the day of the fall of Jerusalem, the *ywm 'p Yhwh* (Lam 2:22) in Study 20.

8. Lam 4:11

In Lamentations 4 as in Lamentations 1 human enemies are the cause of Jerusalem's downfall, but once again the presentation is partly in terms of the-Lord-did-it. V 11 reads:

> The Lord has spent his *ḥmh*;
> he has poured out his *ḥrwn 'p*.
> He kindled an *'š* on Zion
> that has consumed (*'kl*) her foundations.

The noun *ḥmh* is a constant in sirocco contexts (Study 10). The combination *'š* + *'kl* is likewise sirocco vocabulary (Study 12). The Sodom motif (v 6) appears in sirocco contexts (Study 18). With that could fit the thirst of v 4; the hunger of vv 4-5, 9-10; the darkened complexion and shriveled skin (*ṣpd*, *ybš*) of v 8; the comparison of mother Jerusalem to an ostrich in the desert (v 3; Study 15). The presentation is partly made in terms of mythological materials connected with a warrior deity coming in a sirocco.

9. Ps 2:5

The psalm has frequently been tied to the fall interchange period on grounds other than the meteorological considerations of concern here.[19] On the occasion of a world revolution against the Lord and his

---

that is necessary or not is not clear. See *kws ḥmtw* in Isa 51:17, 22. The question is unimportant for present purposes.

[19] J. Gray, *The Biblical Doctrine of the Reign of God* (Edinburgh: Clark, 1979) 79-81.

anointed, vv 5-6 present the Lord announcing to the rebels the appointment of the Israelite king:

> Then he speaks to them *bʾpw*;
> *bḥrwnw* he berates[20] them:
> "I myself have appointed my king
> on Zion, my holy mountain."

The reference here is clearly to "anger," but this is in a context (v 11) where the rebels are threatened with the possibility that the Lord will be angry (*yʾnp*) and his *ʾp* will blaze (*ybʿr*). The combination *ʾp* + *bʿr* is sirocco-connected vocabulary. See *bʿr ʾpw* in Isa 30:27 (Part V, 2) and Study 21.

10. Ps 88:17

The psalmist near death prays for assistance. His difficulties are due to the fact that the Lord's *ḥrwnym* (pl. only here) have passed over (*ʿbr*[21]) him (v 17). In v 8 his difficulties are attributed to the fact that the Lord's *ḥmh* (Study 10) lay heavy (*smk*) upon him.

I think it possible on the basis of this review of the 10 previously undiscussed instances in poetry of *ḥrwn* (*ʾp*) as well as those already treated that even here there is more than just a slight hint more is involved than just "anger" in this phrase—either "anger" with added connections to the sirocco or the sirocco directly. It is clear that something holds this language together. In some cases the argument could be strengthened by an appeal to a broader context or motifs and vocabulary not directly meteorological, but that cannot be gone into here. It should be noted that the operative word in the phrase is *ḥrwn*, as might be expected. For example, Ps 18:16 (= 2 Sam 22:16; Part V, 4) speaks of the Lord's *nšmt rwḥ ʾp* in the midst of a rainstorm; Hab 3:12 describes the Lord coming in a rainstorm as crushing his enemies *bʾp* (Part V, 3).

The following texts referring to the Lord's "hot nose" in sirocco contexts, but without the vocabulary being discussed they are here noted: Deut 32:22 (*ʾš qdḥh bʾpy*; Part III, 4); Isa 30:27 (*bʿr ʾpw*; Part V, 2);

[20] J. VanderKam, "*BHL* in Ps 2:5 and its Etymology," *CBQ* 39 (1977) 245-50.
[21] The verb can be used of the wind. See Study 19.

Ps 18:9 (= 2 Sam 22:9; *ʿlh ʿšn bʾpw wʾš mpyw tʾkl*; Part V, 4). In the same psalm *ḥrh lw* of v 8; *ḥrh . . . ʾp* of Hab 3:8 (Part V, 3); and the *ḥry ʾp* of Lam 2:3 (Part III, 5) were regarded as reflecting *ḥrwn ʾp* and as having sirocco connections because of the context. This language more generally, however, can be used of human beings and does not betray the same connections to the sirocco as *ḥrwn* (*ʾp*).

***

Study 10
ḥmh

The noun *ḥmh* is much more common than *zʿm* (Study 8) or *ḥrwn* (*ʾp*) (Study 9). It occurs over thirty times in Ezekiel alone. In Hos 7:5 *ḥmt myyn* apparently means "heat from wine"; in several texts it means "poison" (e.g., Deut 32:24). For the rest it is generally interpreted as "burning anger" or the like. Unlike *zʿm* and *ḥrwn* (*ʾp*) it can be used of human anger, though more frequently the reference is to divine anger. Like *zʿm* and *ḥrwn* (*ʾp*) it hovers around clear sirocco contexts. It is never attested in a rainstorm context—once in a hailstorm context.[1] It has already been suggested that sometimes it ought to be interpreted concretely as "the hot (sirocco)." In Nah 1:6 (Part II, 2), for example:

> His *ḥmh* was poured out like fire,
> and cliffs were shattered before him.

And in Jer 23:19 (= 30:23; Study 4) "The Lord's *sʿrh*, *ḥmh*, goes forth." Understood as "anger" or the "heat (of the sirocco)" the noun hovers around such contexts with sufficient consistency to serve on its own as an indicator of the nature of the storm.

The following texts have been discussed to this point: Nah 1:2, 6 (Part II, 2); Lam 2:4 (Part III, 5); Isa 34:2 (Part V, 1) Jer 21:5 (Study 2); Ezek 7:8 (Study 2); Isa 66:15 (Study 3); Jer 23:19 (Study 4); Jer 30:23 (Study 4); Zech 8:2 (Study 4, p. 139, n. 10); Isa 63:3, 5, 6 (Study 9); Lam 4:11 (Study 9); Ps 88:8 (Study 9). To these texts ten are added here. It is understood that substitutions could be made, e.g. the four texts listed at the end of this Study and treated in the following Studies.

Study 10

[1] Ezek 13:13: *ʾbny ʾlgbyš bḥmh*. The text was discussed in Study 4.

1. Isa 42:25

In vv 10-12 the Lord comes off the Mediterranean in a rainstorm. As the storm moves west to east the sea, everything in it, the coastlands and their inhabitants resound.[2] As the storm moves inland the *mdbr* (presumably being rained on by the first fall rains) and Kedar add their acclaim; the inhabitants of Sela cheer from the mountain tops and ascribe *kbwd* to the Lord.[3] This happens in a context where the Lord goes forth as a *gbwr* (v 13); pants (*nšm*), gasps (*šʾp*, v 14); withers the vegetation of mountains and hills (*ḥrb*, *ybš*; Study 7) and dries up bodies of water (*ybš*, v 15; Study 1) to save his people (v 16). The imagery here is based on the contrasting storms of the fall interchange period. V 25 explains the people's need for help and the events of 587 in terms of the same sirocco imagery:

> He poured out *ḥmh* upon him,
> his anger and the fury of battle.

The *ḥmh* burned (*lhṭ*) and blazed against (*bʿr*) Jacob (v 25b). Both *lhṭ* (Study 22) and *bʿr* (Study 21) are typical sirocco vocabulary.

2. Ezek 19:12

A royal mother under the figure of a vine is plucked up (*ntš*) *bḥmh*, cast (*šlk*) to the ground, and withered (*ybš*; Study 7) by the *rwḥ hqdym*. It is possible,[4] though hardly necessary, to understand *bḥmh* as "by the hot (east wind)." The sirocco context is, however, clear.

[2] The interpretation presumes *yrʿm* for MT *ywrdy* in the light of Ps 96:11; 98:7 (Part V, 6) with *BHK*. For present purposes MT could just as well be read.

[3] See Ps 29:9. The motif of nature rejoicing at the coming of the first rains was met in Isa 35:1-2 (Part V, 1) and Pss 96:11-12; 98:7-8 (Part V, 6). The mention of the sea first in Psalms 96 and 98 is also dictated by the movement of rainstorms from west to east. See pp. 105-6, n. 79 which also points out the west to east orientation of the rainstorm theophany in Psalm 29. For the same orientation of the rainstorm in Hab 3:8b-15 see Part V, 3.

[4] The sirocco of March 29, 1957 "caused heavy damage, particularly in the Jordan Valley, where it destroyed light buildings, uprooted trees and banana plantations, dried fields and cut telephone and electric wires. . . . Wind velocities reached 75-85 km/hour at 'Ein Gev, Daphnah, Kabri, and Haifa Port," J. Katsnelson, "Meteorology," *IEJ* 7 (1957) 263.

3. Deut 29:22, 27

If Israel is disloyal the moist (land?, *hrwh*) will be swept away (*sph*) with the dry (land?, *hṣmʾh*, v 18). The Lord's nose will smoke (*yʿšn ʾp Yhwh*, v 19; Study 9). The land will end up unsown and unfruitful, a burnt-out waste (*śrph*) and *gpryt* like Sodom, Gomorrah, Admah and Zeboiim (Study 18) which the Lord overthrew in *ḥmh* (v 22). The nations will say: what is this *ḥry hʾp* (v 23; Study 9)? This happened because the Lord's nose burned (*ḥrh* + *ʾp*, v 26; Study 9) against the land. The Lord plucked up (*ntš*) his people *bḥmh* from their *ʾdmh* and cast them off (*šlk*) into another *ʾrṣ* (v 27).[5]

The contrast for this is in chap. 30. If Israel repents (v 2), all the agriculture of the *ʾdmh* will prosper (v 9). That presumes rain. In v 15 the alternatives are described as a choice between *hḥyym* and *hṭwb* on the one hand and *hmwt* and *hrʿ* on the other.

The language and motifs here are sufficiently removed for the modern interpreter from their setting in nature myth that one would be pressed to identify with any degree of precision their source without the background of the texts already seen. But the choice is clearly between rain and no rain, ultimately the east and west wind, and the vocabulary and motifs are so similar to those already seen there can be little doubt where they are coming from. The text is important because it supplies the bridge between poetic texts where the language often enough clearly betrays its origin in nature myth and normal prose texts where it rarely does.

4. Lev 26:28

The prose of Lev 26:27-33 is similar, though it is a somewhat dimmer reflection of these myth-based materials. But again *ḥmh* resurrects the pertinent vocabulary and motifs; and that is the key to the origin of the language here too.

The unit of concern is part of the complex 26:3-45 which contrasts the results of obedience and disobedience. If Israel is obedient, the Lord will send the rains and the agriculture will flourish etc. (vv 3-13). The results of disobedience are spelled out in five paragraphs, each introduced by a protasis referring to the disobedience (vv 14-33). The

[5] The *ntš* + *šlk* combination is the same as in Ezek 19:12, the preceding text.

arrangement is climactic, at least as regards the last. The presentation of the first four threats is such that a modern, at least, would see in them natural catastrophes or war.

The fifth (vv 27-33) is different; here the Lord is not the indirect but the direct protagonist and the language reflects the myth of Yahweh, the warrior, coming in a sirocco:[6]

> I will oppose you with heated defiance (*ḥmt qry*, v 28). . . . You will eat the flesh of your children (hunger, v 29). . . . I will smash high places . . . cut off incense altars . . . heap up your bodies (v 30) . . . make your cities *ḥrbh* (v 31; Study 15) . . . make your land a desert (*hšmty*; Study 15) so that even your enemies will be appalled (v 32). You I will scatter among the nations and I will unsheathe my sword after you. Your land will be a *šmmh* and your cities *ḥrbh* (v 33; Study 15).

5. *Isa 51:20*

In v 3 Zion's *mdbr* and *ʿrbh* become like Eden, the Lord's garden. That presumes rain, the first rains of the fall (see v 11). Though the heavens are dispersed[7] like smoke and the earth wears out, the Lord's people have nothing to fear (v 6). The reference is to the sirocco. The Lord is the one who dried up (*ḥrb*) the sea (v 10; Part IV and Study 1). Before him all men are *ḥṣyr* (which withers in the sirocco,[8] v 12). V 20 reviews the events of 587 and their effects on Jerusalem's sons. They are presented from the Yahweh-did-it point of view. Jerusalem's sons lie faint (Pu. *ʿlp*); the same verb (Hith.) is used in Jonah 4:8 for the effects of the sun on the prophet in an east-wind period (*rwḥ qdym*). They got their full of the *ḥmh* and *gʿrh* of the Lord (*hmlʾym ḥmt Yhwh gʿrt ʾlhyk*). Both *ḥmh* and *gʿrh* could be understood concretely. In the general context that is what is meant in any case.[9] Note how the *qbʿt kws ḥmty* is

[6] For the "paragraphing" of the piece see M. Noth, *Leviticus* (Philadelphia: Westminster, 1965) 195-98. Chap. 26 originally closed out Leviticus; chap. 27 is an appendix. Viewed this way, Leviticus 26 calls to mind the agricultural-new-year closings of Habakkuk (Part V, 3) and Joel (Part VI). The same remark could be made about Deuteronomy 29-30 discussed on p. 161. With chap. 31 the narrative of the Pentateuch resumes. Deut 31:10-11 makes obligatory the reading of the Law at Sukkoth in the sabbatical year.

[7] The verb occurs only here; *kʿšn* suggests the sense. See Isa 34:4 (Part V, 1).

[8] Isa 40:6-8.

[9] The text is like Lamentations 2 etc., in that it presents the events of 587 now past in terms of the Lord's coming in a sirocco.

taken from Jerusalem's hand and put in the hands of the Babylonians (v 22) who are about to be destroyed by Yahweh, the warrior, coming in the sirocco (vv 9-10).

6. Jer 4:4

Jer 4:5-31 was studied in Part III, 2. There Judah was threatened with the invasion of the Babylonian army under the figure of the east wind unless it repents (v 14). The opening of the chapter (vv 1-4) is similar. Vv 1-4a urge repentance. The threat is in v 4b:

> Lest my *ḥmh* come forth like *ʾš*
> and *bʿrh* with none to quench it.

Both *ʾš* and *bʿr* are typical sirocco-context vocabulary (Studies 12 and 21); *ḥmh* could be understood concretely.

7. Jer 21:5, 12

The text of Jer 4:4b cited above is repeated verbatim in 21:12 as part of a complex 21:1-23:8 condemning the kings who closed out the Davidic dynasty starting with Jehoahaz. Jer 21:1-10, though simply juxtaposed to what follows, cannot be separated from the complex in the final redaction. The things said about Zedekiah in vv 1-10 make it clear that, whoever *Yhwh ṣdqnw* (23:6) was supposed to be outside its present context, in the MT it is not Zedekiah. Apart from its general concern with the last kings of the house of David, the complex is held together by the imagery of the fall interchange period which runs through it like a thread.

Yahweh will turn back the weapons of those defending Jerusalem (21:4). He himself will join the Babylonian attack (*nlḥmty*) with his *yd nṭwyh*, his *zrwʿ ḥzqh* in *ḥmh* (v 5). The population will die of *dbr* (v 6, Study 2). Vv 1-10 combine the presentation of Nebuchadnezzar's attack on Jerusalem with the imagery of the Lord coming in the sirocco to indicate Yahweh is the ultimate cause of Jerusalem's fall.

Vv 11-14 continue this imagery pattern. V 12 repeats 4:4b:

> Lest my *ḥmh* come forth like *ʾš*
> and *bʿrh* with none to quench it.

Again *ʾš* and *bʿr* are typical sirocco-context vocabulary; and again *ḥmh* could be understood concretely. In v 14 the Lord threatens to kindle in the "forest" of Jerusalem an *ʾš* which will consume (*ʾkl*) everything round about. The combination *ʾš* + *ʾkl* is sirocco vocabulary (Study 12).

In 22:5 the palace becomes *ḥrbh* (Study 15); in v 6, an uninhabited *mdbr* (Study 15). In v 22 the (east) wind "shepherds" all of Jerusalem's "shepherds" (*kl rʿyk trʿh rwḥ*).

The promise of the ultimate reversal of the fates that concludes the complex speaks of the Lord gathering his *ṣʾn* from all the lands where he scattered them and returning them to their *nwh* where they will prosper (23:3). The Lord will raise up a new "sprout" (*ṣmḥ*) of David as king (v 5) and the exiles will once again dwell on their *ʾdmh* (agricultural land as opposed to *mdbr* of 22:6) (v 8). All of this presumes rain.

Into this imagery pattern as analyzed here fits the mention of trees and mountains throughout the piece in characterizing pre-destruction Jerusalem. Along the Syro-Palestinian litoral the first mountains, met by the moisture-laden winds off the Mediterranean, force them upwards and cause rain to fall. Thus, these mountain areas produce forests which require abundant water and become symbols of lush vegetation—especially the evergreen, cedar forests of the Lebanon. Jer 21:14 speaks of Jerusalem's "forest." The city is compared to Gilead and Lebanon (22:6); it has "cedars" (v 7) and a palace built with cedar (vv 14-15). Jerusalem dwells on Lebanon, nests among the "cedars" (v 23). On a secondary level these images are intended to suggest pre-destruction Jerusalem was well supplied with rain.

8. Ezek 5:13

The Jerusalem temple has been defiled (v 11). So her people will die of *dbr* (Study 2), hunger and the sword and be scattered in every direction. The Lord will unsheathe his sword (v 12) and wreak his *ḥmh* on them (v 13). Jerusalem will be a *ḥrbh* (v 14; Study 15).

9. Ezek 30:15

The prophecy against Egypt in 30:1-19 presents Nabuchadnezzar's invasion of Egypt (vv 10-11) for the most part as the work of Yahweh, the warrior, coming in a sirocco. The day on which Egypt is destroyed is a *ywm lYhwh*, a *ywm ʿnn* (v 3). The *ywm Yhwh* is typically the day of the sirocco; and *ʿnn* (not a rain cloud), typically the blowing dust of the sirocco (Studies 20 and 5). The day will be a day of darkness (rd *ḥāšak*) because of the cloud (*ʿnn*) cover (v 18; Study 16). The Lord fights with a sword (vv 4, 5, 6). Egypt and her cities end up a desert (v 7; rd *nšmh* with the LXX and *ʿryh*; Study 15). The Lord will pour out his *ḥmh* (v 15). He will set Egypt on fire (vv 8, 16; Study 12). The "Niles" will end up a desert (v 12; *ḥārābâ*). The drying up of the "Niles" in particular indicates the nature of the Lord's intervention (Study 1).

10. Prov 16:14

This is a text completely different from those looked at so far; *ḥmh* certainly denotes "anger" directly and it is a question of human wrath. But there is a clear antithesis intended between vv 14 and 15, and the antithesis gives cause to wonder whether below the surface there isn't a literary allusion connecting the language of the proverb to that of the texts being studied here:

> The *ḥmh* of the king is *mlʾky mwt*;
> the wise man will try to pacify it.
> In the light of the king's face there is *ḥyym*,
> and his favor is like an *ʿb mlqwš*.

Does *ḥmh* take on fresh overtones in the light of *ʿb mlqwš*? The situation could be like Job 1:21:

> Naked I came forth from my mother's womb,
> and naked I return there,

where "naked" and "mother's womb" on a secondary level end up meaning something quite different from the plain sense of the words in the light of colon two.

The contrast here between *mwt* and *ḥyym* is the same as that in Deut 30:15 (discussed in no. 3 above) with reference to the choice between no rain and rain. In Ps 78:49 (Study 8) the Lord's *ḥrwn ʾp*, *ʿbrh*, *zʿm* and *ṣrh* (the sirocco) are his embassy of messengers of woe (*mšlḥt mlʾky rʿym*).[10] And in Ps 104:3-4 the east wind is the Lord's messenger:

> He who makes the clouds (*ʿbym*) his chariot,
> and travels on the wings of the wind;

[10] See Ps 35:5.

Who uses the *rwḥwt* as *mlʾkyw*,
ʾš lhṭ[11] as his ministers.

The *ʿbym* are rain clouds[12] and that identifies the storm in the first line. All the indications are that *ʾš lhṭ* (|| *rwḥwt*) has no connections to the rainstorm, but typically to the sirocco (Study 22). The reference to the alternating storms of the fall interchange period is appropriate in a psalm that traces the progress of the agriculture from the coming of the first rains (v 13) through the grass of winter, the grain of spring (v 14), the wine of late summer and the olive oil at the very end of the summer (v 15).

There is a probable reference to the coming of the first rains in vv 29-30. All creatures look to the Lord for food (v 27) and when he gives it to them they have their fill (v 28). Vv 29-30 read:

a. If you hide your face, they are dismayed;
b. if you take away their *rwḥ*, they perish;
they return to the dust.
c. If you send forth your *rwḥ*, they are restored (*ybrʾwn*);
d. and you renew the face of the *ʾdmh*.

I take that to mean in the context of the psalm: a) if you are angry at them and don't send your rain in the fall, they are dismayed; b) if *thereby* you take away their *rwḥ* (life breath), they die; c) but if in the fall you send forth your (west) wind (*rwḥ*) they are restored. The reference is not to those who die in b, but to men and animals still alive waiting for the fall rains to renew the water supply and restart the growth cycle of the plant world; d) the same west wind renews the face of the *ʾdmh*. Of course, the Lord's *rwḥ* denotes more than the west wind here, but it means that too. The alternatives once again are life and death as above.

Vv 31-32 continue:

May the Lord's *kbwd* be forever;
may the Lord rejoice in his creation (*mʿśyw*),
He who can look at the earth and it shakes,
who can touch (*ngʿ*) the mountains and they smoke (*yʿšnw*).

[11] *ʾš* m. ?; < *lōhiṭt* ?; see F. Zorell, *Lexicon hebraicum et aramaicum Veteris Testamenti* (Roma: Pontificium Institutum Biblicum, 1963) s.v. *ʾš*. 11QPs^a *lwhṭt*.

[12] R. B. Y. Scott, "Meteorological Phenomena and Terminology in the Old Testament," *ZAW* 64 (1952) 25.

This, I suspect, is a prayer for the west wind and against the east wind. The Lord's *kbwd* is to be connected with his coming in the rainstorm as in Ps 29:9.[13] The second line where the earth shakes and the mountains smoke is a reference to the possibility that he might come in a sirocco.[14]

In the texts cited in this review the verbs *ntk* and *špk* were used of *ḥmh* in Nah 1:6 (*ntk*); Lam 2:4; Ezek 7:8; Isa 42:25; Ezek 30:15 (*špk*). The usage is paralleled elsewhere. Both verbs are connected primarily to liquids. But secondarily they can be used of *rwḥ*. See *špk* + *rwḥ* in Ezek 39:29; Joel 3:1, 2; Zech 12:10.

See further the following *ḥmh* texts discussed below: Ezek 38:18 (Study 13); Ezek 22:20, 22 (in Study 19); Jer 7:20 (Study 21); Jer 44:6 (Study 21).

* * *

[13] See Isa 42:12 discussed in no. 1 above; and Isa 35:2 (Part V, 1).

[14] It is clear that in attempting to distinguish references to distinct storms in Ps 104:3-4 and 31-32 the limits of what is possible for a modern interpreter have been approached or passed, though the questions asked here are ones any schoolboy in OT times could have answered without hesitation. But the distinction is virtually made in vv 29-30 and on the basis of the available evidence *ʿbym* and *ʾš lhṭ* are incompatible in vv 3-4. V 32 was identified as the sirocco because nominal and verbal *ʿšn* in various ways has connections to the sirocco, not the rainstorm. See, for example: Isa 34:10 (Part V, 1); Isa 51:6 (no. 5 above); Joel 3:3 (Part VI); Ps 18:9 (Part V, 4); Deut 29:19 (no. 3 above).

Ps 144, which is likewise in part a prayer for the success of the agriculture (vv 13-14), presents in vv 5-6 the closest verbal reflection of Ps 104:32b:

O Lord, incline your heavens and come down;
touch (*ngʿ*) the mountains so that they smoke.
Flash forth lightning and scatter them;
shoot your arrows and rout them.

That too I would suggest with necessary reserve is a reference to a sirocco followed by a rainstorm. There is no text to indicate *ngʿ* is ever used of lightning; Ezek 17:10 shows that the verb can be used of the *rwḥ hqdym*. Amos 9:5 is patient of the same explanation. In v 4 the Lord sets his eye on his people for *evil* and not for *good*. He is the one who touches (*ngʿ*) the earth; it shakes/melts (*mwg*); and the people mourn (*ʾbl*) (v 5). That is the *evil*. He is also the one who summons the waters of the sea and pours them out on the earth (v 6). That is the *good*. Note how the epilogue which reverses this situation describes the wonderful success of the agriculture (vv 13-15). That presumes rain. Jer 10:10 + 12-13 as interpreted in the discussion of Part VI is very similar to Amos 9:4-6.

One final remark about Ps 104. The possible influence here of the Aton hymn has been often commented on; see the critical discussion of P. E. Dion, "YHWH as Storm-god and Sun-god: The Double Legacy of Egypt and Canaan as Reflected in Psalm 104," *ZAW* 103 (1991) 43-71. It should be noted that the meteorology, which presumes the agriculture depends on rain, is pure Syro-Palestinian. The Aton hymn does, however, recognize that a Nile has been set in heaven for non-Egyptians (*ANET*, 371).

Study 11
Flying *qš*, *mṣ*, *glgl*, *tbn*

A description of a storm in which mention is made of withered vegetation, flying or otherwise, is a priori not a rainstorm. Withered vegetation is not a phenomenon of the wet period but of the rainless summer; and it does not fly in a rainstorm in any case. A review of the pertinent OT texts makes it immediately clear that they reflect this situation. It is, of course, true that loose *qš* and the like will be blown about by any wind in a dry period, but they do have an immediate connection to the sirocco and the meteorologically related heat waves of the spring insofar as these are prime causes for the withering of the winter green.[1]

This is the situation reflected in a text like Jer 13:24 (discussed in Part IV) where the Lord threatens to scatter people like *qš ʿwbr* before the *rwḥ mdbr*. The picture may be the same in Jer 18:17 where the Lord threatens to scatter people *krwḥ qdym* before the enemy in a context where Judah becomes a *šmh* (v 16; Study 15); here though the picture could be flying dust or sand (Study 6). And in Job 27:21 (Study 3) the *qdym* picks up the prosperous man (apparently under the figure of a plant) and blows (*śʿr*; Study 4) him from his place. For the rest it is necessary to find other pieces of sirocco-related vocabulary or motifs to identify the storm as the east wind. Thus, in Isa 40:24 (Study 4) the Lord blows (*nšp*) on the potentates of the world, they wither (*ybš*; Study 7) and the *sʿrh* (Study 4) carries them away like *qš*.

The texts where the motif of flying *qš* etc. has been identified with certainty or probability in a sirocco context are: Exod 15:7 (Part IV); Jer 13:24 (in Part IV); Isa 29:5 (Part V, 5); Isa. 17:13 (Study 3); Ps 83:14 (Study 3); Job 21:18 (Study 3); Isa 40:24 (Study 4); Isa 41:16 (Study 4); Zeph 2:2 (Study 9; corrected text).

Three further instances are added here:

1. Job 13:25

Job asks the Lord:

> Will you harass a (wind-) driven leaf;
> will you pursue *qš ybš* (Study 7)?

Study 11

[1] G. Dalman, *Arbeit und Sitte* I (Gütersloh: Evangelischer Verlag, 1928) 323-26.

He continues in 14:1-2:

> Man born of woman—
> his life is short and full of trouble.
> Like a blossom he comes forth and withers (*mll* = *ʾml*; Study 7);
> he is fleeting like a shadow, cannot endure.

2. Isa 41:2-3

> 2 Who has stirred up from the *mzrḥ* "Victory (Cyrus),"
> summons him for his retinue?[2]
> To him he hands over nations,
> makes kings subject.[3]
> 3 His (the Lord's) sword makes them like *ʿpr*;
> his bow makes them like *qš ndp*;
> Be pursues them and passes on untouched;
> he travels no path with his feet.

The imagery presents Cyrus' victories as those of Yahweh, the warrior, coming in a sirocco. Cyrus merely follows him. The Lord fights with sword and bow. Those whom he slays are blown away like the *ʿpr* (Study 6) and *qš*. In this way is to be explained the fact that the Lord's feet do not touch the ground. He travels in the wind; whether in a chariot or not is unclear (see the discussion in Study 14). Into this imagery pattern fits the specific mention of the fact that Cyrus comes from the east. The imagery here is related to 40:21 discussed above. See 41:16 (Study 4).[4]

[2] For the sense of *lrgl* see: 1 Sam 25:42; Hab 3:5; Gen 30:30.

[3] Rd with 1QIsa^{a} *yôrîd*.

[4] The sword and bow are generally understood as those of Cyrus who is also regarded as the subject in v 3. But there is no real indication of a change in subject and the explanation this view allows for v 3b favors the Lord as agent in the whole of vv 2-3. It would be possible to interpret the sirocco imagery as applied to Cyrus himself but 40:24 argues against that.

B. Duhm (*Das Buch Jesaia* [5th ed.; Göttingen: Vandenhoeck und Ruprecht, 1968] 302) comes close to the explanation of v 3b suggested here, though he thinks Cyrus is the subject.

3. Ps 1:4

The just man is like a tree planted by streams of water which produces fruit and the leaves of which never wither and fall (v 3). The wicked man is like *mṣ* which *rwḥ* (withers and) drives away (v 4, *ndp*).

***

Study 12
ʾš + ʾkl

The first point to be made in this Study is that the combination, simple *ʾš + ʾkl*, with *ʾš* as the grammatical or logical subject is never used of lightning in *any recognizable meteorological context*. The operative element here is *ʾkl*; *ʾš* without *ʾkl* can denote lightning.[1] The phrase "simple *ʾš*" is used to distinguish *ʾš* from *lhb ʾš* which once in Isa 30:30 combined with *ʾkl* denotes lightning (see below). The phrase "*any recognizable meteorological context*" is meant to eliminate from the discussion texts like the following where there is nothing to indicate a storm is involved and which show little connection to anything like normal meteorology. In Lev 9:23-24 the Lord's *kbwd* appears, *ʾš* comes forth from before him and consumes (*ʾkl*) the oblation. In Lev 10:2 *ʾš* comes forth from before the Lord and consumes (*ʾkl*) Nadab and Abihu. In Job 1:16 an *ʾš ʾlhym* falls (*npl*) from heaven, burns up (*bʿr*) and consumes (*ʾkl*) the flock and the shepherds. In 1 Kgs 18:38 an *ʾš Yhwh* falls (*npl*) and consumes (*ʾkl*) the holocaust.[2] The first two texts one might be tempted to tie ultimately to the picture of the Lord coming in a sirocco. In the second two one might be more inclined to think of lightning. But in none of these texts can one eliminate supranatural fire that has relatively little to do with anything experienced in nature apart from the every-day experience of the destructive force of fire itself.[3]

Study 12

[1] See Exod 9:23, 24; Ps 148:8.

[2] See the discussion of the last two texts in Part V, 6.

[3] There are other prose texts where there are clearer indications where the language is coming from. For instance, in Num 11:1-2 the Lord becomes angry (*ḥrh + ʾp*; Study 9); the *ʾš Yhwh* burns (*bʿr*; Study 21) people; and consumes (*ʾkl*) the edge of the camp. At the prayer of Moses the fire dies down. There is enough here to tie the text with some probability *ultimately* to the picture of the Lord coming in a sirocco, but there is not

The essential thing to note for the purpose of the present discussion is that there are more than a few easily recognizable descriptions of rainstorms and hailstorms in the OT and that in one of these does this vocabulary appear. The other thing to note is that a canvas of the OT occurrences of *ʾš* + *ʾkl* immediately picks up the motifs and vocabulary being isolated in these Studies as typical of the sirocco and they also have nothing to do with rainstorms or hailstorms and lightning. It is clear that these materials including *ʾš* + *ʾkl* are a tidy package and that something is holding them together. Here the claim has been made it is the sirocco as experienced in Palestine. That the combination *ʾš* + *ʾkl* is a natural one in such a setting is made clear by Gen 31:40 where Jacob complains of having been consumed (*ʾkl*) by the scorching heat (*ḥrb*) of the day (as opposed to the *qrḥ* of the night).

It is possible, of course, that in many or all of these texts where *ʾš* + *ʾkl* appears we are dealing with mysterious supranatural fire and that it is a mistake to seek an explanation for them in experienced Palestinian meteorology.[4] This possibility has to be defended against and I return

---

enough in the context of this legendary material to indicate that a meteorological interpretation of the language is necessary. This is most often the case in prose texts.

Though the question cannot be discussed at length, there is a probable, partial explanation for the different relation to nature as experienced, in texts like those just treated and those to be treated immediately below – most clearly Joel 2:3 (Part VI). In the former situation the language has become part of legend for the most part divorced from a seasonal setting and so no longer controlled by nature. Thus it has taken on or is in the process of taking on a supranatural reference. Though one could suspect, for example, that the language of Lev 10:2 is rooted in nature myth derived from meteorology, it has lost its seasonal and meteorological context and it is impossible to know what the writer or his Israelite audience made of it.

Joel 2:3 is different. It is clearly set in the fall interchange period. It talks the language of meteorological nature myth connected with that time period and most probably the feast of Sukkoth which immediately preceded. As the language of the liturgy of that feast it stood under the control of real meteorology and preserved contact with it.

Midway between Lev 10:2 and Joel 2:3 stand Lev 26:27-33 and Deut 29:18-27, both prose texts, discussed in Study 10. There it was argued that echoes of the language of sirocco mythology of the fall interchange period could be heard. But note how both texts presume a temporal reference to that period. There nature is exercising control over the language.

[4] This is the point of view, for example, of P. D. Miller, "Fire in the Mythology of Canaan and Israel," *CBQ* 27 (1965) 256-61. He reviews some of the texts dealt with here, but does not consider the possibility of a meteorological explanation. Behind that position I suspect is the unspoken American and European prejudice that a storm is a rainstorm.

to the two arguments used before as support for the position taken here. The second is the stronger. The first argument is that the combination, *ʾš* + *ʾkl*, fits into contexts where there is also present a storm and/or effects akin to those produced by the sirocco. For illustration sake I use extreme examples. In Amos 1:14 (Study 3) the Lord threatens to kindle an *ʾš* on the wall of Rabbah which will consume (*ʾkl*) her towers. This happens on a day of battle in a *sʿr* on a day of *swph*. Both *sʿr* and *swph* are frequently the sirocco, never a rainstorm (Studies 4 and 3). The text is part of the prophecies-against-the-nations section that runs through Amos 1-2. Six more times (1:4, 7, 10, 12; 2:2, 5) the Lord threatens to start a fire on the walls of cities which will consume their towers. On these occasions the *sʿr* and the *swph* are not mentioned, but in the light of 1:14 they can be inferred there too. The whole is introduced (1:2) by a presentation of the Lord roaring (*šʾg*) from Zion and the pastures and top of Carmel withering (*ʾbl*, *ybš*; Study 7). Throughout the section the Lord is the only agent indicated. There are exaggerations here, of course. No sirocco ever originated on Zion. No sirocco ever of itself started fires, though the sirocco does prepare the conditions under which prairie fires or forest fires become possible in Palestine and such a fire fanned by a sirocco could be a fearsome thing.[5] But if the presentation here is rooted in a nature mythology that is itself rooted in anything experienced in Palestine, the only possible candidate is the sirocco.

Similarly in Amos 7:4 (Part VI, p. 114, n. 17) the prophet sees as his second vision an *ʾš*[6] that consumes (*ʾkl*) the *thwm* (Study 1) and the agricultural land (*ḥlq*; Study 7). The effects are exaggerated again, but if the vision has its roots in nature, the phenomenon can only be the sirocco. This is also suggested by the sequence of the first four visions

[5] Such fires become possible after the siroccos of the spring interchange period. This situation continues through the summer. See G. Dalman, *Arbeit und Sitte in Palästina* II (Gütersloh: Evangelischer Verlag, 1932) 340; G. A. Smith, *The Historical Geography of the Holy Land* (reprint 1931 ed.; London: Collins, 1966) 64.

[6] It may or may not be necessary to read *lhb ʾš* or *lirbīb ʾš* for MT *lārīb bʾš*. See the discussion of W. Rudolph, *Joel, Amos, Obadja, Jona* (KAT 13/2; Gütersloh: Gerd Mohn, 1971) 232. In Ps 103:9 *ryb* used absolutely certainly means "to defend one's rights by punishing." The punishment aspect is at least implied and *ryb* understood this way makes good sense in Amos 7:4. Whatever one reads here is of little import in the context of the present discussion.

which is natural: locusts before the spring interchange period, the sirocco in it, an invasion after it and finally the basket of summer fruit (7:1-8:3).[7]

The second argument is the more important. It springs from texts where the sirocco is played off explicitly or implicitly against the rainstorm. Such texts were treated in Parts V and VI; and more have been added in these Studies. Nobody hesitates in understanding these references to rain for what they are. It is possible, of course, that the texts interpreted here as references to siroccos in such contexts unlike the rain should not be connected to nature. But that seems unlikely—especially in the light of the fact that these storms do alternate in the spring and fall interchange periods.

Of all the texts illustrating both the *ʾš* + *ʾkl* combination and the interplay between the rainstorm and the sirocco, Joel 2:3 (Part VI) is the parade example because the temporal setting and development of Joel 1–2 are crystal clear. The prophet is speaking at the end of a summer which had been an agricultural disaster because of the locusts and insufficient rain during the previous spring and winter. Now at the summer's end, water from any source is in extremely short supply. These signs of the Lord's displeasure Joel interprets as presaging the absence of rain and the coming of the *ywm Yhwh*, the day of the Lord's sirocco, in the imminent fall interchange period (2:1-11). In the course of the description of that day which resurrects the typical vocabulary and motifs treated in these Studies, Joel describes the coming of the Lord and his army using the vocabulary of concern here:

> Before them fire consumes (*ʾš ʾklh*);
>   behind them flame burns (*tlhṭ lhbh*).
> Like the garden of Eden is the land before them;
>   behind them a *mdbr šmmh*. (2:3)

Land being turned into a desert is a typical sirocco motif (Study 15); the combination, *lhṭ* + *lhbh*, is likewise sirocco vocabulary (Study 22). After a mourning ceremony the prophet is able to change his mind and announce the rains are imminent and the agriculture will flourish (2:19-27). The temporal sequence of events in the piece and the contrast

[7] See p. 114, n. 17.

between the imminent sirocco and the benevolent rain make it almost impossible to interpret the *ʾš* + *ʾkl* vocabulary as anything else but a reference to the sirocco. Since qualitatively there is nothing better for linking this vocabulary to the sirocco than the Joel text, I simply list the other texts with this vocabulary discussed to this point that have been interpreted similarly: Deut 32:22 (Part III, 4); Isa 30:27 (Part V, 2); Ps 50:3 (Part V, p. 92, n. 49); Ps 18:9 (= 2 Sam 22:9; Part V, 4); Joel 1:19, 20 (Part VI); Isa 26:11 (Study 8); Lam 4:11 (Study 9); Jer 21:14 (Study 10). In Zeph 1:18 (in Part VI) and 3:8 (Study 8) the combination *ʾš qnʾh* + *ʾkl* was identified in a sirocco context; likewise *ʾš* and *ʾš ʿbrh* without *ʾkl* in Isa 66:15, 16 (Study 3); Lam 1:13 (Study 9); Ps 97:3 (Part V, 6); and in Ezek 22:31 (Study 8); 21:36 (Study 8).

In meteorological texts the combinations *ʾš lhbh/lhb ʾš* + *ʾkl* and *lhby ʾš* without *ʾkl* were *lhb* also identified in sirocco contexts: Lam 2:3 (Part III, 5); Isa 29:6 (Part V, 5); Joel 2:5 (Part VI); Isa 66:15 (Study 3). The problem here is created by the one text, Isa 30:30 (Part V, 2), where *lhb ʾš* + *ʾkl* is clearly lightning. On either side of the phrase the verse speaks of the lowering of the Lord's arm (probably the motion for launching a spear is meant) and shattering rain and hail. Sandwiched in that way, the reference can only be to lightning which *ʾš*[8] alone can denote as well as the combinations *ʾš lhbwt* (Ps 105:32) and *lhbwt ʾš* (Ps 29:7). The distinction between *ʾš* and *lhb/lhbh* is probably the distinction between fire as a mass and the individual flame. As such *lhb/lhbh* comes to denote lightning and the glittering blade of a sword or a spear (Judg 3:22; Job 39:23). But that it can also denote fiery breath (or wind) is made clear by Job 41:13 where Behemoth's *npš* that sets coals afire is a *lhb* that comes out of his mouth.

Studies 21 and 22 will study *bʿr* and *lhṭ* in sirocco contexts. The texts to be met there are very similar to the ones treated here.

See further: Ezek 38:19, 22; 39:6 (Study 13); Ezek 22:21 (in Study 19); Mal 3:2 (Study 20).

***

[8] See p. 170.

Study 13
The Dead or Frightened Fish

The motif of the fish as a reflex of the motif of the drying up of bodies of water (Study 1) in which it is implicit needs no discussion. If a storm is involved it is the sirocco. The motif was identified in: Isa 50:2 (Part II, 4); Zeph 1:3 (in Part VI). The motif can be identified with some probability in Isa 19:6 (Part II, 3).

To these may be added:

1. Hos 4:3

The *dgy hym* perish along with the wild animals and birds in a context where land withers[1] (*ʾbl*; Study 7) and all who dwell on it languish (*ʾml*). It is possible to think here of the meteorologically related heat wave or drought, but probably a super-sirocco is needed to dry up as large a body of water as a *ym*, whether understood as a sea, lake or river.[2] Note the climactic character of *gm dgy hym*.

2. Ezek 38:20

The text is found in the Gog material that runs through chaps. 38-39. The whole has undergone secondary expansions,[3] but what brought the materials together is relatively clear and for present purposes that is sufficient. The Lord alone opposes Gog. It is only after Gog is dead that he employs helpers (39:9-20). In 39:3 Yahweh, the warrior, knocks the bow and arrows from Gog's hands. When Gog comes, the Lord's *ḥmh* (38:18; Study 10) will rise up—as he has promised with *ʾš ʿbrh* (38:19; Studies 12 and 19). There will be a great shaking (*rʿš*) on the land of Israel (38:19). That is frequently interpreted as a reference to an earthquake, but I suspect the shaking is rather the result of the sirocco.

Study 13

[1] Presumably the vegetation is meant. See Amos 1:2.

[2] A. Schwarzenbach, *Die geographische Terminologie im Hebräischen des Alten Testamentes* (Leiden: Brill, 1954) 68-69.

[3] The parts of chaps. 38-39 of concern here and discussed below are, for example, only sporadically represented in what W. Zimmerli (*Ezechiel* [BKAT 13/1-2; Neukirchen-Vluyn: Neukirchener Verlag, 1955-69] 937) regards as the base unit.

At least that presents a unified picture. The *dgy hym*, birds, wild animals, reptiles and men will also tremble (*rʿš*) before the Lord (38:20). Mountains, cliffs and walls will collapse (38:20). The Lord will judge Gog with *dbr* and *dm* (38:22). The first is a reference to disease, especially typical of the sirocco periods in the spring and fall (Study 2); the second, either to the sword with which the Lord fights,[4] or the fighting among Gog's own troops mentioned in 38:21, or both. He will rain down upon Gog *gšm šwṭp wʾbny ʾlgbyš* and *ʾš wgpryt* (38:22).[5] The first is a reference to a combined rain and hailstorm; the fire and brimstone motif is typical of sirocco contexts (Studies 12 and 18) and the reference will be to that storm. What is reflected here are the alternating storms of the interchange periods, and it is the sirocco that the fish fear.[6] In 39:6 the Lord sends down fire (*ʾš*; Study 12) on Magog. The construction, *šlḥ* + *ʾš* + *b*, is the same as in Amos 1:7 discussed in Study 3.

It is difficult to tell whether the text has in mind the spring or fall interchange period or any season at all. There are, however, a few indications that could be read so as to favor the fall. When Gog is defeated, Israel will live on her land in security with no one to frighten her (39:26). There is no direct mention of the coming of the rains, of course, but it is surely presumed. In addition the closest OT echo of 39:26 is 34:28:

39:26	*bšbtm . . .*	*lbṭḥ*	*wʾyn*	*mḥryd*
34:28	*wyšbw*	*lbṭḥ*	*wʾyn*	*mḥryd*

The context in chap. 34 is: the Lord will bring back his sheep (v 13); he will send the rains in due season (v 26) and the agriculture will flourish (v 27). Chap. 34 is clearly under the influence of the motif of the agricultural new year that has been met often to this point.[7] Chaps. 38-39, I

[4] The *ḥrb* of 38:21a might be the Lord's but the text is usually corrected after the LXX. Otherwise the Lord's sword is not mentioned.

[5] The absence of *w* before *ʾš* signals the disjunction here. The second grouping is rather clearly hendiadys, " sulphur." That suggests the first grouping is rather a combined rain and hailstorm.

[6] W. Zimmerli (*Ezechiel*, 960-61) denies that the three groups of afflictions described in 38:22 can be brought together into any rational picture while the *Zweikampfbild* of 33:3 is understandable. If what has been said here against the background of what has preceded is valid, both pictures are equally clear and belong together.

[7] See also *wškbtm wʾyn mḥryd* in Lev 26:6. The agricultural-new-year character of Leviticus 26 was discussed in Study 10.

think, are capable of a similar reading. That sort of close would serve as a fitting introduction to the vision of the new temple and new Israel in chaps. 40-48. It would be possible to be more sure of this if the time of God's coming, *mymym rbym . . . bʾḥryt hšnym* (the latter phrase only here), in 38:8 could be interpreted "after many days . . . at the end of the years"—with the new agricultural year to begin after Gog's death.

There are two further pieces of meteorological imagery in chaps. 38-39 that could be fitted into the imagery of the fall interchange period. In 38:9 Gog and his army come up like a *šʾh*, like an *ʿnn* to cover the land; in 38:16 they come up like an *ʿnn* against Israel to cover the land. Combined with *ʿnn* here, whatever kind of storm *šʾh* is, it is not a rainstorm (Study 5). The picture is that of an army on the march raising dust, and on that basis *šʾh* here could be the sirocco. This calls to mind the Babylonian army of Jer 4:5-31 which advances like *ʿnnym* and the chariots of which are like the *swph* (Jer 4:13) where the advance of the Babylonian army is presented under the figure of the sirocco. This text was discussed in Part III, 2. Note too that Gog comes from *yrkty ṣpwn* (Ezek 38:6, 15; 39:2); the Babylonians from *ṣpwn* (Jer 4:6).[8]

If this *šʾh* – *ʿnn* imagery is to be connected to the rest of the meteorological imagery of chaps. 38-39, it could be done as follows. Gog threatens Israel like a terrible fall sirocco (38:9, 16); he is attacked by the Lord who comes in a combined sirocco-rainstorm of the fall (38:18-22; 39:6). Israel lives happily thereafter (39:25-29). For her the rains are benevolent. The imagery here is, of course, not blatant as in Isaiah 34-35 (Part V, 1) or Habakkuk 3 (Part V, 3); but it is a type of material that a native would pick up easily and a foreigner so often misses.

***

[8] The semantic range of *šʾh* is broad and its interpretation in particular contexts is not agreed upon, as a glance at the standard dictionaries will show. See also: Schwarzenbach, *Geographische Terminologie*, 142; J. Milik, "Deux documents inédits du désert de Juda," *Bib* 38 (1957) 219-50. The best proof that it can denote "storm" is Prov 1:27/Qere where it is used in parallel with *swph*, which is generally the sirocco (Study 3). In Zeph 1:15 (discussed in Part VI) the day of the sirocco is called: *ywm Yhwh* (Study 20), *ywm ʿbrh* (Study 19), *ywm ḥšk* (Study 16), *ywm ʿnn* (Study 5) and *ywm šʾh wmšwʾh*. In Job 38:27 rain comes to enrich *šʾh*, "wasteland" or the like. However the relation between the denotation "wasteland" and "storm" is explained, the former has connections to the sirocco. Cf. Syr. *šhyʾ*, Aram. *šhwʾ* "desert."

Study 14
The Chariot in Sirocco Contexts

The point of this Study is not to distinguish a motif peculiar to sirocco contexts, but simply to show that the chariot belongs in references to both the sirocco and the rainstorm, though in different ways. In no case is the language clear enough to tempt one to draw the scene, but the rainstorm texts where the take-off point is the *distinct* rain cloud present the clearer picture.

Thus in Ps 68:5 the Lord is described as "the one who mounts the clouds (pl.)," *rkb bʿrbwt*, which echoes Baal's title at Ugarit, *rkb ʿrpt*. In Ps 104:3 (Study 10) the Lord makes *ʿbym* his *rkwb* and travels on the *knpy rwḥ*. Whether we are to think of several clouds (= horses) pulling something like a chariot or whether the Lord is thought of as mounted on one cloud (or several, each conceived of as parts of the chariot) is not particularly clear, but the ultimate picture of distinct rain clouds scudding across the heavens is.

Ps 18:11 (= 2 Sam 18:11, rd *wydʾ*; Part V, 4) presents Yahweh as mounting the Cherub (*wyrkb ʿl krwb*), flying and soaring on the wings of the wind (*wyʿp wydʾ ʿl knpy rwḥ*) in a rainstorm. Here the picture may or may not be some cloud-like creature (= the chariot) being pulled by some winged creature representing the wind. It would also be possible to think of the *krwb* itself having wings. Hab 3:8 (Part V, 3) speaks of the Lord mounting (*rkb*) *swsym* and *mrkbt* (pl. of majesty) as his means of transport in a rainstorm theophany. What adaptations of the usual denotations of these words the Israelite imagination made in this particular context cannot be known. But in any case the take-off point for the imagery and its ultimate reference is: distinct rain clouds flying across the heavens.

The *ʿnn*, typically the dust cloud of the sirocco (Study 5), unlike *ʿb* is not a distinct cloud, and it is hard to envision how it could be conceived of as a chariot. Thus, there is no OT text where the Lord is said to mount (*rkb*) an *ʿnn*. It can be guessed that chariots come into sirocco contexts from another direction. The take-off point, I think, is rather real chariots moving swiftly and raising dust—like the sirocco.

In Jer 4:5-31 (Part III, 2), where the Babylonian army is presented under the figure of the sirocco, chariots come up like *ʿnnym* and like the *swph* (v 13). Once that connection is made it is possible to paint the picture of the Lord coming in the *ʾš* of the sirocco and compare his chariot(s) to the *swph* (*kswph mrkbtyw*). The swiftly moving chariot comes into the picture as the explanation of the swiftly moving dust (Isa 66:15, Study 3). Whether the chariot is thought of as touching the ground or not is not clear. Joel 2:4-5 (Part VI) presents a description of the Lord and his army coming in a sirocco:

> Their appearance is like horses;
> like chariot horses they run (Qal *rwṣ*).
> Like the sound of chariots
> they bounce/jolt (Pi. *rqd*) over the mountain tops.

The Lord or his army may or may not be chariot-borne, though Qal *rwṣ* can be used of horses (Amos 6:12); and Pi. *rqd*, of chariots (Nah 3:2). In either case the roar of the wind perhaps blowing things into one another, and the blowing dust occasion the comparison.

This discussion isolates Isa 19:1 (Part II, 3). In vv 5-7 the presentation is made completely in terms of the sirocco. In the previous discussion (Part II, 3) the possibility was raised that the presentation of the Lord coming against Egypt as *rōkēb ʿl ʿb ql* in v 1 was, perhaps, likewise in terms of the sirocco. Against that is the unique use of *ʿb* (typically a rain cloud) for the dust of the sirocco. The present review has also indicated that the picture of the Lord mounted (*rkb*) on a cloud is rather rainstorm language than sirocco language. Against that background the alternate interpretation of Isa 19:1, 5-7 as a combined rainstorm and sirocco attack is probably to be preferred.

***

Study 15
Agricultural Land Becoming a Desert

The designations for desert encountered in the texts treated are: *šmh*, *šmmh*, *mšmh*, *bhw*, *mdbr*, *ṣmʾwn*, *mlḥh*, *ṣyh*, *ʿrbh*, *ḥorbâ*,[1] *ḥārābâ*.

Study 15

[1] For the distinctions among these words for "desert" see A. Schwarzenbach, *Die geographische Terminologie im Hebräischen des Alten Testamentes* (Leiden: Brill, 1954) 91-112. The noun *ḥorbâ* can mean simply "ruin" (Ezra 9:9). But it can also mean "rocky desert" as in Ezek 29:9-10 discussed below. There the *ʾrṣ mṣrym* becomes *šmmh* and

This vocabulary has been met in: Isa 50:2 (Part II, 4); Jer 51:37, 41, 43 (Part II, 5); Isa 13:9 (Part III, 1); Jer 4:7, 23, 26, 27 (Part III, 2); Jer 49:13, 17 (in Part III); Jer 25:38 (Part III, 3); Isa 15:6 (Part III, p. 55, n. 25); Joel 2:3 (Part VI); Joel 4:19 (Part VI); Ps 107:33, 34 (in Part VI); Jer 50:3, 12, 13, 23 (Study 1 and in Part III, 1); Ezek 29:9, 10 (Study 1); Ps 102:7 (Study 8); Zech 7:14 (Study 4, p. 139, n. 10); Zeph 2:4 (Study 9); Lev 26:31, 33, 34, 35 (Study 10) Jer 22:5, 6 (Study 10); Ezek 5:14 (Study 10); Ezek 30:12 (Study 10); Jer 18:16 (Study 11).

In addition verb forms of the following have been interpreted in the sense "to become/make into a desert." Generally one of the words for desert listed above is found in the same context: *šdd* Qal (Jer 25:36, Part III, 3); Pu. (Isa 15:1, Part III, p. 55, n. 25); *dmm/dmh* Niph. (Jer 25:37, Part III, 3; Isa 15:1, Part III, n. 25); *ḥrb* Qal (Isa 34:10, Part V, 1); Hiph. (Zeph 3:6, Study 8); Niph. (Ezek 30:7, Study 10); *šmm* Niph. (Zeph 3:6, Study 8; Zech 7:14, Study 4, p. 139, n. 10; Ezek 30:7, Study 10); Hiph. (Jer 49:20, in Part III; Lev 26:31, 32, Study 10; Ezek 30:12, 14, Study 10); *ṣdh* Niph. (Zeph 3:6, Study 8).

This motif needs little discussion. If there is involved a storm that has anything to do with nature, the only candidate is the sirocco. It is true that many of these texts do not speak of a specific wind. But the texts were not meant for an audience unfamiliar with the implications of this vocabulary and in need of such explicit signposts at every corner—like the modern interpreter. The point to notice is that seeing the sirocco in these texts generally explains other phenomena and makes immediate connections in the context. Thus in Isa 50:2-3 (Part II, 4) the sirocco immediately explains not only how rivers become *mdbr* and waters dry

---

ḥorbâ. Both denotations are involved when it is a question of imagery that presents cities being destroyed by the sirocco. From the opposite direction see Isa 51:3 (discussed below) where the Lord pities Jerusalem's ruins (*ḥrbtyh*) and turns her *mdbr* and *ʿrbh* into a garden of Eden. Schwarzenbach discusses *ḥorbâ* in *Geographische Terminologie*, 107-9. Since both are to be connected to *ʿrb* = "to be dry/withered/ lifeless/ruined" the denotation "rocky desert" is primary. It comes to denote "ruin" because destroyed cities look like rocky deserts.

It is worth noting that Schwarzenbach catalogues 22 distinct words meaning "desert" in one sense or another for which European and American translators are embarrassed to find distinct equivalents in their own languages. This large desert vocabulary reflects and highlights the completely different meteorological situation of Palestine and the keen awareness of that situation so manifest in the OT. That could hardly be otherwise in an agriculturally based society along the Syro-Palestinian litoral. Indeed, this is very much the point of the present study.

up, but also why the heavens are clothed in darkness and sack. And a contrast is immediately forged to 51:3 where Zion's *mdbr* and *ʿrbh* become a garden of Eden. No one is going to seek a supranatural explanation, an explanation other than rain, in a Palestinian context for 51:3; the same approach toward the phenomena in 50:2-3 seems the right one.

In Ezek 29:8-11 (Study 1) the Lord brings a sword against Egypt and kills people and animals (v 8). Egypt becomes a *šmmh* and a *ḥrbh* (v 9). He is against Egypt and the "Niles" and makes Egypt *ḥrbwt ḥrb šmmh* (v 10)[2] which neither man nor beast will pass through and no man will inhabit for forty years (for lack of water, v 11). The whole concatenation of ideas is readily explainable if the picture is Yahweh, the warrior, coming against Egypt with a sword in a sirocco.

In Ps 107:33-31 (discussed in Part VI) the Lord turns *nhrwt*, *mṣʾy mym* and *ʾrṣ pry* into *mdbr*, *ṣmʾwm* and *mlḥh*. The contrast is in v 35 where he turns *mdbr* and *ʾrṣ ṣyh* into *ʾgm mym* and *mṣʾy mym*. V 35 is certainly a reference to rain; in a Palestinian context where a prevailing east wind prevents the west wind from bringing rain in a period when it can reasonably be expected (see Part I), vv 33-34 will be a reference to the sirocco. The whole argument here is: entia non sunt multiplicanda sine necessitate.

The motif of a city or land being turned into a desert by the sirocco is sometimes expanded by turning the newly formed desert into the home of desert beasts or demons.[3] This refinement was met in: Jer 51:37 (Part II, 5); Isa 13:21-22 (Part III, 1); Jer 50:39 (Study 1 and in Part III, 1); Isa 34:11, 13-15 (Part V, 1); and in a modified form Ps 102:7 (Study 8). It is also present in Zeph 2:14-15 where the animals come to inhabit Nineveh after the Lord stretches out his hand, destroys Assur, and makes Nineveh a *šmmh*, a *ṣyh* like a *mdbr* (v 13), a *šmh* (v 15). This happens after Moab and the Ammonites become like Sodom and Gomorrah (Study 18), a salt pit, an eternal *šmmh* (v 9). See the discussion of vv 2-4 in Study 9.

See further: Ezek 32:15 (Study 17); Zeph 1:13 (Study 20); Jer 7:34 (Study 21); Jer 44:6 (Study 21).[4]

***

[2] The LXX probably reflects an original *lḥrbh wšmmh*. See Study 1, p. 131.

[3] See the discussion of H. Wildberger, *Jesaja* (BKAT 10/1-3; Neukirchen-Vluyn: Neukirchener Verlag, 1965-) 523-24.

[4] Worth noting at the close of this Study is the reference of D. Baly (*The Geography of the Bible* [New York: Harper, 1957] 67) to siroccos as "winds ... which bring with them desert conditions to the whole of Palestine."

Study 16
The Darkening of the Heavens

Since in fact and in the texts the sun and the moon are darkened by the sirocco and the rainstorm (1 Kgs 18:45) and since this motif does not serve to distinguish them, a simple listing of the texts where the motif has been encountered is sufficient.

In a rainstorm: Hab 3:10-11 (Part V, 3); Ps 18:12 (= 2 Sam 22:12, Part V, 4); in a sirocco: Nah 1:8 (Part II, 2); Isa 50:3 (Part II, 4); Isa 13:10 (Part III, 1); Jer 4:23, 28 (Part III, 2); Isa 34:4 (Part V, 1); Joel 2:2, 10; 3:4; 4:15 (Part VI); Zeph 1:15 (in Part VI); Amos 5:18, 20 (in Part VI); Exod 10:21-29 (Study 8); Ezek 30:18 (Study 10). Darkness to one extent or another is, of course, implicit when mention is made of *ʿnn* (Study 5).

***

Study 17
tnyn in Sirocco Contexts

Attention has been drawn in the course of this investigation to a whole series of texts that reflect a myth which presumes hostility between a nature god and the sea and in which the nature god dries up the sea with the sirocco. It has been suggested that this myth has to be different from the Baal-Yamm myth known from Ugarit on the grounds that, though Baal's struggle with Yamm is presented more in terms of a human brawl[1] than a clash between nature forces, his clear connections to the rainstorm eliminate Baal here. Rainstorms do not dry up the sea. This conclusion is certain if de Moor's appealing interpretation of the Baal myth from Ugarit which puts the sirocco on the side of Baal's enemy, Mot,[2] is accepted. What has just been said is not meant to deny there is genuine Baal-Yamm material in the OT (e.g., Psalm 29).

The point of this Study is simply to point out on the basis of OT *tnyn*, generally regarded as reflecting Ugaritic *tnn* (= *tunnanu*/

Study 17

[1] KTU. 1.2:IV:8-30.

[2] J. C. de Moor, *The Seasonal Pattern in the Ugaritic Myth of Baʿlu* (AOAT 16; Neukirchen-Vluyn: Neukirchener Verlag, 1971) 115, 173-76, 180, 187-89, 207, 228, 238-39. The prominence of the material about the Lord drying up the sea with the sirocco in the OT could be explained as a manifestation of anti-Baal bias (cf. 1 Kgs 18), but the question is difficult and cannot be pursued here.

tunnānu[3]), that the minor characters met at Ugarit in the presentation of Baal's and Anat's difficulties with Yamm also can appear in this other myth reflected in the OT. Two relevant texts have already been studied. In Jer 51:34-37, 42-45 (Part II, 5), Bel, the king of Babylon, who had devoured all that was dear to Jerusalem is compared to *tnyn* (v 34). The Lord dries up Babylon's *ym* with the sirocco (v 36) and kills Bel (v 44). In Isa 51:9-10 (discussed in Part IV) the Lord is described as the one who dried up *ym* and pierced *tnyn*. Two other *tnyn* texts are added here.

1. Ezek 32:3-15[4]

In this editorial unit the Lord threatens to destroy Egypt. The destruction will be at the hands of the king of Babylon and his army (vv 11-12),[5] but for the rest the presentation is made in terms of Yahweh, the warrior, who fights with a sword (v 10) and comes in a sirocco. No one, of course, is going to see the sirocco in this text by looking at it in isolation. But against the broad background of similar texts already looked at the indirect references to this storm stand out. If the coming of the king of Babylon (vv 11-12) is assigned to the spring as is normal and v 14 is read as a reference to the flow of the Nile beginning to subside in September, then the whole takes on a logical time sequence.

In vv 3-6 the Lord fishes Pharaoh who is compared to *tnym* (= *tnyn*,[6] v 2) out of *ymym* and *nhrwt* (= the Nile and Nile arms, v 2) with a net and Pharaoh dies on dry ground. This is accompanied by the lights of the heavens being darkened by an *ʿnn* (Study 5) in a sirocco of the spring which is in fact in Egypt the worst sirocco period (vv 7-8, Study 16).[7]

The results of the spring invasion in which the Lord (v 10), the king of Babylon (v 11) and the Babylonian army (v 12) fight with swords are described in vv 9-13. There will not be a man or beast left to disturb the *mym rbym* (= the Nile dark with silt in full summer flood during the invasion, v 13) with their feet or hooves. In v 15 Egypt ends up a *šmmh*

[3] *Ugaritica* V, 241, 1. 8'.

[4] For the relation of vv 1-2 and 16 to vv 3-15 see W. Zimmerli, *Ezechiel* (BKAT 13/1-2; Neukirchen Vluyn: Neukirchener Verlag, 1955-69) 765-67,

[5] *bqhl ʿmym rbym* in v 3 is apparently a secondary explanatory gloss. Ibid., 764.

[6] Ibid., 703.

[7] T. Sivall, "Sirocco in the Levant," *Geografiska Annaler* 39 (1957) 122; G. Dalman, *Arbeit und Sitte in Palästina* I (Gütersloh: Evangelischer Verlag, 1928) 320-21.

(Study 15). That could only happen if more is being described in v 14 than the normal slackening of the Nile starting in September which leaves behind the moist silt that made Egypt so fertile. What v 14 really describes is not the normal slackening of the Nile from September through May but the rapid drying up of the Nile (and the fertile land too) as the result of the Lord's coming, this time in a fall sirocco. The Nile is not completely dried out, but almost so, because that fits Egyptian circumstances.[8] V 14 reads:

> Then I will cause their (= *mym rbym*) waters to sink back;
> their *nhrwt* to flow (i.e., trickle) like oil.

It is true that *ʾašîqaʿ* here is usually rendered "I will make clear" with an eye on *mšqʿ* in 34:18[9] and the "disturbed waters" of v 13; but the closest parallels for 32:14 are Amos 8:8 (Qere) and 9:5 where *šqʿ* (Niph. and Qal) in simile is again used of the Nile and the sense required is "to sink back." The oil simile is meant directly to characterize the slow flow of the Nile at dead low rather than the clarity of the water—which seems more natural. Of course, that involves the clearing of the Nile too. The calm waters of the low Nile are not filled with the silt and whatever else the swiftly flowing high Nile drags along.

2. *Ezek 29:1-16*

This text is again an editorial unit.[10] It bears remarkable similarities to 32:1-16 and the two texts can be used to interpret one another. Vv 8-11 were discussed previously in Studies 1 and 15. The Lord announces he is coming at Pharaoh presented as the great *tnym* (= *tnyn*[11]) crouching in the midst of the Niles (v 3). No helpers are mentioned and throughout the whole the only protagonist is Yahweh. The Lord will fish Pharaoh out of the Nile and dump him in the *mdbr* as food for the wild animals and birds (vv 4-5). The Lord is bringing a sword against Egypt to kill every man and beast (v 8). Egypt will end up a *šmmh* and a *ḥrbh* (v 9,

[8] Contrast Isa 19:5-7 which presumes the Nile is completely dried out by the sirocco (pp. 35-37 above). Isaiah 19 also shows a detailed knowledge of Egypt similar to that presumed for Ezek 32:3-15 (see p. 37, n. 34).

[9] Zimmerli, *Ezechiel*, 765.

[10] Ibid., 705-6.

[11] Ibid., 703.

Study 15). The Lord is coming up against Egypt and the Niles; the land becomes a *ḥrbwt ḥrb šmmh*[12] (Study 15) from the delta to Assuan and even to the frontier of Ethiopia (v 10). That presumes the Nile has been dried up—so completely dried up that no man or beast will pass through her (because Egypt has become an absolute desert, v 11). The whole presentation becomes clear if it is in terms of Yahweh, the warrior, who comes in the sirocco.

***

Study 18
The Sodom and *gpryt* Motifs

The analysis of the Sodom (-Gomorrah-Admah-Zeboiim) and *gpryt* (- *zpt*) motifs will not begin with the Gen 19:24-28 account because Gen 19:24-28 does not afford enough context out of which to interpret with confidence the phenomena involved and because in any case it is not necessary that the same phenomena are involved when the motifs appear elsewhere. If the results are the same or similar, specifically land ending up a barren desert, that could be the justification for the appearance of these motifs in other contexts. Having said that, I put aside for the moment any direct discussion of Gen 19:24-28 and pass on to the other texts which contain the Sodom and *gpryt* motifs. The only aspect of the Gen 19:24-28 story that is allowed to influence this initial discussion is the fact that the Lord rained down upon Sodom and Gomorrah hot *ʾš wgpryt* (19:24).

It is clear that if there is a Palestinian storm that might make any sort of immediate connections to fiery sulphur (*ʾš wgpryt*) it is the sirocco. It is simply impossible to think of a rainstorm here. That presumption is borne out by a survey of the texts apart from Gen 19:24-28 where the Sodom and *gpryt* motifs occur. Neither motif is found in a context that goes near a drop of rain; they are found in storm contexts and consistently resurrect other motifs and vocabulary sufficiently noted already as typical of presentations of the sirocco. Now it is possible that with sulfur falling from the sky and the like we have lost all contact with nature and have entered the realm of the supranatural

[12] This should probably be corrected to *ḥrbh wšmmh* (ibid., 704), but for present purposes either reading will do. See p. 131, n. 11.

that has no basis in experienced meteorology. It is, consequently, possible that we are not dealing here with the sirocco presented in exaggerated dress and that the attempt to analyze these texts on the basis of experienced meteorology is simply a mistake and methodologically flawed from the start. There is only one defense against this possibility—texts where rain is played off against the sirocco. If the rain is to be given a natural interpretation, that argues for interpreting the other storm in a similar way—especially when the texts suggest a temporal setting in the fall interchange period when rain and the sirocco do alternate.

There are no new texts to be added here; the clear or relatively clear ones have been exhausted. The discussion will simply advert to two texts where the wind is directly mentioned and give a complete list of those texts already identified where the sirocco is played off against the rain. The discussion is abbreviated in view of the previous treatment.

In Ps 11:6 (Study 8) the Lord rains down upon the wicked *paḥămê*[1] *ʾš wgpryt*; their portion is a *rwḥ zlʿpwt*. In Jer 23:14 (Study 4) the prophets and the people of Jerusalem are like Sodom and Gomorrah. Consequently there comes the Lord's *sʿrh* and *sʿr* (v 19). This happens in the *šnt pqdtm* (v 12) which could be a reference to the agricultural year beginning in the fall interchange period.

In Isaiah 34 (Part V, 1) the Lord has a *ywm nqm*, a *šnt šlwmym* in defense of Zion (v 8). Edom's wadis become bitumen (*zpt*); her dust, sulfur (*gpryt*); her land, burning bitumen (*zpt bʿrh*, v 9). She ends up a desert (*tḥrb*, v 10). The contrast is in Isaiah 35 where the first fall rains come to Judah's *mdbr*, *ṣyh* and *ʿrbh* and the flowers blossom (v 1), etc.

In Deuteronomy 29 (Study 10) if Israel is disloyal, the Lord threatens to sweep away (*sph*) the wet and the dry (v 18) and the land will end up a burnt out waste (*śrph*), *gpryt* and *mlḥ* like Sodom, Gomorrah, Admah, Zeboiim (v 22). The Lord will exile Israel (v 27). The contrast is in chap. 30. If Israel repents, the Lord will bring Israel back from exile (v 3) and all the agriculture of the *ʾdmh* will prosper (v 9). That presumes abundant rain starting in the fall interchange period.

Isa 30:27-33 (Part V, 2) presents the Lord coming in an alternating

Study 18

[1] MT *pḥym*.

rainstorm and sirocco. V 30 speaks of lightning, shattering rain and hail. In v 33 the Lord's breath (*nšmh*) like a wadi of *gpryt* sets the pyre of Assyria afire. These alternating storms are characteristic of the spring and the fall; the editorial context supplied by the preceding vv 23-26 favors the fall.

In Isaiah 13 (Part III, 1) as a result of the attack of the Lord and human helpers, Babylon ends up like Sodom and Gomorrah (v 19). The presence of the sirocco in the picture is indicated by the darkening of the heavens (v 10), the shaking of heaven and earth (v 13) and the fact that Babylon becomes a home of *ṣyym* (v 21).

Isaiah 13 viewed in isolation gives no indication as to whether one should attempt to locate the sirocco in the spring or the fall—or even whether one should think of any particular period at all. Babylon did in fact open its gates to the Persians on Oct. 12, 539 and Cyrus entered the city seventeen days later.[2] In view of the fact that armies usually marched after the close of the rainy season, one might be tempted to think of the spring as in Hos 13:14-15 (Part II, 1). On the other hand, if the connection to the agricultural-new-year close of Isaiah 1-12, i.e. Isaiah 11-12, suggested in the discussion of Isa 11:15 (Study 1), is valid,[3] a fall setting is the one wanted.

In Ezek 38:22 (Study 13) the Lord rains down upon Gog *gšm šwṭp wʾbny ʾlgbyš* (combined rainstorm and hailstorm) and *ʾš wgpryt* (the sirocco). The evidence is slight, but in the previous discussion a case was made for locating these storms in the fall.

The other texts treated in which these motifs appear in a sirocco context are: Jer 49:18 (in Part III); Jer 50:40 (Study 1) Hos 11:8 (Study 9); Job 18:15 (Study 9); Lam 4:6 (Study 9); Zeph 2:9 (Study 15); see also Deut 32:32 in the light of the discussion of Deut 32:21-25 (Part III, 4).

What really happened at Sodom and Gomorrah is of no particular import in the present investigation. That some biblical writers used the Sodom and Gomorrah tradition (at times with direct connections to the Genesis form and at times not[4]) in describing the sirocco is clear.

[2] R. A. Parker and W. H. Dubberstein, *Babylonian Chronology 626 B.C. - A.D. 75* (Brown University Studies 19; Providence: Brown University, 1956) 14.

[3] See especially Study 1, p. 130.

[4] C. Westermann, *Genesis* II (BKAT 1/1-3+; Neukirchen-Vluyn: Neukirchener Verlag, 1966-) 363-64.

So far as Gen 19:24-28 is concerned, that agriculture based on irrigation was practiced in the Dead Sea area in the Bronze Age is a fact.[5] This was, perhaps, known in biblical times (Gen 13:10). The destruction of the cities and the explanation of the text of Gen 19:24-28 as the result of volcanic activity has been ruled out by Harland (and others) on the grounds that historical Palestine knew no volcano;[6] and the tradition is unlikely to have wandered in from someplace else; it fits the geography of the area too well (see below). Besides, a volcano goes up before anything comes down and the text of Gen 19:24 says the Lord rained down (*hmṭyr*) fire and sulfur. The explanation of Harland (and others) is as follows:

> A great earthquake, perhaps accompanied by lightning, brought utter ruin and a terrible conflagration to Sodom and the other communities in the vicinity. The destructive fires may have been caused by the ignition of gases and of seepages of asphalt emanating from the region, through lightning or the scattering of fires from hearths.[7]

The first sentence is a clearly plausible explanation for what may have happened; the second reads like pseudo-scientific historicism. The introduction of lightning is clearly ad hoc and besides igniting gas likewise goes up before anything comes down.

No matter what the real explanation for the abandonment of the Dead Sea area is, on the basis of the way the Sodom tradition is used elsewhere it is easier to see a storm in the presentation of Genesis 19 too. Whether completely supranatural or one with ties to the sirocco is another question. Bringing a storm into the picture fits the verb *sph* (19:15) and *mṭr* (19:24). The *gpryt* which burns gets into the tradition because it is found in the area[8]—as is the *zpt* of Isa 34:9.[9] The same is true of the salt of Gen 19:26 and Deut 29:22. The latter probably reflects an awareness of the results of ground salt tending to rise to the surface in areas of deficient rainfall unless the ground is washed in other

[5] J. P. Harland, "Sodom and Gomorrah," *The Biblical Archaeologist Reader* I (ed. G. E. Wright and D. N. Freedman; Garden City: Doubleday, 1961) 51-53, 66 (= *BA* 5 [1942] 26-28; 6 [1943] 47).

[6] Ibid., 61.

[7] Ibid., 67.

[8] M. Blanckenhorn, "Entstehung und Geschichte des Todten Meeres," *ZDPV* 19 (1896) 44-46.

[9] Ibid., 48-51.

ways.[10] That the Dead Sea area experienced some terrible siroccos is made clear by the description of the sirocco in that area cited from W. F. Lynch in Part I.[11] I would tend to regard Gen 19:24-28 as at base an etiology of the peculiar geography and of the sparse habitation of the Dead Sea area rooted in geography and the mythology of the god who comes in a sirocco. The material, of course, is used in Genesis 19 for other purposes.

***

Study 19
ʿbrh

In Studies 8-10 were examined three well attested terms which the dictionaries for all practical purposes regard as synonyms denoting "anger" or the like: *zʿm*, *ḥrwn* (*ʾp*), *ḥmh*. The term *ḥrwn* (*ʾp*) is used exclusively of the Lord's anger, hovers around sirocco contexts and never is attested in conjunction with a rainstorm. The same is true of *zʿm* with two exceptions. Once *zʿm* is not the Lord's anger; once it appears in a rainstorm context (Hab 3:12). While *ḥmh* is generally divine anger, it is often enough human anger. It too, however, consistently hovers around sirocco contexts, appearing once in conjunction with a hailstorm (Ezek 13:13). It was suggested that these terms have more than a casual connection with the sirocco and that in some cases a concrete interpretation was perhaps indicated: the roaring (sirocco), the heat of the Lord's nose, the hot (sirocco). The best case can be made for *ḥrwn* (*ʾp*) which sounds like terminology with a story behind it. This would afford a ready explanation for its tightly circumscribed usage pattern.

The usage pattern for *ʿbrh*, which likewise denotes "anger," is very similar—especially to that of *ḥmh*. While generally used of divine anger, it can be used of human anger. It hovers around sirocco contexts and never goes near a rainstorm. Thus, it too can be used to identify that storm. The dictionaries sometimes distinguish between *ʿbrh* I = arrogance (Heb. *ʿbr* = Arab. *ʿbr* = to cross over) and *ʿbrh* II = anger

[10] D. Baly, *The Geography of the Bible* (New York: Harper, 1957) 84.

[11] W. F. Lynch, *Narrative of the United States' Expedition to the River Jordan and the Dead Sea* (Philadelphia: Lea and Blanchard, 1849) 312-16.

(Heb. *ʿbr* = Arab. *ǵbr* = to be angry), but whether that is necessary or not is unclear.[1] The second group is the one of concern here.

Verbal forms of *ʿbr* in Qal can be used with the wind as subject. Nah 1:8 speaks of the *šṭp ʿbr* (storm bursting/rushing forth; a sirocco, Part II, 2). Job 37:21 speaks of a *rwḥ ʿbrh* which clears the heavens. In Prov 10:25 when the storm passes (*kʿbwr swph*) the wicked man is no more. In view of *swph* (Study 3) and the next example the storm is probably the sirocco. In Ps 103:15-16 man's days are described as being like those of grass; man blooms like a flower of the field. When the *rwḥ* sweeps over (*ʿbr*) him, he is no more. The *rwḥ* here is clearly the sirocco (Study 7). In addition Isa 29:5 speaks of chaff flying (*ʿbr*) in a sirocco (Part V, 5); Jer 13:24, of stubble flying (*ʿbr*) before the *rwḥ mdbr* (in Part IV). In Gen 8:1 God causes a *rwḥ* to sweep over (Hiph. *ʿbr*) the waters.

Like its synonyms already discussed, *ʿbrh* in sirocco contexts sometimes totters on the brink of suggesting a concrete interpretation, "outburst/eruption/surge (of the wind)." That would connect to the verbal occurrences of *ʿbr* with the wind as subject, would favor relating *ʿbrh* = "anger" to Heb. *ʿbr* = Arab. *ʿbr*, and would parallel the semantic development of *ḥrwn* (*ʾp*) from "the heat of the Lord's nose" to "anger."

As instances of *ʿbrh* where the concrete interpretation is suggested by the context can be cited the following. In Habakkuk 3 (Part V, 3) the prophet sees the Lord coming in a sirocco from Teman (v 3) and threatening the Mediterranean. He asks whether the Lord's anger/nose (*ʾp*) burns (*ḥrh*, Study 8), whether his wrath/outburst (*ʿbrh*) burns against the rivers and sea (v 8). The storm switches directions and the Lord comes in a tremendous rainstorm to annihilate the enemies of his people (v 13).

In Ps 78:49 (Study 8) the Lord sends forth the heat of his nose (*ḥrwn ʾp*), outburst (*ʿbrh*), roar (*zʿm*) and trouble (*rʿh*), an embassy of messengers of woe, to level a path for his anger (*ʾp*). Note how the concrete interpretation immediately explains the leveling of the path. In Isa 13:9 (Part III, 1) the day of Yahweh (Study 20) comes—*ʿbrh* and *ḥrwn ʾp* too—to make Babylon a *šmh* (Study 15). The concrete effect suggests a concrete interpretation of both *ʿbrh* and *ḥrwn ʾp*. In Ezek 21:36 the

Study 19

[1] GB, s.v., has the clearest statement of the problem; contrast BDB, s.v.

Lord pours forth (*špk*) his *zʿm* (Study 8) and blows (*pwḥ*) with his *ʾš ʿbrh* against the Ammonites. The phraseology here, *wšpkty ʿlyk zʿmy* and *bʾš ʿbrty ʾpyḥ ʿlyk*, seems to imply a story every bit as much as *ḥrwn ʾp*.

Also worth noting here is the phrase *ʾš ʿbrh*, attested four times, only in Ezekiel (21:36, Study 8; 22:31, Study 8; 38:19, Study 13; 22:21) and always the Lord's anger. The sirocco context of the first three has already been discussed. The fourth, Ezek 22:21, will be similar. Israel will be gathered into Jerusalem in *ḥmh* (Study 10; see v 22) and smelted (*ntk*) just as[2] metal is gathered into the furnace (vv 19-20). The Lord will blow (*npḥ*) upon Israel with the fire of his wrath (*bʾš ʿbrty*) and he will be smelted (*ntk*) in the midst of the city (v 21).[3]

At the same time it is clear that the old problem persists. Even if one grants for the sake of the argument that *ʿbrh* like *zʿm*, *ḥrwn* (*ʾp*) and *ḥmh* was originally language with connections to a myth about some god capable of breathing forth the sirocco and that this is the explanation why this language is so consistently met in sirocco contexts, it is not clear what overtones the language had at the stage in which it is met in its various OT attestations. Some texts more or less strongly suggest the concrete interpretation, but it is possible to survive everywhere with "anger" or the like (metonymy of cause for effect). The one thing that can be insisted on is that *ʿbrh* with a remarkable consistency avoids rain contexts and turns up in clear sirocco contexts. In a text where a storm is involved it helps to identify that storm.

Apart from Ezek 22:21 discussed above, no new texts are added here. The clear or relatively clear ones have already been treated: Isa 13:9, 13 (Part III, 1); Lam 2:2 (Part III, 5); Hab 3:8 (Part V, 3); Zeph 1:15, 18 (in Part VI); Ezek 7:19 (Study 2); Ps 78:49 (Study 8); Ezek 22:31 (Study 8); Ezek 21:36 (Study 8); Ps 85:4 (Study 9); Ezek 38:19 (Study 13); see Hos 13:11 in the light of 13:14-15 (Part II, 1).

***

[2] Rd *kqbṣt*.

[3] See the discussion of Ezek 22:23-31, the continuation of vv 17-22, in Study 8.

Study 20
The *ywm Yhwh*

The purpose of this Study cannot be and is not to present a complete treatment of this much discussed phrase. That would involve a treatment of many matters other than weather which is the concern here. In a sense this discussion of the *ywm Yhwh* is out of place in the present study insofar as a *ywm* is a unit of time and in itself indifferent to weather. The excuse for the discussion is simply that a *ywm* like the weather is a part of nature and that frequently the *ywm Yhwh*, among other things, is a day of storm, specifically the sirocco. The rainstorm can appear in the same context with it in the fall interchange period, but by way of contrast. Whenever a text makes this contrast, the *ywm Yhwh* is the day of the sirocco in that period.

The point of view just expressed, though arrived at from a completely different direction, comes close to the view of those who connect the *ywm Yhwh* motif to the autumn festival. It was for this reason that the discussion has been delayed to almost the end—to make sure that the other pieces of vocabulary and motifs identified as typical of sirocco texts searched out the *ywm Yhwh* texts and not vice versa. That that has in fact happened will become immediately clear below. Most of the relevant texts have already been discussed. All the texts will be reviewed; the analysis will be summary in the case of those already given fuller treatment. To guarantee that the argument is not prejudiced from the start, I work with the list of texts isolated by Černý[1] who rejects the autumn-festival connection.

Černý's analysis of the motif begins with a list of 29 instances of the pertinent vocabulary: *ywm Yhwh; ywm . . . Yhwh; ywm lYhwh; ywm . . . lYhwh;* and *ywm . . . ʾlhym* (Isa 61:2). From this original list he eliminates Isa 61:2 and 58:5.[2] The remainder of Černý's list is catalogued below. The number of texts dealt with is fewer than 27 because of repetitions in some texts.

In the first four instances the *ywm Yhwh* is clearly the day of the sirocco which is contrasted with the coming of the first rains in the fall interchange period.

Study 20

[1] L. Černý, *The Day of Yahweh and Some Relevant Problems* (Prague: Universitas Carolina, 1948) 17-18.

[2] Ibid., 20.

1. Joel 1:15; 2:1, 11 (Part VI)

The previous discussion made clear that the three references are to a sirocco period in the fall which is contrasted with the beneficent rain.

2. Joel 3:4; 4:14 (Part VI)

It is readily admitted that it would be impossible to interpret the second half of Joel with any degree of certainty without the first. But with chaps. 1-2 as the model, both references to the *ywm Yhwh* are to the sirocco in the fall interchange period. The nations, in particular Egypt and Edom, receive the sirocco; Judah, the rain.

3. Isa 34:8 (Part V, 1)

In Isaiah 35 the first rains fall in Judah and the eastern desert to ease the return of the exiles. In Isaiah 34 Yahweh, the warrior, comes in a sirocco to destroy the nations (v 2) and especially Edom (vv 5-17) which ends up a desert (*tḥrb*, v 10). This happens on the *ywm nqm lYhwh* which is (the opening of) a *šnt šlwmym* for Zion (v 8).

4. Mal 3:23

The reference to the *ywm Yhwh hgdwl whnwr'*, occurs in what is generally regarded as a final addition to the book, vv 22 and 23-24.[3] It simply says: before the *ywm Yhwh* comes the Lord will send Elijah the prophet. The text by itself gives practically no information about the day, save that it is great and terrible, a day of doom (*ḥrm*, v 24). The present discussion, however, has already given the hint why vv 23-24 were added to the book and suggests once again that the *ywm Yhwh* was a day of sirocco in the fall interchange period.

The mention of Elijah coming before the *ywm Yhwh* (3:23) is a reference to the messenger of 3:1, the *ywm* of the Lord's coming in 3:2 and the *ywm* that comes in 3:19. Thus, the context for the understanding of the *ywm Yhwh* of 3:23 is supplied by the closing units of the book: 2:17-3:5; 3:6-12; 3:13-21.

2:17-3:5 speak of the coming of the Lord to remove varieties of evildoers after he has sent his messenger. No one will be able to endure[4]

[3] E.g., R. C. Dentan, "Malachi," *IB* (1956) 1143-44.

[4] Pilp. *kwl*. The same verb in Hiph. is used in exactly the same way and with language reminiscent of Mal 3:23 in Joel 2:11.

that day; for the Lord will come like a refiner's *ʾš* (3:2; Study 12), like a fuller's lye.

Mal 3:6-12 offer an alternative. If Israel returns to the Lord (v 7) and presents the whole tithe (v 10; and does in general what is expected), the Lord will open up the windows of the heavens and pour down a blessing (rain) in abundance (through the winter, v 10). The locust (*ʾōkēl*) will not come (in the spring) to destroy the *pry ʾdmh* and the vine will not be barren (in the late summer, v 11). The sequence reflects the agricultural year starting in the fall interchange period. That agricultural success beyond the ordinary is meant is indicated by v 12: all the nations will call Israel blessed and she will be an *ʾrṣ ḥpṣ*.

Mal 3:13-21 speak of the Lord judging justly and making a clear distinction between the just and the wicked. Those who fear the Lord are written down in a record book (v 16) and when the Lord takes action they will be protected (v 17). The day is coming, blazing (*bʿr*, Study 21) like an oven. Sinners are *qš*, and the day that is coming will set them afire (*lhṭ*, v 19; Study 22). After sinners are destroyed the sun of justice will shine for those who fear the Lord (v 20).

V 20 goes on to describe the just as going out (from the stalls) and gamboling (*pwš*) like calves of the stall (*kʿgly mrbq*). The image here I would take as a reference to stall-fed calves being let out to graze on the first grass of winter after the coming of the rains (v 10). Jer 50:11[5] with the same verb presents a similar picture from the opposite direction. The Babylonians rejoice and exult; they gambol (*pwš*) like calves on the green.[6] But Babylon will become a *mdbr*, *ṣyh*, *ʿrbh*, *šmmh* (Study 15) never more to be inhabited (vv 12-13). Both situations are reflected in Joel 1:18 and 2:22 (Part VI). In 1:18 the *bhmh* at the end of the summer groan because there isn't any pasture; in 2:22 the *bhmwt śdy* are told not to fear because (the fall rains will come and) the pastures will be green.

I suspect that the rain of Mal 3:10 and the sirocco of 3:2, 19 are thought of as coming in the same fall interchange period; and that the whole of 2:17-3:21 is another instance of an agricultural-new-year close for a prophetic book like Habakkuk 3 (Part V, 3) and Joel 3-4 (Part VI).[7]

[5] The whole of Jeremiah 50(-51) is filled with the language and motifs being treated in these Studies.

[6] Rd *kʿgly bdšʾ* with LXX and Vg.

[7] The other instances of the agricultural-new-year close of prophetic books or sec-

In any case the way rain is contrasted with 3:2 and 19 isolates the latter as the sirocco and makes the *ywm Yhwh* of 3:23 the day of the sirocco in the fall interchange period.

5. Isa 13:6, 9 (Part III, 1)

Isaiah 13 contains for all practical purposes as complete a catalogue of the vocabulary and motifs identified as characteristic of the sirocco as any text in the OT. The *ywm Yhwh* is near; it comes like *šd* from *šdy* (v 6). The *ywm Yhwh* is coming—cruel—*ʿbrh* (Study 19) and *ḥrwn ʾp* (Study 9) too (v 9). If the connection to Isaiah 11-12 is valid, the text presumes the sirocco is in the fall interchange period (Study 1, p. 130).

In the following three texts the *ywm Yhwh* is clearly the day of the sirocco, but meteorological grounds are lacking for thinking in terms of a fall or spring sirocco.

6. Zeph 1:7, 8, 14, 14, 18; 2:2, 3

The *ywm Yhwh* sections of Zeph are 1:2-18 and 2:1-3. The first announces the destruction of Judah; the second, the possibility of safety for those who seek the Lord (2:3). The destruction of Judah is attributed to an army—most clearly 1:13, 7 (cf. Isa 13:3). But the presentation is in large part made in terms of Yahweh-did-it and the effects clearly surpass the possibilities of an ordinary army. No army ever removed[8] the birds of the air or the fish of the sea 1:3, Study 13). The imagery here is in the familiar terms of Yahweh, the warrior, coming in a sirocco. The sirocco language of 1:2-2:3 has been discussed piecemeal at several points in the preceding discussion (in Part VI; Studies 8, 9 and 13, p. 177, n. 8). It is brought together here in summary fashion.

The *ywm Yhwh* is near (1:7). The Lord will stretch forth his hand against Judah and the inhabitants of Jerusalem (1:4). The Lord has organized his *zbḥ* and consecrated his guests (= army, 1:7). The houses

---

tions of prophetic books singled out for discussion are: Isaiah 34-35 (Part V, 1); Isaiah 11-12 (Study 1, 1; see Study 18 and Study 20, 5); Isa 66:11-16 (Study 3, 5); Amos 9:4-15 (in Part VI, p. 127, n. 47; see Study 3, 2 and Study 10, p. 167, n. 14); Hos 13:12-14:9 (Part II, pp. 26-27, n. 7); Ezekiel 38-39 (Study 13, 2). It would seem that we are dealing here with a convention in the editing of prophetic materials.

[8] Rd *ʾōsēp*.

of Judah will become *šmmh* (1:13, Study 15). This *ywm Yhwh* is a *ywm ʿbrh* (Study 19), a *ywm ḥšk wʾplh* (Study 16), a *ywm ʿnn* (15, Study 5). On the *ywm ʿbrt Yhwh* (Study 19) all the land/earth will be consumed by fire (1:18; *ʾš* + *ʾkl*, Study 12). The *ḥrwn ʾp Yhwh* (Study 9) is coming (2:2).[9]

The way in which this text picks up the language and motifs of other sirocco texts betrays its connection to them. In addition, the text clearly reflects in a special way the phraseology of other *ywm Yhwh* texts and particularly Joel 1-2:

Zeph 1:14	*qrwb*	*ywm*	*Yhwh*	*hgdwl*
Joel 2:11		*gdwl*	*ywm*	*Yhwh*
Joel 1:15	*qrwb*	*ywm*	*Yhwh*	

*

Zeph 1:15	*ywm*	*ḥšk*	*wʾplh*	*ywm*	*ʿnn*	*wʿrpl*
Joel 2:2	*ywm*	*ḥšk*	*wʾplh*	*ywm*	*ʿnn*	*wʿrpl.*

There are sufficient differences between the texts to indicate that this is not a case of dependency of one text upon another. Rather, both are reflecting the traditional language of the mythological day of Yahweh, the warrior, who comes in the sirocco.

7. Ezek 7:19 (Study 2)

The phrase here is *ywm ʿbrt Yhwh* (Study 19).

8. Ezek 30:3 (Study 10)

The *ywm lYhwh* is a *ywm ʿnn* (Study 5).

9. Lam 2:22 (Part III, 5)

In the previous discussion it was pointed out that, despite the poet's knowledge of the progression of events leading up to the fall of

[9] The way in which *mṣ ʿbr* (Study 11) fits sirocco contexts makes the *BHK/BHS* reading in 2:2a probable: *bṭrm lʾ tiddāḥēqû kmṣ ʿōbēr*. See the LXX and the discussion of H. Irsigler, *Gottesgericht und Jahwetag* (St. Ottilien: Eos, 1977) 62-64. Admittedly *dḥq* in this context is unparalleled. The verbs that normally appear in this contest (see Study 11) do not approximate the consonants of MT.

Jerusalem in August 587, these events are presented in terms of Yahweh-did-it, in terms of the myth of Yahweh, the warrior, who comes in the sirocco. All the Babylonians are allowed to do is shout in the temple after the victory (v 7). The myth-based presentation endeavors to interpret the events of 587 religiously; the Babylonians fall into the background because they are the mere instruments of the Lord's purpose.

About this *ywm Yhwh* text there are two peculiarities. This is the one *ywm Yhwh* text identified by Černý, the focus of which is the past.[10] This fact was noted in the previous discussion as important because it shows this package of mythological materials was understood as imagery in Israelite circles. In the second place this *ywm Yhwh* text has lost contact with a time period in which the sirocco is to be reckoned with. The *ywm ʾp Yhwh* of v 22 is probably to be understood as the day of the fall of Jerusalem in August 587. This is unlike the situation in the first four texts discussed which presume a sirocco in the fall interchange period. Lamentations 2 makes it clear that this imagery is not tied to that period.

At the same time from another direction there is another possible reference to be noted in v 22 which may make the connection to the fall interchange period or, better, Sukkoth which immediately preceded it:

> You invited (*qrʾ*) as on a/the *ywm mwʿd*
> terrors against me from all sides.
> There was not on the *ywm ʾp Yhwh*
> fugitive or survivor.

The verb *qrʾ* can be used in the sense "to invite to a sacrificial banquet, feast" and the usage is illustrated by Zeph 1:7 discussed above. Granted that fact and the clear fall setting presumed in the first four texts discussed above, it would be easy to understand *kywm mwʿd* as a specific reference to Sukkoth and to connect this mythological presentation of Yahweh, the warrior, coming in the sirocco specifically to that feast. This immediately connects to the Babylonians cheering in the temple *kywm mwʿd* (v 7) after having entered the city.

The presence of this *ywm Yhwh* imagery here and the reference to the feast of Sukkoth (v 22) could easily be explained if Lamentations 2 were regarded as written for a liturgical mourning ceremony among

[10] Černý, *The Day of Yahweh*, 20.

the ruins of Jerusalem at the time of the autumn festival. The situation would be similar to the mourning ceremony to which the "eighty men with beards shaved off, clothes in rags, and with gashes on their bodies came from Shechem, Shilo and Samaria, bringing food offerings and incense for the house of the Lord" (Jer 41:5) in the seventh month of 587 (41:1). Lam 2:6 says that feast (*mwᶜd*) and sabbath have been forgotten on Zion. Lam 2:10 speaks of the old men of Zion clothed in sack, sitting on the ground and strewing dust on their heads. The bitter irony involved would be clear. No real Sukkoth can be celebrated on Zion this year because the Lord conducted a Sukkoth feast (*mwᶜd*) on Zion in August 587 with his invited pilgrims, the Babylonians (Lam 2:22). See the discussion of Lamentations 1 in Study 9.

What has just been said is, of course, speculative and outside the purview of this study. Attention is drawn to the possible connection between this imagery and Sukkoth in Lamentations 2 because the body of materials brought together in this Study suggest it and because on other grounds the connection of the *ywm Yhwh* to Sukkoth is made more generally.[11]

The final eight *ywm Yhwh* texts on Černý's list present little or no meteorological evidence for or against viewing it as the day of the sirocco. In a few cases there are elements that could be understood as pointing in that direction.

10. Amos 5:18, 18, 20

The *ywm Yhwh* is a day of darkness and not light (Study 16).

11. Ezek 13:5

The prophets did not build a proper stone wall for Israel to withstand the *mlḥmh bywm Yhwh*. Note the meteorology of the fall interchange period in the next unit, 13:10-16 (Study 4).

12. Isa 2:12

One can try to hide in the rocks or in the ground (v 10) from the terror of the Lord on the *ywm lYhwh ṣbʾwt* (v 12). The day is also a threat to mountains (v 14), Tarshish ships (v 16), the cedars of Lebanon and the oaks of Bashan (v 13). It is easy here to think of a storm-and one that

[11] J. Gray, *The Biblical Doctrine of the Reign of God* (Edinburgh: Clark, 1979) 217-20.

endangers the vegetation would most readily be the sirocco (Study 7). See Ps 48:8.[12]

The other three texts in Černý's list are: Jer 46:10; Obad 15; Zech 14:1. The whole tenor of the discussion to this point, I think, makes clear that it is possible to have a *ywm Yhwh* without direct mention of the phrase. For example, there is just as much reason to consider the *ywm ḥrwn ʾpw* and the *ywm qrʾt* in Lam 1:12 and 21 (Study 9) a *ywm Yhwh* as the *ywm ʾp Yhwh* of Lam 2:22.[13] It is worth noting that in Jer 25:33 the LXX reflects *bywm Yhwh* rather than MT *bywm hhwʾ*. The sirocco imagery of Jer 25:30-38 was discussed in Part III, 3.

***

[12] K. J. Cathcart has devoted a study to Isa 2:6-22, "Kingship and the 'Day of Yahweh' In Isaiah 2:6-22," *Hermathena* 125 (1978) 48-59. Because of its publication in *Hermathena* it is noted here. He, like others, understands the poem as a speech delivered by Isaiah on the occasion of "the autumnal New Year festival which celebrated the kingship of Yahweh" (p. 53). The direction of the remarks to this point in the Study makes it clear that I can only be sympathetic with that assessment, though the approach to the text has been completely different—as is my analysis of the implied meteorology.

[13] As part of a discussion of Isa 42:15, S. Mowinckel criticizes H. Gressmann for precisely the naturalistic view of the *ywm Yhwh* just outlined (*Psalmenstudien II. Das Thronbesteigungsfest Jahwäs und der Ursprung der Eschatologie* [reprint of 1982 ed.; Amsterdam: Schippers, 1961) 252, n. 1.). Actually Gressmann's view is broader (*Der Ursprung der israelitisch-jüdischen Eschatologie* [Göttingen: Vandenhoeck und Ruprecht, 1905] 141-58), but in context Mowinckel cites fairly. He writes:

"Wenn hier, wie Gressmann, Ursprung S. 27, will, das Ausdörren der Berge und Hügel usw. als durch einen Glutwind verursacht gedacht wird, so ist es nicht eine Theorie von dem Tag Jahwä's als einem Tag des Schirokkos, der im Hintergrunde liegt, sondern der Zug geht zuletzt auf den Wirbelwind (*Imḫullu*) zurück, den Marduk in den Rachen der Tiamat hineinjagt. . . . Der Zug ist somit aus babylonischen, nicht aus kanaʿanitischen Naturverhältnissen zu erklären."

The defense against Mowinckel is the group of four texts with which this Study opened. Everyone of them presumes the agriculture depends exclusively on rain which is not the situation in heartland Mesopotamia. In addition, all four texts presume a setting in the fall when rainstorms and siroccos alternate on the Syro-Palestinian litoral. The whole situation is so genuinely Palestinian and un-Mesopotamian, there is no reason whatsoever to view this material as imported from there. In fairness to Mowinckel, in 1922 he did not know Ugarit or the western counterpart to Marduk vs Tiamat. T. Jacobsen has tentatively reversed the direction of the borrowing and views Marduk vs Tiamat as Baal vs Yamm in Mesopotamian dress (*The Treasures of Darkness* [New Haven: Yale, 1976] 168). Admittedly the suggestion is quite speculative, but there is support from a Mari text (which was unavailable to Jacobsen); see M. S. Smith, *The Ugaritic Baal Cycle: Volume I. Introduction with Text, Translation and Commentary of KTU 1.1-1.2* (VTSup 55; Leiden: Brill, 1994) 108-12.

Study 21
bʿr

It is from the start clear that a storm which can be described as burning (*bʿr*), in Palestine is the sirocco. It is true most of the sirocco texts in which *bʿr* appears presume that it starts real fires. The sirocco doesn't do that, though it does set the circumstances favorable to brush fires or the like. That even in this situation we are dealing with a sirocco in a theophany context being turned into a super-sirocco is indicated once again by the way the sirocco in these texts is played off against the rainstorm. Thus, for example, in Isa 34:9 (Part V, 1) Edom ends up *zpt bʿrh*, which contrasts with the flowers blossoming in 35:1 after the first rains of the fall interchange period. In Isa 30:27 (Part V, 2) the Lord's nose burns (*bʿr*), his lips are full of *zʿm* (Study 8), his tongue is like an *ʾš ʾklt* (Study 12). In v 33 the *nšmt Yhwh,* like a wadi of *gpryt* (Study 18), sets afire (*bʿr*) the pyre of Assyria. This contrasts with the lightning, shattering rain and hailstorm of v 30. The imagery of this text probably presumes a fall setting too. These three instances of *bʿr* also serve to illustrate the typical ways in which the verb is used in the other texts.

The texts in which *bʿr* has been identified in a sirocco context are the following: Lam 2:3 (Part III, 5); Isa 30:27, 33 (Part V, 2); Ps 18:9 (= 2 Sam 22:9; Part V, 4, p. 98, n. 60); Ps 83:15 (Study 3); Hos 11:9 (corrected text, Study 9); Ps 2:12 (Study 9); Isa 42:25 (Study 10); Jer 4:4 (Study 10); Jer 21:12 (Study 10); Mal 3:19 (Study 20).

To these can be added:

1. Jer 7:20

My *ḥmh* (Study 10) will be poured out on this place—man, beast, the trees of the field and the fruit of the agricultural land. It will burn (*bʿr*) and not be quenched. The text presumes harm to trees and crops. That is most readily explained as due to the Lord's sirocco. The land will become *ʿrbh* (v 34, Study 15).

2. Jer 44:6

This text like Lamentations 2 describes the destruction of Judah and Jerusalem, already an accomplished fact, in terms of the Lord's sirocco. The role of the Babylonians is ignored. The Lord's *ḥmh* (Study 10) was poured forth. It blazed (*bʿr*) through the cities of Judah and Jerusalem. They became *ʿrbh* and *šmmh* (Study 15).

A review of all the instances of *bʿr*, apart from two slight problems (2 Sam 22:13; Job 1:16), uncovers no connection with lightning in a rainstorm. The *bʿrw* in the rainstorm context of 2 Sam 22:13 is probably a mistake for *ʿbrw* of the Ps 18:13 version.[1] In any case, both the Sam and Ps versions of the text at this point are too problematic to base any conclusions on them. In Job 1:16 what the *ʾš ʾlhym* which falls from heaven and consumes (*bʿr*) the flocks and the shepherds is, is not clear. See the discussion in Study 12 and Part V, 6.

***

Study 22
lhṭ

This verb is so similar to *bʿr* (Study 21) with which it is lined up in context four times (Isa 42:25; Mal 3:19; Ps 83:15; Ps 106:18) that no preliminary discussion is needed. It occurs 11 times in all. The problematic Ps 57:5 stands apart and *HALAT*, s.v., sets this occurrence under a *lhṭ*-2.[1] Eight of the remaining instances have already been identified in sirocco contexts: Deut 32:22 (Part III, 4); Ps 97:3 (Part V, 6); Joel 1:19 (Part VI); Joel 2:3 (Part VI); Ps 83:15 (Study 3); Isa 42:25 (Study 10); Ps 104:4 (in Study 10); Mal 3:19 (Study 20). There are no new examples to add. This fact, here again as progressively throughout these Studies, indicates the tight package of materials being dealt with—a package of materials completely foreign to rainstorm contexts.

The other two instances of *lhṭ* are Ps 106:18 and Job 41:13. In Ps 106:18 the reference is to the events of Numbers 16 and there is nothing to suggest that the text ought to be analyzed meteorologically. Job 41:13 speaks of Behemoth's breath as setting afire (*lhṭ*) coals and of flame (*lhb*) issuing from his mouth. The text makes the wind-fire connection evidenced in all the sirocco texts in which *lhṭ* appears.

***

Study 21

[1] G. Schmuttermayr, *Psalm 18 und 2 Samuel 22* (SANT 25; München: Kösel, 1971) 73-76.

Study 22

[1] Contrast F. Zorell, *Lexicon hebraicum et aramaicum Veteris Testamenti* (Roma: Pontificium Institutum Biblicum, 1963) s.v.

Conclusion

This investigation started with the question whether it is proper to use the meteorology of Palestine as described by modern geographers in the attempt to analyze descriptions of storms, in significant part theophanies, in OT texts. In general the geographers presume the process is legitimate and they do so. The exegetes are more hesitant in treating OT texts in this fashion. When it is a question of the rainstorm, there are fewer differences between the approach of the geographers and the exegetes. Both immediately recognize, for example, that the theophany of Psalm 29 is modeled on the rainstorm and interpret the psalm on that basis. It is with the other common storm in Palestine, the sirocco, that the serious division of opinions begins. The geographers are consistent and tend to identify this storm in OT texts, though it is clear that the identifications have never been based on a systematic analysis of the language in which these literary presentations of the sirocco are made. The exegetes will, of course, recognize that a text like Isa 40:7,

> The grass withers (*ybš*), the flower wilts (*nbl*),
> when the wind (*rwḥ*) of the Lord blows upon it,

is a reference to the sirocco. But when it comes to a text like Nah 1:2-8, the geographers and the exegetes go their own ways. G. Dalman,[1] as

[1] G. Dalman, *Arbeit und Sitte in Palästina* I (Gütersloh: Evangelischer Verlag, 1928) 108.

was indicated in the Introduction, consistently analyzes the details of this theophany description on the basis of the sirocco as experienced in modern Palestine. In the Introduction and in the discussion of Part II, 2 there was contrasted the approach to this text of J. Jeremias[2] and W. Rudolph.[3] Though there are differences between their analyses, neither consistently uses nature as experienced in Palestine for the interpretation of the text. Both presume we are dealing here with the supranatural, the irrational, the product of prophetic or poetic imagination or the like and that the text is not patient of consistent meteorological analysis. Nature may appear in the text, but the presentation is not made under the control of nature.

The position of the exegetes is at first glance reasonable, easily justified and understandable. There are exaggerations, for example, in Nah 1:2-8 that are clearly in a sense unnatural. No sirocco experienced in Palestine ever dried up the sea (Nah 1:4), shook mountains (v 5) or knocked over cliffs (v 6). And Joel 2:1-11, which in Part VI was identified as modeled on the sirocco, contains even more fantastic elements.

The question at issue between Jeremias and Rudolph on the one hand and Dalman on the other is essentially: do these exaggerations in the presentation of the sirocco mean that the texts are no longer in a significant way under the control of experienced meteorology and that consequently it is a mistake to analyze them on the basis of meteorology as described by the geographers? Or, are the exaggerations to be regarded as consistent with the nature of that storm and to be explained by the fact that a text like Nah 1:2-8 is not a simple meteorological statement like Isa 40:7, but is rather a statement about nature presented as theophany in which sirocco becomes super-sirocco; a statement about nature mediated through the exaggerated language of a nature myth only in part represented in the OT about some god who once dried up the sea (Nah 1:4) with the sirocco?

It is worth noting in this regard that there are fantastic elements in OT descriptions of rainstorm theophanies too. No rainstorm ever made the Lebanon range dance like a calf (Ps 29:6), though exegetes in general are content enough simply to describe the theophany here as a

[2] J. Jeremias, *Theophanie* (WMANT 10; Neukirchen-Vluyn: Neukirchener Verlag, 1965) 32-33.

[3] W. Rudolph, *Micha-Nahum-Habakuk-Zephanja* (KAT 13/3; Gütersloh: Gerd Mohn, 1975) 155-56.

rainstorm theophany. It is true that J. Jeremias,[4] consistent with his approach to theophany texts in general, attributes the dancing of Lebanon to an earthquake. But that is hardly necessary. Houses shake in the wind of a severe rainstorm; houses struck by lightning shake. It is easy to imagine how the poet of Psalm 29 could present mountains doing the same thing in a rainstorm that is presented as theophany. That is surely what is intended in a psalm that otherwise betrays the characteristics of a tremendous thunderstorm, has that storm travel west to east over the Mediterranean and finally reach the desert beyond the Anti-Lebanon, distinguishes the evergreens from the deciduous trees and presents the storm as stripping the deciduous trees of their leaves which would locate the storm in the fall interchange period.[5] The whole picture is too true to nature to require anything other than Palestinian meteorology to analyze it.

The present attempt to resolve these questions began with the supposition that there can be no secure answers to the questions just outlined without a rigid analysis of the language in which meteorology is presented in the OT. It started with the hypothesis that the Dalman approach to a text like Nah 1:2-8 ought to be the right one. The OT was written by members of an agriculturally based society in which prosperity or disaster was to no small degree determined by the weather. As such, it was written by people like the Palestinian farmers whom Dalman is so fond of quoting. They show genuine concern for meteorology, know the weather of Palestine well and reflect it accurately. This study set out to test that hypothesis on the basis of the presentation of the sirocco in the OT. That storm was chosen because of the more radical divergence of views between the geographers and the exegetes in interpreting such texts.

It became immediately evident that any attempt to analyze the language in which this storm is presented could not limit itself to immediately meteorological language like words for clouds and winds. The investigation had to be broadened to include the effects of such storms like the drying up of water sources or the withering of the vegetation and even other pieces of vocabulary like *ḥrwn* (*ʾp*) that initially did not suggest they had any sort of meteorological connections.

[4] Jeremias, *Theophanie*, 31.

[5] See p. 106, n. 79.

After a brief summary of the characteristics of the sirocco as experienced on the Syro-Palestinian litoral and a discussion of the periods in which it blows in Part I, Part II set out to analyze a series of five texts which seem to reflect characteristics of the sirocco as described in Part I and in which storms occur that dry up bodies of water. It was assumed that if any motif was to isolate the sirocco and the language in which it is described, the drying up of bodies of water would serve that purpose. A consistent series of motifs and vocabulary began to emerge in the course of this investigation—a series of motifs and vocabulary that never occur in any rainstorm. In Parts III and IV six more apparent sirocco texts were added in which the same vocabulary and motifs appear.

At this point it was clear that a consistent series of vocabulary and motifs was emerging in texts apparently dealing with storms in which not a drop of rain fell. They certainly betrayed characteristics of the sirocco, but often enough described in such exaggerated terms that it was possible to wonder whether in fact it was that storm which was being described.

To resolve the dilemma the peculiar characteristics of Palestinian weather that presents us with siroccos and rainstorms alternating in the fall interchange period was called upon. In Parts V and VI were studied a series of seven texts in which rainstorms and siroccos alternate. These texts in which the sirocco is presented with the same vocabulary and motifs that were met in the siroccos of Parts II-IV on purely meteorological grounds could for the most part be assigned to the fall interchange period. The manner in which the sirocco is combined with the easily recognizable rainstorm in these texts in a way that so clearly reflects the peculiar meteorology of the fall interchange period along the Syro-Palestinian litoral guarantees that not only the sirocco descriptions in the texts of Parts V and VI but also those of Parts II-IV, which reflect the same vocabulary and motifs, are precisely that. We are not limited here simply to the texts discussed in Parts V and VI. Numerous other texts that certainly or with some probability contrast siroccos and rainstorms in the fall interchange period or at least contrast the sirocco with a situation that presumes rain were discussed in the course of the Studies of Part VII. Texts similar to these in a more limited way were already met in Parts II-IV or discussed briefly as part of the discussion of the principal texts treated in Parts V-VI. All these texts are not equally demonstrative, of course, but it is clear that the texts are so similar they ought to be allowed to interpret one another. Since these texts are the linchpin of the whole argument of this investigation they are gathered here in a summarizing footnote.[6]

The questions with which this investigation opened are thus to be answered affirmatively. Yes, it is legitimate to use Palestinian meteorology as described by the geographers to analyze OT texts, including theophanies. Yes, it is legitimate to identify texts like Nah 1:2-8 as crafted on the model of the sirocco and to explain the exaggerations in the text as due to the fact that the sirocco interpreted as theophany has become super-sirocco. The exaggerations were meant by the OT writers as exaggerations consonant with the nature of that storm.

Part VII, Vocabulary and Motif Studies, gathered the principal results of this investigation, the language characteristic of sirocco descriptions that does not appear in rainstorm descriptions and consequently serves to distinguish references to the sirocco and the rainstorm, the other common Palestinian storm. The OT presents the sirocco as a storm that dries up bodies of water (Study 1), is a threat to the fish (Study 13), withers vegetation (Study 7), turns agricultural land into a desert (Study 15) and brings disease (Study 2). It is a hot storm which can be described with the vocabulary *ʾš* + *ʾkl* (Study 12), *bʿr* (Study 21), *lhṭ* (Study 22). This explains the fact that the Sodom and *gpryt* motifs (Study 18) regularly appear in its description. The sirocco is presented as blowing about withered vegetation (Study 11) or dust (Study 6). The dust cloud of the sirocco is referred to as an *ʿnn* (never a

[6] Omitted from this list are the principal texts studied in Parts V-VI: Hos 13:12-14:9 (in Part II, pp. 26-27, n. 7; see Hos 11:9, Study 9, 1); Isa 19:1, 5-7 (Part II, 3; see Study 14); Deut 32:21-25, 13-14 (Part III, 4); Exod 15: 1b-18 + 21b (Part IV); Isa 42:10-25 (in Part V, pp. 105-6, n. 79; see Study 10, 1); Deut 28:12, 23-24 (in Part V, 6); Jer 10:10, 12-13 (in Part VI, p. 127, n. 47); Amos 1:2-2:16 and 9:4-15 (in Part VI, p. 127, n. 47); see Study 3, 2 and Study 10, p. 167, n. 14.); Ps 107:33-34 (in Part VI; see Study 15); Ezek 17:24 (in Part VI); Job 38:23-24 (in Part VI); Isa 11-12 (Study 1, 1; see Study 18 and Study 20, 5); Isa 66:12-16 (Study 3, 5); Jer 30-31 (Study 4, 1); Zech 9:14-17 (Study 4, 3); Isa 41:16-19 (Study 4, 5); Zech 7:14-8:13 (in Study 4, n. 10); Ps 78:47-49 (Study 8, 2); Zeph 3:6-13 (Study 8, 3); Ezek 22:17-31 (Study 8, 4); Prov 25:23 (in Study 8); Isa 32:9-20 (in Study 9); Ps 85 (Study 9, 5); Deut 29-30 (Study 10, 3); Lev 26:3-13, 27-33 (Study 10, 4); Isa 51:3-22 (Study 10, 5; see Study 15); Jer 21:1-23:8 (Study 10, 7); Prov 16:14 (Study 10, 10); Ps 104: 3-4, 29-32 (in Study 10); Ps 144:13-14 (in Study 10, p. 167, n. 14); Ezek 38-39 (Study 13, 2); Mal 2:17-3:24 (Study 20, 4); Ezek 13:1-16 (Study 20, 11; see Study 4, 4).

rain cloud, Study 5) which darkens the heavens (Study 16). The darkening of the heavens is, however, not a discriminating motif since that can be the result of the *ʿbym* of the rainstorm. The sirocco is referred to as a *swph* or a *sʿr* (Studies 3 and 4). None of this is particularly surprising, if it is kept in mind that R. B. Y. Scott[7] had already connected the *ʿnn* and the *swph* to the sirocco. He did, however, fail to distinguish *sʿr* adequately from the rainstorm.[8] More surprising is the fact that *zʿm* (Study 8), *ḥrwn* (*ʾp*) (Study 9), *ḥmh* (Study 10) and *ʿbrh* (Study 19) avoid rainstorms and concentrate in sirocco contexts.

In the course of the discussion it was speculated that these common words for "anger" or the like perhaps all originated in a myth about a nature god whose breath was the sirocco and that sometimes they seem to require a concrete interpretation: the roaring sirocco, the hot sirocco issuing from the nose, the hot sirocco, the gust of the sirocco. That is most clearly suggested by *ḥrwn ʾp* which has the appearance of a phrase with a story behind it, and on this basis it would be possible to explain why *ḥrwn ʾp* and *zʿm* are used almost exclusively of divine anger. However that may be, whether these terms are interpreted concretely or abstractly, they still avoid rainstorms, concentrate in sirocco contexts and serve to identify that storm. Finally, the *ywm Yhwh* is the day of the sirocco. On purely meteorological grounds it is four times clearly the day of the sirocco in the fall interchange period.[9]

That the vocabulary and motifs collected in the Studies of Part VII are a tidy package of materials is made clear by the fact that each of these Studies consistently resurrects the vocabulary and motifs analyzed in the other Studies and by the way all of this material consistently avoids presentations of rainstorms. This combined with the fact that siroccos are often contrasted with rain in such a way as to indicate that what is being described is the meteorology of the fall interchange period along the Syro-Palestinian litoral is important evidence for the

[7] R. B. Y. Scott, "Meteorological Phenomena and Terminology in the Old Testament," *ZAW* 64 (1952) 24.

[8] Ibid.

[9] There are two other Studies, 14 and 17. The first attempts to explain how the chariot fits into both rainstorm and sirocco descriptions in different ways. The second calls attention to the fact that *tnyn* appears in OT texts that reflect the hostility between the sea and a god who comes in a sirocco. This *tnyn* rather contrasts with *tnn* who appears at Ugarit in the presentation of Baal's and Anat's difficulties with Yamm.

correctness of the conclusion of this investigation: OT reflections of the weather of Palestine are crafted under the control of nature and ought to be analyzed on that basis.

This investigation has concerned itself almost exclusively with meteorology and the language in which it is described. It has given a certain cogency to the view that OT meteorology, the sirocco in particular, as presented in the OT can be analyzed on the basis of Palestinian meteorology as observed and described by the geographers. The investigation ends at this point.

At the same time it is clear that only the groundwork for the essential following steps in the investigation has been laid. On the grounds that there is so much of this meteorological material, that it is so stereotyped and that so much of it reflects the contrasting storms of the fall interchange period, it has been suggested several times that the language analyzed here almost has to have a common *Sitz* and that its *Sitz* in significant part at least is the liturgy of the feast of Sukkoth, temporally situated immediately prior to the fall interchange period. This raises the question of the relation of the materials isolated here to the texts that S. Mowinckel and his followers connect to Sukkoth.[10] Since the question involves a good deal more than meteorology, the narrow scope of this investigation prohibited extended discussion of the matter. One significant exception to this approach was made at the end of Part V in an attempt to call attention to the potential relevance of the material treated here for the discussion of the autumn festival. In Part V, 6 it was shown that Psalms 96-97 (and 98), all of which for reasons completely different from mine Mowinckel assigns to Sukkoth, meteorologically reflect the contrasting storms of the fall interchange period. The reader will have noticed not a few other texts treated in this study which Mowinckel has connected to Sukkoth. The task to be undertaken is to run this meteorological material into the discussion of the Israelite New Year. In the course of working through the meteorological material, I have become convinced that the marriage will be mutually supportive of Mowinckel's views and the analysis of OT meteorological texts defended in this study.

The second task is likewise a product of the narrow parameters which governed the ordering of this study. The prime intention here

[10] John Gray's *The Biblical Doctrine of the Reign of God* (Edinburgh: Clark, 1979) presents a convenient review of Mowinckel's position and the subsequent discussion.

was to isolate the vocabulary and motifs in which the sirocco is described and to gather these materials in the Studies of Part VII. That necessitated the comprehensive but more or less superficial review of the numerous texts treated, especially in Part VII. It is nonetheless clear that the attempt to read texts meteorologically throughout this investigation yielded the best results in treating in depth texts of some length like Isaiah 34-35 (Part V, 1), Habakkuk 3 (Part V, 3) and Joel (Part VI). That I think can be done for other similar texts by using the materials isolated here. If it is done successfully, it will be the ultimate proof that the results of this investigation are valid.

Bibliography of Works Cited

The abbreviations used in this study and in the bibliography below are those of the *CBQ*. To that list are added:

GB: F. Buhl, *Wilhelm Genesius' hebräisches und aramäisches Handwörterbuch über das Alte Testament* (15th ed.; Leipzig: Vogel, 1910).

KTU: M. Dietrich, O. Loretz and J. Sanmartín, *Die keilalphabetischen Texte aus Ugarit* (AOAT 24/1; Neukirchen-Vluyn: Neukirchener Verlag, 1976).

Lexikon der Ägyptologie: W. Helck and E. Otto, eds., *Lexikon der Ägyptologie* (4 + vols.; Wiesbaden: Harrassowitz, 1975-).

Joüon: P. Joüon, *Grammaire de l'hébreu biblique* (Rome: Institut Biblique Pontifical, 1947).

Ugaritica V: J. Nougayrol et al., *Ugaritica* V (Mission de Ras Shamra 16; Paris: Geuthner, 1968).

WdM: H. W. Haussig, ed., *Wörterbuch der Mythologie* I, *Götter und Mythen im Vorderen Orient* (Stuttgart: Klett, 1965).

***

Abel, F.-M. *Géographie de la Palestine* (2 vols.; Paris: Gabalda, 1933-38).

Albright, W. F. "The Psalm of Habakkuk," *Studies in Old Testament Prophecy Presented to Prof. Theodore H. Robinson* (ed. H. H. Rowley; Edinburgh: Clark, 1950) 1-18.

Ashbel, D. *Bio-Climatic Atlas of Israel* (Hebrew and English; Jerusalem: Hebrew U., n.d. [1950?]).

Baly, D. *The Geography of the Bible* (New York: Harper, 1957).

Barnett, R. D. *A Catalogue of the Nimrud Ivories* (2nd ed.; London: British Museum, 1975).

Bascom, W. *Deep Water, Ancient Ships* (Garden City: Doubleday, 1976).

Bauer, L. "Die Heuschreckenplage in Palästina," *ZDPV* 49 (1926) 168-71.

Bewer, J. *Obadiah and Joel* (ICC; New York: Scribner, 1911).
Blanckenhorn, M. "Entstehung und Geschichte des Todten Meeres," *ZDPV* 19 (1896) 1-59.
Blau, J. "Über homonyme und angeblich homonyme Wurzeln II," *VT* 7 (1957) 98-102.
Böhl, F. M. Th. "Babylon, die heilige Stad," *JEOL* 3 (1944-48) 491-525.
Bourke, J. "Le Jour de Yahvé dans Joël," *RB* 66 (1959) 5-31, 191-212.
Bright, J. *Jeremiah* (AB 21; Garden City: Doubleday, 1965).
Butterworth, E. A. S. *The Tree at the Navel of the Earth* (Berlin: de Gruyter, 1970).
Campbell, E. F. *Ruth* (AB 7; Garden City: Doubleday, 1975).
Casanowicz, I. M. *The Collection of Ancient Oriental Seals in the United States National Museum* (Proceedings of the United States National Museum 69/4; Washington: Government Printing Office, 1926).
Cassuto, U. *A Commentary on the Book of Exodus* (Jerusalem: Magnes, 1967).
Cathcart, K. J. "Kingship and the 'Day of Yahweh' in Isaiah 2:6-22," *Hermathena* 125 (1978) 48-59.
Cazelles, H. "Le Nouvel An en Israël," *DBSup* 6 (1960) 620-45.
Černý, L. *The Day of Yahweh and Some Relevant Problems* (Prague: Universitas Carolina, 1948).
Chaplin, T. "Observations on the Climate of Jerusalem," *PEFQS* (1883) 8-40.
Childs, B. S. "A Traditio-historical Study of the Reed Sea Tradition," *VT* 20 (1970) 406-18.
______. *The Book of Exodus* (Philadelphia: Westminster, 1974).
Coats, G. W. "The Traditio-historical Character of the Reed Sea Motif," *VT* 17 (1967) 253-65.
Coogan, M. D. "A Structural and Literary Analysis of the Song of Deborah," *CBQ* 40 (1978) 143-66.
Cross, F. M. *Canaanite Myth and Hebrew Epic* (Cambridge: Harvard University, 1973).
______ and Freedman, D. N. *Studies in Ancient Yahwistic Poetry* (SBLDS 21; Missoula: Scholars Press, 1975).
Dahood, M. "Some Northwest-Semitic Words in Job," *Bib* 38 (1957) 306-20.
______. *Psalms* (AB 16-17a; Garden City: Doubleday, 1966-70).
Dalman, G. *Arbeit und Sitte in Palästina* (7 vols.; Gütersloh: Evangelischer Verlag, 1928-42).
de Moor, J. C. *The Seasonal Pattern in the Ugaritic Myth of Baʿlu* (AOAT 16; Neukirchen-Vluyn: Neukirchener Verlag, 1971).
______. *New Year with Canaanites and Israelites* (2 parts; Kampen: Kok, 1972).

Dentan, R. C. "Malachi," *IB* 6 (1956) 1115-44.

de Vaux, R. *Ancient Israel* (New York: McGraw-Hill, 1961).

Dhorme, P. *Le livre de Job* (Paris: Lecoffre, 1926).

Dion, P. E. "YHWH as Storm-god and Sun-god: The Double Legacy of Egypt and Canaan as Reflected in Psalm 104," *ZAW* 103 (1991) 43-71.

Driver, G. R. "Linguistic and Textual Problems: Ezekiel," *Bib* 19 (1938) 60-69.

Duhm, B. *Das Buch Jesaia* (5th ed.; Göttingen: Vandenhoeck und Ruprecht, 1968).

Eaton, J. H. "The Origin and Meaning of Habakkuk 3," *ZAW* 76 (1964) 144-71.

Eissfeldt, O. *Baal Zaphon, Zeus Kasios und der Durchzug der Israeliten durchs Meer* (Halle: Niemeyer, 1932).

_______. *Das Lied Moses Deuteronomium 32:1-43 und das Lehrgedicht Asaphs Psalm 78 samt einer Analyse der Umgebung des Mose-Liedes* (Berlin: Akademie, 1958).

_______. *The Old Testament: An Introduction* (Oxford: Blackwell, 1965).

Ewald, H. *Ausführliches Lehrbuch der hebräischen Sprache* (8th ed.; Göttingen: Dieterich, 1870).

Fitzgerald, A. "*BTWLT* and *BT* as Titles for Capital Cities," *CBQ* 37 (1975) 167-83.

Fohrer, G. *Das Buch Jesaja* (3 vols.; Zürich/Stuttgart: Zwingli, 1960-64).

Freedman, D. N. "Strophe and Meter in Exodus 15," *A Light unto my Path, Old Testament Studies in Honor of Jacob N. Myers* (ed. H. N. Bream et al.; Philadelphia: Temple, 1974) 163-203.

Good, R. M. "Cloud Messengers?" *UF* 10 (1978) 436-37.

Goodenough, E. R. *Jewish Symbols in the Greco-Roman Period* (Bollingen Series 37; 13 vols.; New York: Pantheon, 1953-68).

Gray, J. *The Biblical Doctrine of the Reign of God* (Edinburgh: Clark, 1979).

Gressmann, H. *Der Ursprung der israelitisch-jüdischen Eschatologie* (Göttingen: Vandenhoeck und Ruprecht, 1905).

Hallo, W. W. and Moran, W. L. "The First Tablet of the SB Recension of the Anzu Myth," *JCS* 31 (1979) 65-115.

Harland, J. P. "Sodom and Gomorrah," *The Biblical Archaeologist Reader* I (ed. G. E. Wright and D. N. Freedman; Garden City: Doubleday, 1961) 41-75 (= *BA* 5 [1942] 17-32; 6 [1943] 41-52).

Hartman, L. F. and DiLella, A. A. *The Book of Daniel* (AB 23; Garden City: Doubleday, 1978).

Hiebert, T. *God of My Victory: The Ancient Hymn in Habakkuk 3* (HSM 39; Atlanta: Scholars, 1986).

Hillers, D. R. *Lamentations* (AB 7a; Garden City: Doubleday, 1972).

Hruška, B. *Der Mythenadler Anzu in Literatur und Vorstellung des alten Mesopotamien* (Assyriologia 2; Budapest: Eotvös-Loránd-Unirversität, 1975).

Irsigler, H. *Gottesgericht und Jahwetag* (St. Ottilien: Eos, 1977).
Jacobsen, T. *The Treasures of Darkness* (New Haven: Yale, 1976).
Jahnow, H. *Das hebräische Leichenlied* (BZAW 36; Giessen: Töpelmann, 1923).
Janzen, J. G. *Studies in the Text of Jeremiah* (HSM 6; Cambridge: Harvard, 1973).
Jaroš, K. "Des Mose 'strahlende Haut,'" *ZAW* 88 (1976) 275-80.
Jenni, E. *Das hebräische Piᶜel* (Zürich: EVZ, 1968).
Jeremias, J. *Theophanie* (WMANT 10; Neukirchen-Vluyn: Neukirchener Verlag, 1965).
Jirku, A. "Die Gesichtsmaske des Mose," *ZDPV* 67 (1945) 43-45.
Kaiser, O. *Isaiah 13-39* (London: SCM, 1974).
Kallner-Amiran, D. H. "A Revised Earthquake-Catalogue of Palestine," *IEJ* 1 (1950-51) 223-46; 2 (1952) 48-65.
Katsnelson, J. "Meteorology," *IEJ* 7 (1957) 262-63.
Klein, H. "Das Klima Palästinas auf Grund der alten hebräischen Quellen," *ZDPV* 37 (1914) 217-49, 297-337.
Köhler, L. "Zum hebräischen Wörterbuch des Alten Testamentes," *Studien zur semitischen Philologie und Religionsgeschichte, Festschrift Julius Wellhausen* (BZAW 27; ed. K. Marti; Giessen: Töpelmann, 1914) 243-62.
Kraus, H.-J. *Psalmen* (BKAT 15/1-2; 2nd ed.; Neukirchen: Neukirchener Verlag, 1961).
______. *Klagelieder* (BKAT 20; 3rd ed.; Neukirchen-Vluyn: Neukirchener Verlag, 1968).
Lambert, W. G. and Millard, A. R. *Atra-ḫasīs, The Babylonian Story of the Flood* (Oxford: Clarendon, 1969).
Landsberger, B. "Einige unerkannt gebliebene oder verkannte Nomina des Akkadischen," *WZKM* 57 (1961) 1-23.
Lauha, A. "Das Schilfmeermotiv im Alten Testament," *Congress Volume, Bonn 1962* (VTSup 9; ed. G. W. Anderson et al.; Leiden: Brill, 1963) 32-46.
Levy-Tokatly, Y. "Easterly Storms – November 1958," *IEJ* 10 (1960) 112-17.
Lugt, H. "Wirbelstürme im Alten Testament," *BZ* 19 (1975) 195-204.
Lutz, H.-M. *Jahwe, Jerusalem und die Völker* (WMANT 27; Neukirchen-Vluyn: Neukirchener Verlag, 1968).
Lynch, W. F. *Narrative of the United States' Expedition to the River Jordan and the Dead Sea* (Philadelphia: Lea and Blanchard, 1849).
Mann, T. W. "The Pillar of Cloud in the Reed Sea Narrative," *JBL* 90 (1971) 15-30.
Margulis, B. "The Psalm of Habakkuk: A Reconstruction and Interpretation," *ZAW* 82 (1970) 409-42.
Masterman, E. W. G. "Hygiene and Disease in Palestine in Modern and in Biblical Times," *PEFQS* (1918) 13-20, 56-71, 112-19, 156-71; (1919) 27-36.

McKane, W. *Proverbs* (Philadelphia: Westminster, 1970).

Mendenhall, G. E. *The Tenth Generation* (Baltimore: Johns Hopkins, 1973).

Meyers, C. *The Tabernacle Menorah: A Synthetic Study of a Symbol from the Biblical Cult* (ASOR Dissertation Series 2; Missoula: Scholars Press, 1976).

Milik, J. "Deux documents inédits du desert de Juda," *Bib* 38 (1957) 245-68.

Miller, P. D. "Fire in the Mythology of Canaan and Israel," *CBQ* 27 (1965) 256-61.

Moran, W. L. "Some Remarks on the Song of Moses," *Bib* 43 (1962) 317-27.

Mowinckel, S. *Zum israelitischen Neujahr und zur Deutung der Thronbesteigungspsalmen* (Oslo: Dybwad, 1952).

______. *Psalmenstudien* (2 vols.; reprint of 1921-24 ed.; Amsterdam: Schippers, 1961).

Muilenburg, J. "The Linguistic and Rhetorical Usages of the Particle *ky* in the Old Testament," *HUCA* 32 (1961) 135-60.

Müller, D. H. "Der Prophet Ezechiel entlehnt eine Stelle des Propheten Zephanja und glossiert sie," *WZKM* 19 (1905) 263-70.

Nir, D. "Whirlwinds in Israel in the Winters 1954/55 and 1955/56," *IEJ* 7 (1957) 109-17.

Norin, S. I. L. *Er spaltete das Meer* (ConBOT Series 9; Lund: Gleerup, 1977).

Noth, M. *Leviticus* (Philadelphia: Westminster, 1965).

Oliver, F. W. "Dust-Storms in Egypt and their Relation to the War Period, as Noted in Maryut, 1939-45," *The Geographical Journal* 106 (1945) 26-49.

Parker, R. A. and Dubberstein, W. H. *Babylonian Chronology 626 B.C. - A.D. 75* (Brown University Studies 19; Providence: Brown University, 1956).

Pedersen, J. *Der Eid bei den Semiten in seinem Verhältnis zu verwandten Erscheinungen sowie die Stellung des Eides im Islam* (Strassburg: Trübner, 1914).

Pettinato, G. "Die Lesung von AN.IM.DUGUD.MUŠEN nach einem Ebla-Text," *JCS* 31 (1979) 116-17.

Picardi, L. "Lithological Map," *Atlas of Israel* (ed. D. H. K. Amiran et al.; Jerusalem: Ministry of Labour/Amsterdam: Elsevier, 1970) no. III, 4.

Porada, E. *Corpus of Ancient Near Eastern Seals in North American Collections: I, The Collection of the Pierpont Morgan Library* (Bollingen Series 14; New York: Pantheon, 1948).

Propp, W. H. "The Skin of Moses' Face—Transfigured or Disfigured?" *CBQ* 49 (1987) 375-86.

Rahner, H. *Greek Myths and Christian Mystery* (New York: Harper and Row, 1963).

Reymond, P. *L'eau, sa vie, et sa signification dans l'Ancien Testament* (VTSup 6; Leiden: Brill, 1958).

Robertson, D. A. *Linguistic Evidence in Dating Early Hebrew Poetry* (SBLDS 3; Missoula: SBL, 1972).

Robinson, E. *Biblical Researches in Palestine, Mount Sinai and Arabia Petraea* (3 vols.; Boston: Crocker and Brewster, 1841).

Rudolph, W. *Das Buch Ruth. Das Hohe Lied. Die Klagelieder* (KAT 17/1-3; Gütersloh: Gerd Mohn, 1962).

_______. *Jeremia* (HAT 12; 3rd ed.; Tübingen: Mohr, 1968).

_______. *Joel, Amos, Obadja, Jona* (KAT 13/2; Gütersloh: Gerd Mohn, 1971).

_______. *Micha-Nahum-Habakuk-Zephanja* (KAT 13/3; Gütersloh: Gerd Mohn, 1975).

Schmuttermayr, G. *Psalm 18 und 2 Samuel 22* (SANT 25; München: Kösel, 1971).

Schoors, A. *I am God your Saviour* (VTSup 24; Leiden: Brill, 1973).

Schwarzenbach, A. *Die geographische Terminologie im Hebräischen des Alten Testamentes* (Leiden: Brill, 1954).

Scott, R. B. Y. "Meteorological Phenomena and Terminology in the Old Testament," *ZAW* 64 (1952) 11-25.

Sivall, T. "Sirocco in the Levant," *Geografiska Annaler* 39 (1957) 114-42.

Skehan, P. W. "The Structure of the Song of Moses in Deuteronomy (Deut. 32:1-43)," *CBQ* 13 (1951) 153-63 (= *CBQMS* 1 [1971] 67-77).

Smith, G. A. *The Historical Geography of the Holy Land* (reprint 1931 ed.; London: Collins, 1966).

Smith, M. S. *The Ugaritic Baal Cycle: Volume I. Introduction with Text, Translation and Commentary of KTU 1.1-1.2* (VTSup 55; Leiden: Brill, 1994).

Talmon, S. "The Gezer Calendar and the Seasonal Cycle of Ancient Canaan," *JAOS* 83 (1963) 177-87.

_______. "The 'Desert Motif' in the Bible and in Qumran Literature," *Biblical Motifs* (ed. A. Altmann; Cambridge: Harvard, 1966) 31-63.

Thomson, W. M. *The Land and the Book* (3 vols.; New York: Harper, 1880-85).

Unger, E. *Babylon* (reprint of 2nd ed., 1931; Berlin: de Gruyter, 1970).

Van Buren, E. D. *Symbols of the Gods in Mesopotamian Art* (AnOr 23; Rome: Pontificium Institutum Biblicum, 1945).

_______. "The Dragon in Ancient Mesopotamia," *Or* 15 (1946) 1-45.

_______. "A Further Note on the Dragon in Ancient Mesopotamia," *Or* 16 (1947) 252-53.

VanderKam, J. "*BHL* in Ps 2:5 and its Etymology," *CBQ* 39 (1977) 245-50.

van der Ploeg, J. "Prov. XXV 23," *VT* 3 (1953) 189-91.

Volz, P. *Das Neujahrsfest Jahwehs (Laubhüttenfest)* (Tübingen: Mohr, 1912).

von Rad, G. "The Origin of the Concept of the Day of Yahweh," *JSS* 4 (1959) 97-108.

Weiser, A. "Zur Frage nach den Beziehungen der Psalmen zum Kult: Die Darstellung der Theophanie in den Psalmen und im Festkult," *Festschrift Alfred Bertholet* (ed. W. Baumgartner et al.; Tübingen: Mohr, 1950) 513-31.

Westermann, C. *Genesis* (BKAT 1/1-3+; Neukirchen-Vluyn: Neukirchener Verlag, 1966-).

Whiting, J. D. "Jerusalem's Locust Plague," *The National Geographic Magazine* 28 (1915) 511-50.

Wildberger, H. *Jesaja* (BKAT 10/1-3; Neukirchen-Vluyn: Neukirchener Verlag, 1965-).

Wolff, H. W. *Dodekapropheton 1, Hosea* (BKAT 14/1; Neukirchen-Vluyn: Neukirchener Verlag, 1961).

______. *Dodekapropheton 2, Joel und Amos* (BKAT 14/2; Neukirchen-Vluyn: Neukirchener Verlag, 1969).

Yadin, Y. *The Art of Warfare in Biblical Lands* (2 vols.; New York: McGraw-Hill, 1963).

Zimmerli, W. *Ezechiel* (BKAT 13/1-2; Neukirchen-Vluyn: Neukirchener Verlag, 1955-69).

Zohary, M. "Flora," *IDB* (1962) 284-302.

Zorell, F. *Lexicon hebraicum et aramaicum Veteris Testamenti* (Roma: Pontificium Institutum Biblicum, 1963).

Index of Passages

OLD TESTAMENT

Genesis

8:1 190
8:6 119
9:13 86n.30, 140
9:14 140
13:10 188
19:15 58n.28, 188
19:17 58n.28
19:24-28 185, 188, 189
19:24 185, 188
19:26 188
30:30 169n.2
31:40 109n.88
40:10 125n.42
41:6 109n.87, 109n.88
41:35 89n.44
44:4 41n.40
50:20 41n.40

Exodus

9:23 170n.1
9:24 98n.62, 99n.63, 170n.1
10:21-29 146, 182
14-15 67n.4
14:20 84
14:21 67, 69, 129, 146
14:24 140n.3
15 70, 146
15:1-21 69, 70
15:1-18 35, 65
15:1-2 66n.1
15:1 67
15:1b-18 66, 66n.1, 206n.6
15:3-18 66n.1
15:3 66
15:4 67
15:6 66
15:7 151, 168
15:7b 67
15:8 66, 151
15:10 66, 67n.2, 151
15:21 65, 66n.1, 67
15:21b 66, 66n.1, 206n.6
16:21 106n.80
19:4 51n.17
25:7 152
34:29 92n.49
34:30 92n.49
34:35 92n.49

Leviticus

9:23-24 170
10:2 170, 171n.3
25:34 53
26 162n.6, 176n.7
26:3-45 161
26:3-13 161, 206n.6
26:4-33 161
26:4-5 90n.46
26:6 176n.7
26:16 108n.84
26:27-33 162, 171n.3, 206n.6
26:28 161, 162
26:29 162
26:30 162
26:31 162, 180, 180
26:32 162, 180
26:33 162, 180
26:34 180
26:35 180
27 162n.6

Numbers

11:1-2 170n.3
16 201
23:7-8 142

Deuteronomy

11:10-11 123
11:10 37n.34
11:11-17 90
11:14-15 37n.34
28:12 46n.4, 107, 109n.88, 206n.6
28:21-22 108
28:21 107, 108, 131
28:22-24 109n.88
28:22 107, 108
28:23-24 107, 206n.6
28:24 107, 141
29-30 162n.6, 206n.6
29 186
29:18-27 171n.3
29:18 58n.28, 161, 186
29:19 161, 167n.14
29:22 161, 161, 186, 188
29:23 161
29:26 161
29:27 161, 186
30 161, 186
30:2 161
30:3 186
30:9 161, 186
30:15 161, 165
31 162n.6
31:10 162n.6
32 70
32:1-43 57
32:11 51n.17
32:13-14 59, 65, 206n.6
32:21-25 56, 57, 59, 65, 187, 206n.6
32:21 57
32:22 158, 174, 201
32:22-23 57, 58
32:22 (Tg. Onq.) 58n.27
32:23 58
32:24 57, 58, 131, 159
32:25 57
32:32 89n.43, 187
32:41-42 59
33:2 90n.47, 91n.47, 92n.49

Joshua

2:10 68, 69
10:42 53n.19
23:5 53n.19

Judges

3:22 174
5:4 86n.31, 90n.47, 91n.47
6:37 109n.88
6:39 109n.88
6:40 109n.88
8:7 154n.10
8:16 154n.10
14:5 52n.18
15:14 108n.83
20:38 80
20:40 80

Ruth

1:10 87n.33

1 Samuel

17:44 113n.14
25:42 168
28:18 150, 151, 152

2 Samuel

5:24 86n.31
6:13 86n.31
11:1 26n.6
15:33-34 94n.56
18:11 78
21:1 100
21:1-14 99
21:9 99, 100
21:10 99, 100
21:14 100
21:15-22 99, 100
22 98n.61, 99n.62
22:1-51 99
22:1 99
22:8-10 97
22:9 151n.3, 159, 174, 200
22:11 51, 51n.17
22:12 182
22:13 201
22:15 85n.30
22:16 30n.15, 158
23:1-7 99
23:8-39 99, 100
24:1-25 99
24:13 100
24:15 100
24:20 100

1-2 Kings

100n.64

1 Kings

5:5 78
8:37 109n.86
9:6-8 40n.38
12:11 58n.28
12:14 58n.28
18 109, 182n.2
18:38 109, 170
18:44-45 109
18:44 85n.29
18:45 182
19:11-12 64n.43
19:12 80

2 Kings
2:1 139
2:11 139
13:17 119
17:25 57
18:35 53n.19
19:17 53n.19
19:26 89n.43
23:4 89n.43

1 Chronicles
14:15 86n.31
20:1 26n.6

2 Chronicles
6:28 109n.86
7:19-21 40n.38
19:7 155
36:11-21 64

Ezra
9:9 179n.1

Nehemiah
8:8-12 78n.19
9:11 69
13:18 58n.28, 150

Job
1:14 109
1:16 109, 170, 201
1:19 143
1:21 95, 165
4:16 80
6:4 58n.29
9:9 136
9:17 139
13:25 142, 168
14:1-2 169
15:33 61n.38
16:2 60
18:15 155, 156, 187
18:16 142
20:23 155
21:18 135, 168
26:8 140
27:20-21 139n.10
27:20 135
27:21 135, 168
37:9 135
37:17 136
37:21 136, 190
38:1 139
38:22 46n.4
38:23-24 128, 206n.6
38:27 177n.8
39:23 174
40:6 139
41:13 98n.60, 174, 201
41:23 39n.36

Psalms
1:3 170
1:4 170
2:5-6 158
2:5 157
2:11 158
2:12 200
11:6 143, 186
18 97, 98n.61, 99
18:7 97
18:8-20 99
18:8-17 97
18:8-10 97
18:8-9 97, 98, 99
18:8 119, 151n.3, 159
18:9 97, 98, 98n.60, 99n.62, 151n.3, 159, 167n.14, 174, 200
18:9b 98
18:10-17 97, 98, 99
18:10a 97
18:11 51, 51n.17, 178
18:12 182
18:13 98, 99n.62, 201
18:14 98n.61
18:15 85n.30
18:16 30n.15, 158
18:34 61n.39
29 62, 106n.79, 160n.3, 182, 204
29:3 106n.79
29:5 106n.79
29:6 106n.79, 203
29:7 174
29:8 106n.79
29:9 106n.79, 155, 160n.3, 167
29:10 35, 86, 106n.79
35:5 165n.10
38:3 58n.29
38:4 149
46:7 41n.40
48:8 139n.8, 199
50:2-3 92n.49, 107n.81
50:3 112, 112n.11, 118, 139n.10, 149n.20, 174
50:3 (Targ.) 143
55:9 139
57:5 201
58:10 150n.1
68:3 108n.83
68:5 178
68:8-9 91n.47
68:8 86n.31
68:9 90n.47
69:25 149, 152
72:8 88
73:16 28n.10

Psalms (*cont.*)
77:16-21 69
77:16 69n.9
77:17-20 69
77:16 69n.9
77:18 85n.30, 119
77:19-20 88n.37
77:21 69n.9
78:13 69
78:44-51 144, 145
78:44 145
78:45-46 145
78:45 145
78:46 145
78:47-49 206n.6
78:47-48 144, 145
145, 146
78:49-50a 144, 145, 146
78:49 144, 152, 165, 190, 191
78:50b-51 145, 146
78:51 146
83:2-9 134
83:14 134, 168
83:15 134, 200, 201
83:16 134, 136
83:16a 134
83:16b 134
85 206n.6
85:4 154, 191
85:13 155
88:8 158, 159
88:17 158
91:4 51n.17
91:5-6 58n.29
96-98 106n.79
96-97 104, 104n.78, 138, 208
96 104, 105, 106, 106n.79, 107, 127n.46, 160n.3
96:10 104, 106n.79
96:11 105, 160n.2
96:11-12 106n.79, 160n.3
96:12 105
96:13 105
97 104, 106, 106n.79, 107, 127n.46
97:1 104
97:2-5 106, 108n.83
97:2-3 108n.83
97:2 106, 141
97:3-5 108n.83
97:3 106, 107n.81, 112, 112n.11, 118, 174, 201
97:4-5 108n.83
97:4 22, 107, 108n.83
97:5 106
98 106n.79, 160n.3
98 208
98:7-8 106n.79, 160n.3
98:7 106n.79, 160n.2
98:8 106n.79
98:9 106n.79
102:4 144
102:5 142, 144
102:7 144, 180, 181
102:11 144
102:12 142, 144
103:9 172n.6
103:15-16 144, 190
103:16 148n.18
104 167n.14
104:3-4 165, 167n.14, 206n.6
104:3 51, 178
104:4 201
104:13-15 90n.46
104:13 74n.7
104:29-32 206n.6
104:29-30 167n.14
104:31-32 167n.14
104:32 167n.14
104:32b 167n.14
105:32 98n.62, 99n.63, 174
106:9 68, 129
106:18 201
107:25 139
107:29 139
107:31-33 181
107:33-35 127
107:33-34 181, 206n.6
107:33 180
107:34 180
107:35 181
114:3 68
114:4 68
114:5 68
118:10-12 41n.40
119:51 41n.40
119:61 41n.40
135:7 46n.4
144 167n.14
144:5-6 167n.14
144:5 97
144:13-14 167n.14, 206n.6
148:8 99n.63, 138, 170n.1

Proverbs
1:27 136, 177n.8
7:8 86n.31
10:25 136, 190
16:13 166
16:14 165, 166, 206n.6
16:15 165, 166
16:27 166

16:28 166
16:29-30 166
16:31-32 166
25:23 149, 206n.6
30:27 116n.24

Qoheleth
11:3 140n.6

Sirach
43:17 143
50:7 1n.2

Isaiah
1-35 130n.5
1-12 130n.5, 187
1:8 61
2:4 118
2:6-22 199n.12
2:10 198
2:12 198
2:13 198
2:14 198
2:16 198
3:7 28
4:4 94n.56
4:6 109n.88
5:28 135, 141
6:11 94n.56
8:7-8 41n.39
11-12 130n.5, 187, 195, 195n.7, 206n.6
11:1-12:6 130, 130n.5
11:15 130, 130n.2, 187
12:3 130
13-35 72
13-23 130n.5
13 65, 103, 117n.27, 187
13:2-22 44, 46
13:2-4 44, 46
13:2-3 46
13:3 195
13:4 46
13:5 143
13:5b 46
13:6 45, 84, 117, 118, 195
13:8 118
13:9 44, 45, 129, 132, 152, 180, 191, 195
13:10 45, 119, 182, 187
13:13 45, 119, 152, 187, 191
13:14-18 44
13:17 65
13:19-22 44, 45
13:19 44, 187
13:20-22 40n.38
13:20 44
13:21-22 44, 181
13:21 187
14:12-19 76n.15
14:12 76n.15
14:19 76n.15
15:1-6 130n.5
15:1 55n.25, 180, 180
15:6 55n.25, 129, 141, 180
15:9 130n.2
16:8 89n.43
16:9 125n.42
17:13 133, 168
18:4 36, 140
18:5 125n.42
19 184n.8
19:1-7 27, 130n.5
19:1 35, 36, 42, 44, 47, 61, 179, 206n.6
19:4 36, 47
19:5-7 35, 36, 42, 44, 47, 179, 184n.8, 206n.6
19:5-6 129
19:5 39n.36
19:6-7 141
19:6 36, 37, 175
19:7 141
19:8a 36
21:1 134
26:11 174
26:20 148
26:21 148
28:2 133, 138
29:1-8 100, 103, 104
29:1-5b 100n.66, 101n.66, 103n.76
29:1 101, 101n.66, 102, 103n.76
29:2 103n.76
29:2-3 102
29:3 102
29:4-5b 101n.66
29:4 61n.39, 102
29:5 141, 168, 190
29:5ab 102, 103, 103n.76
29:5c-8 101n.66, 103
29:5c-6 100, 101, 103
29:5c 102n.74
29:6 133, 136, 174
29:7 101n.66, 102, 103n.76
29:8 101n.66, 102, 104
29:13-14 102n.71
29:13 102n.71
30:23 81

Isaiah (*cont.*)
30:23-26 81, 82, 95, 104, 187
30:25 81
30:25b 82
30:27-33 79, 80, 82, 95, 97, 104, 104, 186
30:27-30 81
30:27-28 81
30:27 81, 81n.24, 143, 158, 158, 174, 200
30:28 81, 81n.24, 104
30:28b 80
30:29 80, 81n.25
30:30-31 81, 82
30:30 80, 99n.63, 174, 187, 200
30:31 81
30:32 80, 81
30:33 81, 81n.24, 86n.30, 103n.76, 109, 187, 200
31:5 51n.17
32:9-20 206n.6
32:12-13 154
32:15-16 126n.43
34-35 8, 71, 72, 74, 78, 79n.21, 82, 95, 104, 130n.5, 177, 195n.7, 208
34 74, 77, 78, 82, 95, 104, 105n.79, 108n.83, 186, 193
34:2-3 72, 74
34:2 74, 75, 104, 159, 193
34:3 108n.83
34:4-5 74
34:4 75, 76n.15, 77, 141, 162n.7, 182
34:5-17 72, 74, 193
34:5-7 74
34:6 74
34:8 77, 186, 193, 193
34:9 75, 186, 188, 200
34:10 75, 167n.14, 180, 186, 193
34:11-17 75
34:11 74, 181
34:13-15 181
34:13 74n.6, 75
35 72, 73, 74, 75, 76n.13, 77, 95, 104, 106n.79, 186, 193
35:1-2 73, 105n.79, 106n.79, 160n.3
35:1 200
35:2 73, 74, 74, 155, 167n.13
35:4 73
35:6-8 74, 106n.79
35:6 74
35:6b 73
35:7 74, 75
35:9 75
35:10 72, 73, 78
36:8 89n.43
36:18 53n.19
36:20 53n.19
37:18 53n.19
37:27 89n.43
40:6-8 68, 162n.8
40:7 203
40:24 137, 141, 168, 168, 169n.4
40:78 142
41:2-3 169, 169n.4
41:2 141
41:3 169n.4
41:3b 169n.4
41:16-19 206n.6
41:16 138, 168, 169
42:10-25 206n.6
42:10-17 68n.7, 105n.79
42:10-12 160
42:10-11 106n.79
42:10 105n.79
42:11 106n.79
42:12 167n.13
42:13 160
42:14 160
42:15 106n.79, 129, 141, 199n.13
42:16 160
42:25 160, 167, 200, 201, 201
42:25b 160
44:3-4 126n.43
44:27 68
50:2-3 27, 37, 42, 47, 68, 180, 181
50:2 54n.23, 129, 175, 180
50:3 182
51:3-22 206n.6
51:3 61, 118, 162, 181
51:6 162, 167n.14
51:9-10 62, 163
51:9a 68
51:9b 68
51:10 68, 69, 129, 162

51:11 162
51:12 68, 162
51:17 157n.18
51:19-20 68
51:20 162, 162
51:22 157n.18, 163
58:5 192
61:2 78n.18, 192
61:3 78n.18
61:4 78n.18
61:5 78n.18
63 156
63:1-2 54n.24
63:2 61n.39, 156
63:3 156, 159
63:5 156, 159
63:6 156, 159
63:12 69
66:11-16 195n.7
66:12-16 206n.6
66:12 134
66:14 134, 135, 144
66:15-16 135
66:15 134, 144, 159, 174, 174, 179
66:16 174

Jeremiah
1:3 114
1:5 114
2:32 29n.11
4:1-4 163
4:1-4a 163
4:4 163, 200
4:4b 163
4:5-6:30 47
4:5-31 46, 48, 49 50, 64, 163, 177, 178
4:6 47, 177
4:7 47, 48, 49, 53, 56, 180
4:8 48, 50, 152
4:11-12 47
4:13 47, 49, 133, 140, 140n.3, 141, 177, 178
4:14 163
4:15 47
4:16 47
4:17 49
4:23-26 48
4:23 48, 180, 182
4:24 48
4:25 48
4:26 32n.18, 48, 48n.10, 152, 180
4:27 48, 180
4:28 48, 141, 182
4:29 48
4:31 47
5:6 52n.18
5:24-25 155n.13
6:22 56
7:20 167, 200
7:34 181, 200
10 127n.47
10:1-16 126
10:5 86n.31, 127
10:10-13 46n.3
10:10 126, 127, 127n.47, 143, 167n.14, 206n.6
10:11 127n.47
10:12-16 46n.3, 127n.47
10:12-13 126, 127n.47, 167n.14, 206n.6
10:13 46n.4
12:10 148n.16, 153
12:12 153
12:13 153
12:15 154
13:24 67, 168, 168, 190
14:1-10 114
15:17 149
17:8 155
18:16 40n.38, 168, 180
18:17 141, 168
19:8 40n.38
21:1-23:8 163, 206n.6
21:1-10 163
21:4-7 132
21:4 132, 163
21:5 132, 159, 163
21:6 132, 133, 163
21:7 132
21:11-14 163
21:12 163, 200
21:14 163, 164, 174
22:5 164, 180
22:6 164, 180
22:7 164
22:8 164
22:14-15 164
22:22 164
22:23 164
23:3 164
23:5 164
23:6 163
23:10 137
23:12 137, 186
23:13 137
23:14 137, 186
23:17 137
23:19-20 137
23:19 136, 136n.1, 159, 186
23:20 136n.2
23:27 137
25:15-38 53n.20

Jeremiah (*cont.*)
25:29 53
25:30-38 52, 53, 54, 56, 59, 119, 151, 199
25:30 53n.19, 54, 56, 119, 124, 151, 156
25:31 53, 53n.19, 54, 56
25:32 53, 53n.19, 54, 55, 56, 58, 136, 151, 154
25:33 53, 53n.19, 54, 56, 199
25:34 54
25:35 54
25:36-38 151
25:36 54, 55, 180
25:36b-37 55
25:37 55, 152, 180
25:38 52, 54, 55, 56, 151, 152, 180
26 53n.20
30-31 206n.6
30 137
30:6 137
30:7 137
30:10 137
30:18-21 137
30:23-24 136, 137, 137
30:23 136, 159, 159
30:24 152
31 137
31:5 137
31:9 137
31:12 137
31:40 89n.43
36:30 109n.88
41:1 198
41:5 198
44:6 167, 181, 200
46:10 199
46:16 53
47:2 41n.39
49:7-22 52
49:13 52, 180
49:17-18 52
49:17 40n.38, 180
49:18 52, 187
49:19 52
49:20 52, 180
49:22 52
49:36 154
49:37 154
50 130n.6
50-51 50, 127n.47, 194, 194n.5
50:1-51:58 39, 46n.3
50:3 131, 180
50:12 131, 180
50:13 40n.38, 46, 131, 180
50:16 53, 125n.42
50:23 46, 131, 180
50:25 46, 143
50:33-34 41n.40
50:35-37a 130
50:37b 130
50:38 109n.88, 130
50:38a 131
50:39-40 131
50:39 181
50:40 187
51 130n.6
51:1 50
51:9-10 183
51:12-45 41
51:14 156
51:15-19 46n.3, 127n.47, 156
51:16 46n.4
51:21 130n.7
51:34-37 38, 44, 46n.3, 47, 61, 127n.47, 130n.6, 156, 183
51:34-45 42
51:34-35 27, 39
51:34 39, 40, 42, 183
51:35 39
51:36-45 39
51:36 39, 39n.36, 129, 131, 183
51:37-45 63, 64
51:37 40, 180, 181
51:39 40
51:41 40, 180
51:42-45 38, 44, 46n.3, 47, 61, 127n.47, 130n.6, 156, 183
51:42-43 41, 41n.40
51:42 40, 41, 42
51:43 40, 41, 180
51:44 39, 42, 183
51:45 39, 40, 152
51:55 41n.40

Lamentations
1 156, 157, 198
1:4 157
1:4a 157
1:6b 156
1:11 156
1:12 156, 199
1:12c 156
1:13 174
1:13a 156
1:15 54n.24
1:15b 157

1:15c 157
1:21 156
2 49, 59, 62, 63, 64, 68, 132, 147, 154, 162n.9, 198, 200
2:1-12 60
2:2-5 60
2:2 191
2:2a 61
2:2b 60
2:3 159, 174, 200
2:3a 60
2:4 159, 167
2:4a 60
2:4c 60
2:6-9 60
2:6 143, 148n.16, 198
2:6a 60, 61
2:6b 60
2:7 197
2:10 198
2:13-19 60
2:13 129
2:13b 62
2:20-22 60
2:22 157, 196, 197, 198, 199
4 157
4:3 157
4:4-5 157
4:4 157
4:6 157, 187
4:8 157
4:9-10 157
4:11 157, 159, 174
4:18 84

Ezekiel
1 139n.9
1:4 139
5:12 133, 164
5:13 164
5:14 164, 180
5:16 58n.28
7 132
7:7 132
7:8 132, 159, 167
7:10 132
7:12 132, 150n.2
7:14 132, 150n.2
7:15 132
7:19 132, 132, 191, 196
7:21 132
13:1-16 206n.6
13:5 198
13:10-16 198
13:11 138
13:13 138, 159n.1, 189
17:10 142, 167n.14
17:24 128, 141, 206n.6
19:12 142, 160, 161n.5
21:36 148, 174, 190, 191
22:17-31 206n.6
22:19-20 191
22:20 167
22:21 174, 191
22:22 191
22:23-31 147, 191n.3
22:24 142n.4, 147, 148
22:30 148
22:31 147, 148, 174, 191, 191
26:9 131n.8
27:26 139n.8
29:1-16 184
29:3 184
29:4-5 184
29:8-11 181, 184
29:8 131, 181, 184
29:9 131, 131n.11, 180, 181, 184
29:10 131, 131, 180, 181
29:11 181
30:1-19 164
30:2-3 117, 118
30:3 141, 164, 196
30:4 165
30:5 165
30:6 165
30:7 165, 180
30:8 165
30:10-11 164
30:12 129, 131, 165, 180, 180
30:14 180
30:15 164, 165, 167
30:16 118, 165
30:18 140, 141, 165, 182
32:1-16 184
32:1-2 183n.4
32:2 39n.36, 183
32:3-15 183, 183n.4, 184
32:3-6 183
32:3 183n.5
32:7-8 183
32:7 141
32:9-13 183
32:10 183, 185
32:11-12 183
32:11 183
32:12 183
32:14 183, 184

Ezekiel (*cont.*)
32:15 181, 183
32:16 183n.4
32:18 184
33:3 176n.6
34 176
34:13 176
34:25-27 148
34:26 176
34:27 176
34:28 176
36:35 61
38-39 175, 175n.3, 176, 177, 195n.7, 206n.6
38:6 177
38:8 177
38:9 141, 177
38:15 177
38:16 141, 177
38:18-22 177
38:18 167, 175
38:19 174, 175, 191, 191
38:20 175, 176
38:21 176
38:21a 176n.4
38:22 133, 174, 176, 176n.6, 187
39:2 177
39:3 175
39:6 174, 177
39:9-20 175
39:25-29 177
39:26 176
39:29 147n.11, 167
40-48 177

Daniel
4:7-12 76n.15
4:7-8 76n.15
7:4 51
8:19 149
11:36 149

Hosea
4:3 142, 175
4:19 51
6:4 140
7:5 159
7:16 142
8:7 136
11:8 153, 187
11:9 153, 200, 206n.6
13:11 191
13:12-14:9 195n.7, 206n.6
13:12-14:1 25, 26n.7
13:14-15 24, 25, 27, 30, 37, 47, 49, 55, 65, 153, 187, 191
13:14 131
13:15 30, 129
14:2-9 26n.7, 65
14:5 153
14:6 153

Joel
1-4 6, 110, 111
1-2 173, 193, 196
1 111, 114, 114n.17, 116
1:4-20 120n.35
1:4-7 111, 112n.8, 113, 117n.26
1:6 116
1:10-12 111, 112, 113
1:10 55n.25, 112
1:11 112
1:12 112, 117
1:14 111
1:15 112n.99, 114, 117, 118, 123, 193, 196
1:18-20 113
1:18-19 112n.11
1:18 117, 194
1:19-20 112, 112n.11, 113, 118, 137n.5
1:19 174, 201
1:20 112n.11, 113, 129, 174
1:20 (Tg. Jon.) 58n.27, 113n.13
2:1-22 124
2:1-11 114, 115, 116, 117, 117n.27, 119, 121, 123, 124, 125, 173, 203
2:1-2 118, 123
2:1 114, 115, 193
2:2 116, 118, 126, 140n.3, 141, 182, 196
2:3 60, 107n.81, 112, 112n.11, 115, 117, 118, 123, 171n.3, 173, 180, 201
2:4-5 118, 179
2:4 116
2:5 174
2:6 115, 118
2:7-9 119
2:7-8 116
2:9 119
2:10 115, 118, 119, 124, 126, 182
2:11 114, 119, 123, 124, 143n.7, 193, 193n.4, 196

2:12-17 120, 125
2:17 120n.31
2:18-27 125
2:18 120
2:19-27 115, 120, 121, 173
2:20 117
2:21-24 120
2:22 120, 194
2:23 120
2:24 120
2:25 111n.4, 112n.8, 117n.26, 120
2:26 120
2:27 121
3-4 110n.1, 121, 124, 125, 194
3:1-4:21 72
3:1-5 121, 124, 125
3:1-2 126, 126n.43, 147n.11
3:1 32n.19, 121, 167
3:2 121
3:3-4 126
3:3 119n.29, 141, 167n.14
3:4 182, 193
3:5 29n.12, 85n.27, 124, 126, 137n.4
4:1-3 121, 124
4:2 124
4:4-8 110
4:7 112n.9
4:9-14a 121, 124
4:9-13 124
4:9-11 125
4:9 124
4:10 118
4:11 124
4:11b 124
4:12 124
4:13 54n.24, 125, 156
4:14 121, 123, 123, 193
4:14a 124, 125
4:14b-21 121, 122
4:14b-16a 124
4:14b 123, 124, 125
4:15-16 124, 125, 125
4:15 126, 182
4:16 56, 119, 122n.36, 123, 124, 125
4:17 122n.36, 123, 123n.38
4:18 121, 123, 124, 126n.43
4:19 123, 124, 125, 129, 180
4:20-21 122n.36
4:21 123

Amos
1-2 172
1:2-2:16 206n.6
1:2 51, 56, 92n.49, 119, 124, 133, 141, 175n.1
1:4 134, 172
1:7 134, 172, 176
1:10 134, 172
1:12 134, 172
1:14 133, 134, 136, 172
2:2 134, 172
2:5 134, 172
2:16 133
4:9 109n.86
5:18 118, 182, 198
5:20 182, 198
6:12 179
7:1-8:3 173
7:1-9 114n.17
7:4 172, 172n.6
8:1-3 114n.17
8:8 184
9:4-15 195n.7, 206n.6
9:4-6 127n.47
9:4 167n.14
9:5 167n.14, 184
9:6 167n.14
9:13-15 134, 167n.14

Obadiah
15 199

Jonah
1:4 139
1:12 139
1:15 143
4:8 68, 162
4:10 112n.9

Micah
1:3-4 108n.83
1:4 108n.83
4:3 118
4:4 78

Nahum
1:2-2:3 28
1:2-8 1, 27, 28, 29, 29n.13, 32, 33, 34, 35, 42, 44, 47, 63, 64, 202, 203, 204, 206
1:2 32, 159
1:3 4, 31, 133, 136, 140, 141
1:3f. 1, 33

Nahum (*cont.*)

1:4 31, 35, 86, 129, 203, 141
1:5 30n.15, 203
1:6 31, 32n.19, 46, 60, 143, 152, 159, 167, 203
1:7-8 85n.27
1:7 137n.4
1:8 182, 190
1:9 28
3:2 179
3:8 39n.36
3:17 119n.30

Habakkuk

1-3 95
1-2 96
1:2-4 96
1:5-11 96
1:6 88n.39
1:12-17 96
2 96
2:1-5 96
2:3 96
2:4 96
2:6b-20 96
2:20 96
3 85, 95, 95n.57, 96, 97, 104, 177, 190, 194, 208
3:2-19 82-84
3:2 29n.12, 85, 85n.28, 89, 93, 93, 94, 94n.54, 104, 137n.4
3:3-16 115n.20
3:3-15 87, 93, 94
3:3-7 85, 85n.29, 86, 87, 90, 91, 97
3:3-4 92n.49
3:3 88, 190
3:3c-4 91
3:4 87, 92n.49
3:5 91, 131, 169n.2
3:6 91
3:7 88, 91
3:8-15 85n.29, 90, 91, 97
3:8-11 85, 85n.28, 86
3:8-9 91n.47
3:8 85, 86, 88, 94, 94n.54, 135, 159, 178, 190, 191
3:8a 87, 91
3:8b-15 87, 88, 160n.3
3:8b-14 88
3:8b-11 86
3:8b 87, 88n.36, 97
3:9-11 86
3:9 93, 108n.83
3:10-11 91, 182
3:10 91n.47
3:12-15 85, 85n.28, 86, 94
3:12-14 88, 88n.36, 95
3:12 86, 86n.31, 88, 88n.39, 104, 142, 149, 158, 189
3:13 86, 88n.39, 190
3:14 86, 139n.10, 142n.3
3:15 85, 88, 88n.39
3:16-19 85, 89
3:16 89, 94
3:17-19 94
3:17 87n.33, 89, 89n.44, 93, 94, 95, 95n.57, 96
3:18-19 95

Zephaniah

1:2-2:3 195
1:2-18 195
1:3 175, 195
1:4 195
1:7-8 147
1:7 117, 195, 197
1:8 195
1:13 181, 195, 196
1:14-18 147
1:14-15 117, 118
1:14 153, 195, 196
1:15 132, 140n.3, 141, 177n.8, 182, 191, 196, 196
1:18 132, 132n.1, 153, 174, 191, 195, 196
2:1-3 195
2:2 153, 168, 195, 196
2:2a 153n.7, 196n.9
2:3 153, 195
2:4 153, 180
2:9 181, 187
2:13 181
2:14-15 153, 181
2:15 181
3:1-8 147, 147
3:6-13 206n.6

3:6 146, 180
3:8 146, 147, 152, 153, 174
3:13 147

Haggai
2:17 109n.86

Zechariah
7:3 139n.10
7:12 139n.10
7:14-8:13 206n.6
7:14 139n.10, 180
8:2 159
9:9-17 137
9:9-10 138
9:14-17 206n.6
9:14 22, 137, 138
9:17 138
12:10 167
14:1 199

Malachi
2:17-3:24 206n.6
2:17-3:21 194
2:17-3:5 193
3:1 193
3:2 174, 193, 194, 195
3:6-12 193, 194
3:7 194
3:10 194
3:11 194
3:12-13 194
3:12 194
3:13-21 193, 194
3:16 194
3:17 194
3:19 193, 194, 195, 200, 201
3:20 194
3:22 193
3:23-24 193
3:23 193, 193n.4, 195
3:24 193

NEW TESTAMENT
Luke
12:54 85n.29

Rev
6:13 76

DEAD SEA SCROLLS
1QpHab
7:1-2 96

Index of Authors

Abel, F.-M., 34n.24, 149n.19
Albright, W. F., 85n.29, 92n.49
Ashbel, D., 14, 14n.11, 22n.13

Baly, D., 11n.1, 14, 14n.10, 15n.12, 33n.23, 181n.4, 189n.10
Barnett, R. D., 51n.16
Bascom, W., 139n.8
Bauer, L., 111n.7, 120n.33
Bewer, J. A., 110n.1, 118n.28
Blanckenhorn, M., 188n.8
Blau, J., 138n.7
Böhl, F. M. Th., 42n.41
Bourke, J., 110n.1
Bright, J., 47n.5, 47n.7
Butterworth, E. A. S., 76n.15

Campbell, E. F., 87n.33
Casanowicz, I. M., 77n.15
Cassuto, U., 92n.49
Cathcart, K. J., 199n.12
Cazelles, H., 9n.14, 103n.78
Černý, L., 192, 192n.1, 197, 197n.10, 199
Chaplin, T., 18, 113n.12
Childs, B. S., 68n.3, 68n.4, 69n.11, 70n.14
Coats, G. W., 68n.4, 69n.11
Coogan, M. D., 91n.47
Cross, F. M., 73n.3, 91n.47, 98n.60, 98n.61, 99n.62

Dahood, M., 51n.17, 69n.9, 92n.49, 155, 155n.12, 155n.13, 155n.14, 172n.5
Dalman, G., 1, 1n.1, 1n.2, 2, 2n.5, 3, 3n.7, 4, 10, 11n.1, 12, 12n.2, 13, 14, 14n.8, 14n.14, 22n.13, 22n.15, 23, 26n.4, 33, 33n.20, 33n.21, 34, 34n.24, 35, 36n.30, 37n.33, 55n.25, 67n.3, 73n.4, 75n.10, 79, 79n.21, 80n.23, 89n.41, 90n.45, 93n.50, 94n.53, 98n.60, 102n.73, 105n.78, 107, 107n.82, 109, 109n.85, 109n.87, 109n.88, 111n.4, 111n.5, 111n.7, 114, 114n.15, 119n.29, 119n.30, 127n.48, 136n.3, 138n.6, 138n.7, 139n.8, 140n.5, 140n.6, 149n.19, 150n.21, 154, 154n.9, 168n.1, 183n.7, 202, 202n.1, 203, 204
de Moor, J. C., 6n.11, 14, 14n.9, 78n.18, 102n.69, 140n.6, 182, 182n.2
de Vaux, R., 26n.6
Dentan, R. C., 193n.3
Dhorme, P., 61n.38, 98n.60, 135n.2, 136n.4
DiLella, A. A., 76n.15

Dion, P. E., 167n.14
Driver, G. R., 142n.4
Dubberstein, W. H., 187n.2
Duhm, B., 169n.4

Eaton, J. H., 6n.11, 78n.20, 84, 84n.26, 93, 93n.52, 94n.54
Eissfeldt, O., 59, 59n.31, 70n.13
Ewald H., 41n.40

Fitzgerald, A., 47n.6
Fohrer, G., 72, 72n.1, 74n.9, 76n.14
Freedman, D. N., 66n.1, 70n.14, 98n.61, 99n.62

Georgii, W., 13
Good, R. M., 140n.6
Goodenough, E. R., 51n.16, 65, 65n.45, 76n.15
Gray, J., 157n.19, 198n.11, 208n.10
Gray, John, 9n.13, 9n.14
Gressmann, H., 10, 10n.15, 199n.13

Hallo, W. W., 51n.15
Harland, J. P., 188n.5, 188
Hartman, L. F., 76n.15
Hiebert, T., 84n.26
Hillers, D. R., 60, 60n.35, 60n.37, 61n.39
Hruška, B., 51n.15

Irsigler, H., 196n.9

Jacobsen, T., 51n.15, 64n.42, 199n.13
Jahnow, H., 40n.38
Janzen, J. G., 39n.35
Jaroš, K., 92n.49
Jenni, E, 28n.10
Jeremias, J., 1, 2, 2n.3, 3n.6, 4, 64n.43, 69n.9, 69n.10, 86n.32, 92n.49, 203, 203n.2, 204, 204n.4
Jirku, A., 92n.49

Kaiser, O., 37n.32, 72, 72n.1, 100n.65, 102n.69
Kallner-Amiran, D. H., 33n.23
Katsnelson, J., 160n.4
Klein, H., 87n.35
Köhler, L., 40n.38
Kraus, H.-J., 60n.37, 61n.39, 69n.9, 89n.40, 155n.12

Lambert, W. G., 51n.15
Landsberger, B., 51n.15
Lauha, A., 68n.4, 69n.11, 70n.14
Levy-Tokatly, Y., 30n.14
Lugt, H., 133n.1
Lutz, H.-M., 79n.21, 100n.65, 147n.13
Lynch, W. F., 20, 189, 189n.11

Mann, T. W., 140n.6
Margulis, B., 84n.26
Masterman, E. W. G., 19
McKane, W., 150n.21
Mendenhall, G. E., 140n.3
Meyers, C. L., 76n.15
Milik, J., 177n.8
Millard, A. R., 51n.15
Miller, P. D., 171n.4
Moran, W. L., 36n.31, 50n.14, 51n.15
Mowinckel, S., 9, 9n.13, 9n.14, 99, 104, 104n.77, 105n.78, 105n.79, 130n.5, 155n.12, 199n.13, 208
Muilenburg, J., 87n.33
Müller, D. H., 147n.14

Nir, D.,30n.14
Norin, S. I. L., 66n.1
Noth, M., 162n.6

Oliver, F. W., 37n.33

Parker, R. A., 187n.2
Pedersen, J., 142n.1

Pettinato, G., 51n.15
Porada, E., 50n.14
Propp, W. H., 92n.49

Rahner, H., 151n.4
Reymond, P., 3, 3n.8, 108n.83, 139, 139n.2
Robertson, D. A., 59n.31, 70n.14
Robinson, E.,15, 16, 28, 28n.8, 33, 33n.22, 34, 47n.5, 47n.7, 54n.21, 59n.33, 60, 60n.36, 61n.39, 74n.9, 84n.26, 86n.32, 87n.35, 88n.39, 94n.54, 95n.57, 96, 110n.1, 110n.2, 115n.22, 116n.23, 120n.31, 131n.9, 147n.12, 156n.15, 179n.5, 203, 203n.3

Schmuttermayr, G., 51n.17, 87n.34, 98n.61, 99n.62, 201n.1
Schoors, A., 126n.43
Schwarzenbach, A., 35n.27, 48n.8, 73n.2, 74n.8, 102n.72, 103n.75, 127n.48, 141n.1, 146n.9, 175n.2, 177n.8, 179n.1, 180n.1
Scott, R. B. Y., 3, 4, 4n.9, 36n.28, 133n.1, 139, 139n.1, 140n.3, 140n.4, 166n.12, 207, 207n.7
Sivall, T., 183n.7
Skehan, P. W., 57n.26
Smith, G. A., 19, 112n.11, 172n.5
Smith, M. S., 70n.13, 199n.13

Talmon, S., 37n.34, 40n.37
Thomson, W. M., 16, 17, 22, 22n.14, 49n.11, 119n.29, 126n.44

Unger E., 42n.41, 42n.43

Van Buren, E. D., 42n.42, 50n.14, 77n.15, 150n.21
VanderKam, J., 158n.20
Volz, P., 9, 9n.12
von Rad, G., 77n.17

Weiser, A., 33n.20
Westermann, C., 187n.4
Whiting, J. D., 111n.7, 119n.30, 120, 120n.34
Wildberger, H., 40n.38, 44n.1, 72n.1, 81n.25, 100n.65, 102n.69, 103n.76, 130n.3, 181n.3
Wolff, H. W., 89n.40, 110n.1, 114n.19, 115n.21, 115n.22, 116n.25, 117n.27, 25n.1

Yadin, Y., 74n.9
Zimmerli, W., 58n.28, 147n.14, 175n.3, 176n.6, 183n.4, 184n.9

Zohary, M., 73n.4
Zorell, F., 58n.28, 89n.44, 166n.11, 201n.1

Index of Hebrew Words

ʾbl, 31, 48, 51, 56, 112, 133, 137, 141, 172, 175
ʾbq, 27, 31, 103, 107, 141
ʾkl, 57, 58, 60, 67, 79, 81, 97, 98, 109, 112, 113, 117, 133, 134, 142, 143, 147, 148, 151, 153, 157, 159, 164, 170, 171, 172, 173, 174, 196, 200, 206
ʾml, 27, 28, 31, 112, 141, 156, 169, 175
ʾrṣ ṣyh, 38, 40, 41, 181
ʾš, 57, 58, 60, 79, 80, 81, 84, 97, 98, 101, 106, 109, 112, 113, 115, 117, 118, 133, 134, 135, 138, 143, 144, 147, 148, 153, 156, 157, 158, 159, 163, 164, 166, 170, 171, 172, 173, 174, 175, 176, 179, 185, 186, 187, 191, 194, 196, 200, 201, 206

bhw, 48, 179
blʿ, 38, 39, 61
bʿr, 60, 81, 97, 98, 134, 153, 158, 160, 163, 170, 174, 178, 186, 194, 200, 201, 206
bʿš, 37, 191
brq, 106, 107, 138

glgl, 67, 133, 134, 168
glym, 38, 40, 75
gʿr, 27, 30, 37, 68, 162
gʿrh, 37, 68, 162
gpryt, 80, 81, 143, 156, 161, 176, 185, 186, 187, 188, 200, 206

dbr, 107, 108, 109, 131, 132, 163, 164, 168, 176
dg, 175, 176
dll, 36
dmm, 53, 55, 80, 151, 180

zʿm, 27, 28, 31, 46, 60, 79, 81, 127, 142, 143, 144, 145, 146, 147, 148, 149, 159, 165, 189, 190, 191, 200, 207

ḥmh, 28, 31, 32, 60, 66, 68, 75, 132, 134, 135, 137, 43, 149, 156, 157, 158, 159, 160, 161, 162, 163, 164, 165, 167, 175, 189, 191, 198, 200, 207
ḥrb, 27, 30, 35, 36, 37, 38, 39, 53, 54, 56, 68, 75, 117, 129, 130, 131, 141, 144, 160, 162, 164, 171, 180, 181, 184, 185, 186, 193
ḥrh, 83, 87, 97, 107, 109, 159, 161, 190
ḥrwn ʾp, 7, 27, 31, 38, 40, 45, 48, 50, 53, 55, 56, 86, 87, 97, 137, 143, 144, 145, 146, 147, 149, 150, 151, 152, 153, 154, 155, 156, 158, 159, 165, 189, 190, 191, 195, 196, 199, 204, 207

ḥrm, 130, 193

ybš, 25, 26, 27, 30, 35, 36, 37, 38, 39, 51, 53, 56, 68, 112, 113, 128, 129, 131, 133, 137, 141, 144, 156, 157, 160, 168, 172, 202
ym Yhwh, 45, 56, 77, 114, 115, 116, 117, 118, 121, 123, 132, 147, 153, 156, 164, 173, 192, 193, 195, 196, 197, 198, 199, 207

kly zʿm, 46, 143

lhbh, 60, 112, 115, 134, 173, 174
lḥt, 57, 58, 106, 107, 112, 115, 134, 142, 160, 166, 173, 174, 194, 201, 206

mdbr, 25, 37, 38, 48, 67, 73, 123, 131, 143, 144, 148, 153, 154, 160, 162, 164, 168, 173, 179, 180, 184, 186, 190, 194
mlḥh, 179, 181
mṣ, 67, 103, 133, 135, 138, 168, 170
mšmh, 179

nbl, 75, 76, 141, 155, 202
ndp, 36, 169, 170
nšt, 35, 36

swph, 4, 27, 31, 47, 48, 50, 101, 133, 134, 135, 136, 144, 172, 176, 178, 179, 190, 207
sʿr, 52, 54, 58, 86, 134, 136, 137, 138, 139, 151, 154, 172, 186, 207
sʿrh, 101, 136, 137, 138, 139, 159, 168, 186
sph, 57, 58, 161, 186, 188

ʿb, 35, 36, 69, 140, 165, 166, 178, 179, 207
ʿbrh, 45, 60, 83, 86, 117, 145, 146, 148, 153, 154, 155, 165, 174, 175, 189, 190, 191, 195, 196, 201, 207
ʿnn, 2, 4, 27, 31, 36, 47, 48, 50, 106, 117, 118, 137, 139, 140, 141, 164, 165, 177, 178, 180, 182, 196, 206, 207
ʿpr, 102, 107, 141, 169
ʿrbh, 38, 40, 41, 73, 131, 132, 162, 179, 181, 186, 194, 200

ṣyh, 38, 40, 41, 73, 131, 179, 181, 186, 194
ṣmʾwn, 179

qdym, 24, 25, 25n.3, 26, 30, 67, 128, 135, 142, 160, 162, 168
qṭb, 131, 138
qml, 36, 141
qṣp, 127, 144
qš, 67, 118, 134, 137, 151, 168, 169, 194

rwḥ Yhwh, 25, 142
rkb, 35, 36, 97, 135, 178, 179
rʿš, 30, 48, 101, 115, 123, 175, 176
ršp, 131

śʿr, 136, 138, 168
śʿrh, 27, 31, 136, 143
śrq, 1n.2

šʾg, 52, 54, 56, 151, 172
šdd, 53, 54, 55, 112, 151, 180
šmh, 38, 40, 41, 44, 45, 46, 48, 49, 50, 53, 55, 131, 165, 168, 179, 181, 190
šmmh, 46, 48, 123, 131, 153, 162, 173, 179 181, 183, 184, 185, 194, 196, 200

tbn, 135, 168
tnyn, 38, 39, 40, 43, 44, 182, 183, 184

The Catholic Biblical Quarterly Monograph Series (CBQMS)

1. Patrick W. Skehan, *Studies in Israelite Poetry and Wisdom* (CBQMS 1) $9.00 ($7.20 for CBA members) ISBN 0-915170-00-0 (LC 77-153511)
2. Aloysius M. Ambrozic, *The Hidden Kingdom: A Redactional-Critical Study of the References to the Kingdom of God in Mark's Gospel* (CBQMS 2) $9.00 ($7.20 for CBA members) ISBN 0-915170-01-9 (LC 72-89100)
3. Joseph Jensen, O.S.B., *The Use of tôrâ by Isaiah: His Debate with the Wisdom Tradition* (CBQMS 3) $3.00 ($2.40 for CBA members) ISBN 0-915170-02-7 (LC 73-83134)
4. George W. Coats, *From Canaan to Egypt: Structural and Theological Context for the Joseph Story* (CBQMS 4) $4.00 ($3.20 for CBA members) ISBN 0-915170-03-5 (LC 75-11382)
5. O. Lamar Cope, *Matthew: A Scribe Trained for the Kingdom of Heaven* (CBQMS 5) $4.50 ($3.60 for CBA members) ISBN 0-915170-04-3 (LC 75-36778)
6. Madeleine Boucher, *The Mysterious Parable: A Literary Study* (CBQMS 6) $2.50 ($2.00 for CBA members) ISBN 0-915170-05-1 (LC 76-51260)
7. Jay Braverman, Jerome's Commentary on Daniel: A Study of Comparative Jewish and Christian Interpretations of the Hebrew Bible (CBQMS 7) $4.00 ($3.20 for CBA members) ISBN 0-915170-06-X (LC 78-55726)
8. Maurya P. Horgan, *Pesharim: Qumran Interpretations of Biblical Books* (CBQMS 8) $6.00 ($4.80 for CBA members) ISBN 0-915170-07-8 (LC 78-12910)
9. Harold W. Attridge and Robert A. Oden, Jr., *Philo of Byblos,* The Phoenician History (CBQMS 9) $3.50 ($2.80 for CBA members) ISBN 0-915170-08-6 (LC 80-25781)
10. Paul J. Kobelski, *Melchizedek and Melchirešaʿ* (CBQMS 10) $4.50 ($3.60 for CBA members) ISBN 0-915170-09-4 (LC 80-28379)
11. Homer Heater, *A Septuagint Translation Technique in the Book of Job* (CBQMS 11) $4.00 ($3.20 for CBA members) ISBN 0-915170-10-8 (LC 81-10085)
12. Robert Doran, *Temple Propaganda: The Purpose and Character of 2 Maccabees* (CBQMS 12) $4.50 ($3.60 for CBA members) ISBN 0-915170-11-6 (LC 81-10084)
13. James Thompson, *The Beginnings of Christian Philosophy: The Epistle to the Hebrews* (CBQMS 13) $5.50 ($4.50 for CBA members) ISBN 0-915170-12-4 (LC 81-12295)

14. Thomas H. Tobin, S.J., *The Creation of Man: Philo and the History of Interpretation* (CBQMS 14) $6.00 ($4.80 for CBA members) ISBN 0-915170-13-2 (LC 82-19891)
15. Carolyn Osiek, *Rich and Poor in the Shepherd of Hermes* (CBQMS 15) $6.00 ($4.80 for CBA members) ISBN 0-915170--14-0 (LC 83-7385)
16. James C. VanderKam, *Enoch and the Growth of an Apocalyptic Tradition* (CBQMS 16) $6.50 ($5.20 for CBA members) ISBN 0-915170-15-9 (LC 83-10134)
17. Antony F. Campbell, S.J., *Of Prophets and Kings: A Late Ninth-Century Document (*1 *Samuel* 1-2 *Kings* 10*)* (CBQMS 17) $7.50 ($6.00 for CBA members) ISBN 0-915170-16-7 (LC 85-12791)
18. John C. Endres, S.J., *Biblical Interpretation in the Book of Jubilees* (CBQMS 18) $8.50 ($6.80 for CBA members) ISBN 0-915170-17-5 (LC 86-6845)
19. Sharon Pace Jeansonne, *The Old Greek Translation of Daniel* 7-12 (CBQMS 19) $5.00 ($4.00 for CBA members) ISBN 0-915170-18-3 (LC 87-15865)
20. Lloyd M. Barré, *The Rhetoric of Political Persuasion: The Narrative Artistry and Political Intentions of* 2 *Kings* 9 -11 (CBQMS 20) $5.00 ($4.00 for CBA members) ISBN 0-915170-19-1 (LC 87-15878)
21. John J. Clabeaux, *A Lost Edition of the Letters of Paul: A Reassessment of the Text of the Pauline Corpus Attested by Marcion* (CBQMS 21) $8.50 ($6.80 for CBA members) ISBN 0-915170-20-5 (LC 88-28511)
22. Craig Koester, *The Dwelling of God: The Tabernacle in the Old Testament, Intertestamental Jewish Literature, and the New Testament* (CBQMS 22) $9.00 ($7.20 for CBA members) ISBN 0-915170-21-3 (LC 89-9853)
23. William Michael Soll, *Psalm* 119*: Matrix, Form, and Setting* (CBQMS 23) $9.00 ($7.20 for CBA members) ISBN 0-915170-22-1 (LC 90-27610)
24. Richard J. Clifford and John J. Collins (eds.), *Creation in the Biblical Traditions* (CBQMS 24) $7.00 ($5.60 for CBA members) ISBN 0-915170-23-X (LC 92-20268)
25. John E. Course, *Speech and Response: A Rhetorical Analysis of the Introductions to the Speeches of the Book of Job, Chaps.* 4 - 24 (CBQMS 25) $8.50 ($6.80 for CBA members) ISBN 0-915170-24-8 (LC 94-26566)
26. Richard J. Clifford, *Creation Accounts in the Ancient Near East and in the Bible* (CBQMS 26) $9.00 ($7.20 for CBA members) ISBN 0-915170-25-6 (LC 94-26565)
27. John Paul Heil, *Blood and Water: The Death and Resurrection of Jesus in John* 18 – 21 (CBQMS 27) $9.00 ($7.20 for CBA members) ISBN 0-915170-26-4 (LC 95-10479)
28. John Kaltner, *The Use of Arabic in Biblical Hebrew Lexicography* (CBQMS 28) $7.50 ($6.00 for CBA members) ISBN 0-915170-27-2 (LC 95-45182)

29. Michael L. Barré, S.S., *Wisdom, You Are My Sister: Studies in Honor of Roland E. Murphy, O.Carm., on the Occasion of His Eightieth Birthday* (CBQMS 29) $13.00 ($10.40 for CBA members) ISBN 0-915170-28-0 (LC 97-16060)
30. Warren Carter and John Paul Heil, *Matthew's Parables: Audience-Oriented Perspectives* (CBQMS 30) $10.00 ($8.00 for CBA members) ISBN 0-915170-29-9 (LC 97-44677)
31. David S. Williams, *The Structure of 1 Maccabees* (CBQMS 31) $7.00 ($5.60 for CBA members) ISBN 0-915170-30-2
32. Lawrence Boadt and Mark S. Smith (eds.), *Imagery and Imagination in Biblical Literature: Essays in Honor of Aloysius Fitzgerald, F.S.C.* (CBQMS 32) $9.00 ($7.20 for CBA members) ISBN 0-915170-31-0 (LC 2001003305)
33. Stephan K. Davis, *The Antithesis of the Ages: Paul's Reconfiguration of Torah* (CBQMS 33) $11.00 ($8.80 for CBA members) ISBN 0-915170-32-9 (LC 2001007936)
34. Aloysius Fitzgerald, F.S.C., *The Lord of the East Wind* (CBQMS 34) ISBN 0-915170-33-7

Order from:

The Catholic Biblical Association of America
The Catholic University of America
Washington, D.C. 20064